WHY DOES EVERYTHING HAVE TO BE ABOUT RACE?

WHY DOES EVERYTHING HAVE TO BE ABOUT RACE?

25 Arguments That Won't Go Away

KEITH BOYKIN

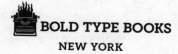

BOLD TYPE BOOKS

NEW YORK

Bold Type Books
Hachette Book Group
1290 Avenue of the Americas, New York, NY 10104
www.boldtypebooks.org
@BoldTypeBooks

Printed in the United States of America

First Edition: January 2024

Published by Bold Type Books, an imprint of Hachette Book Group, Inc. Bold Type
Books is a co-publishing venture of the Type Media Center and Perseus Books.

The Hachette Speakers Bureau provides a wide range of authors for speaking events.
To find out more, go to hachettespeakersbureau.com or
email HachetteSpeakers@hbgusa.com.

Bold Type books may be purchased in bulk for business, educational, or promotional
use. For more information, please contact your local bookseller or the Hachette Book
Group Special Markets Department at special.markets@hbgusa.com.

The publisher is not responsible for websites (or their content) that are
not owned by the publisher.

Print book interior design by Linda Mark.

Library of Congress Cataloging-in-Publication Data
Names: Boykin, Keith, author.
Title: Why does everything have to be about race? : 25 arguments
that won't go away / Keith Boykin.
Description: First edition. | New York : Bold Type Books, [2024] | Includes
bibliographical references and index. | Identifiers: LCCN 2023019505 | ISBN
9781541703315 (hardcover) | ISBN 9781541703339 (ebook)
Subjects: LCSH: Race—United States. | Racism—United States.
Classification: LCC HT1521 .B65 2024 | DDC 305.800973—
dc23/eng/20230424
LC record available at https://lccn.loc.gov/2023019505

ISBNs: 9781541703315 (hardcover), 9781541703339 (ebook)

LSC-C

Printing 3, 2024

To Derrick Bell,
my law school professor and critical race theory pioneer,
who inspired me to fight for justice,
To the Tennessee Three and the many unsung activists
who continue that tradition today,
And to all those
who seek truth and knowledge.

Contents

Contents

A Brief Chronology of Race in America

1526   Enslaved Africans escape from a Spanish settlement in South Carolina and "set it aflame" in a revolt.

1619   Enslaved Africans arrive in Virginia on a ship called the *White Lion*.

1739   Enslaved Black people revolt in the Stono Rebellion in South Carolina.

1770   **Crispus Attucks**, a free Black man, dies in the Boston Massacre, becoming what author William Cooper Nell described as "the first martyr of the American Revolution."

1775   **Lord Dunmore**, the royal governor of Virginia, offers freedom to enslaved Black people who defend the British crown. Virginia's white colonists respond by threatening to execute those who accept his offer.

1776   **Thomas Jefferson** authors the Declaration of Independence, declaring that "all men are created equal," while forty-one of the fifty-six men who signed the document, including Jefferson, enslaved Black people.

1788   The newly ratified US Constitution, signed by **George Washington** and thirty-eight others, counts enslaved Black Americans as only three-fifths of a person.

1790   The Naturalization Act allows immigrants to become citizens only if they are a "free white person" of "good character."

1791   **Toussaint Louverture** leads a successful Black uprising against French colonial rule in the Haitian Revolution.

1808   Congress outlaws the importation of enslaved people from outside the country but allows slavery to continue inside the country.

1820   The Missouri Compromise allows Missouri to be admitted as a slave state and Maine as a free state to maintain the balance of power in the United States Senate.

1829   Mexican president **Vicente Guerrero** abolishes slavery, angering American settlers in the Mexican state of Texas.

1830   Democratic president **Andrew Jackson** signs the Indian Removal Act, authorizing the government to take Native American land and forcibly remove Indigenous people. Thousands of Cherokee people later die on the Trail of Tears.

1831   **Nat Turner** leads a revolt of enslaved Virginians.

1833   The British government abolishes slavery. The United States does not.

1836   The new Texas Constitution bans the presence of free Black people and prohibits "any slave-holder" from emancipating their enslaved people.

1850   The Compromise of 1850 allows California to be admitted as a free state but requires northern states to return formerly enslaved Black people to their enslavers in the South.

1852   Black abolitionist **Frederick Douglass** condemns the "hypocrisy" of the Fourth of July as a celebration to "to cover up crimes which would disgrace a nation of savages."

1857   The Supreme Court rules against **Dred Scott** in his fight for freedom from slavery and declares that African Americans are not citizens of the United States.

1860   Republican **Abraham Lincoln** elected president.

1861   Eleven southern states secede from the union. The Civil War begins.

1863   Lincoln issues the Emancipation Proclamation, "freeing" enslaved people only in states already in rebellion against the union. **Harriet Tubman** leads 150 Black Union soldiers in the Combahee River Raid, which liberates more than 700 enslaved people.

1865   The Civil War ends. Lincoln is assassinated. Slavery ends in Texas on Juneteenth. The Thirteenth Amendment abolishes slavery. Reconstruction begins. The Ku Klux Klan forms.

1868   The Fourteenth Amendment gives citizenship to Black people in America.

1870   The Fifteenth Amendment gives Black men the right to vote. Republican senator **Hiram Rhodes Revels** of Mississippi becomes the first Black person to serve in Congress.

1875   Congress passes the Civil Rights Act of 1875.

1877   After the disputed presidential election of 1876, Republicans agree to end federal protection for Black people in the former Confederate states in the South in return for Republican **Rutherford B. Hayes** becoming president. Reconstruction ends.

1882   Republican president **Chester Arthur** signs the Chinese Exclusion Act, banning Chinese laborers from immigrating to the United States for ten years.

1883   The Supreme Court strikes down the Civil Rights Act of 1875.

1896   The Supreme Court upholds the "separate but equal" doctrine in *Plessy v. Ferguson*.

1898   White supremacists overthrow the multiracial government in Wilmington, North Carolina, killing dozens of Black people and forcing hundreds of Black families to flee.

1909   **Ida B. Wells-Barnett, Mary Church Terrell, W. E. B. Du Bois**, and other leaders form the National Association for the Advancement of Colored People in the aftermath of a race riot in Springfield, Illinois, the year before.

1915   A new film, *The Birth of a Nation* by **D. W. Griffith**, depicts the KKK as heroes fighting to defend white people from Black oppression. Democratic president **Woodrow Wilson** screens the film for an audience in the White House.

1919   White mobs lead a series of race massacres killing hundreds of Black people in cities across the nation in the Red Summer of 1919.

1921   White residents in Oklahoma kill dozens of Black people and destroy a thriving African American community known as "Black Wall Street" in the Tulsa Race Massacre. Republican president **Warren G. Harding** signs the Emergency Quota Act of 1921, setting strict racial limits on immigration to the United States.

1926   Historian Carter G. Woodson launches the first Negro History Week, which would later become Black History Month.

1935   Democratic president **Franklin D. Roosevelt** signs the Social Security Act of 1935, providing federal payments for retirees and unemployment insurance for workers.

1939   Opera star **Marian Anderson** sings before seventy-five thousand people at the Lincoln Memorial after the Daughters of the American Revolution refuse to allow her to perform at Constitution Hall.

1942   Roosevelt signs Executive Order 9066, leading the government to incarcerate more than one hundred thousand Japanese Americans in prison camps.

1945   Democratic president **Harry Truman** gives the order to drop atomic bombs on Hiroshima and Nagasaki, killing tens of thousands of Japanese civilians.

1948   Truman signs Executive Order 9981, abolishing racial segregation in the military.

1954   The Supreme Court's decision in *Brown v. Board of Education* orders public schools to be integrated by race and overturns *Plessy v. Ferguson*.

1955   Fourteen-year-old **Emmett Till** is murdered in Mississippi. **Rosa Parks** refuses to give up her seat on a city bus in Montgomery, Alabama. Black residents lead a bus boycott.

1957   United States marshals escort Black children to Little Rock Central High School in Arkansas as racial integration of schools begins.

1960   **Ella Baker** forms the Student Nonviolent Coordinating Committee and recruits **Diane Nash**, **John Lewis**, and other young leaders to join.

1961   Civil rights activist John Lewis and others are beaten at the Edmund Pettus Bridge in Selma, Alabama, as they lead a march for voting rights. Angry white mobs attack civil rights activists, known as Freedom Riders, who are traveling by bus across the South to protest racial segregation.

1963   Mississippi civil rights leader **Medgar Evers** is assassinated. Dr. **Martin Luther King Jr.** delivers his "I Have a Dream" speech at the March on Washington. Four Black girls are killed by a bomb in a church in Birmingham, Alabama. Democratic president **John F. Kennedy** is assassinated in Dallas, Texas.

1964   Democratic president **Lyndon Johnson** signs the Civil Rights Act of 1964. The Twenty-Fourth Amendment bans poll taxes as a requirement for voting. **Fannie Lou Hamer**, Ella Baker, and **Bob Moses** cofound the Mississippi Freedom Democratic Party and challenge the all-white Mississippi delegation at the 1964 Democratic National Convention.

1965   President Lyndon Johnson signs the Voting Rights Act of 1965; the Immigration and Nationality Act, which eliminates racial quotas in immigration; and a new law creating Medicare for seniors. **Malcolm X** is assassinated in New York City.

1967   **Thurgood Marshall** becomes the first Black person to sit on the Supreme Court.

1968   Rev. Martin Luther King Jr. is assassinated in Memphis, Tennessee. Democratic presidential candidate Robert Kennedy is assassinated in Los Angeles. President Lyndon Johnson signs the Fair Housing Act.

1969   **Marsha P. Johnson**, a Black drag queen, and **Sylvia Rivera**, a Latina drag queen, help lead a rebellion against police brutality at the Stonewall Bar in New York City.

1972   Thousands of Black leaders convene in Gary, Indiana, for the first National Black Political Convention. Democrat **Shirley Chisholm**, the first Black woman in Congress, runs for president.

1985   Police in Philadelphia drop a bomb on the home of the MOVE organization, a Black liberation group, killing eleven people, including five children, and destroying sixty-one homes in two city blocks.

1986   Martin Luther King Jr. Day becomes a federal holiday. Republican president **Ronald Reagan** vetoes antiapartheid sanctions on South Africa. Congress overrides him.

1989   Five Black and Latino teenagers are wrongly accused of raping a white woman in New York City's Central Park. **Donald Trump** calls for their execution.

1992   Black residents in Los Angeles lead a weeklong uprising after an all-white jury acquits four white police officers for the videotaped beating of **Rodney King**.

1998   **James Byrd Jr.**, a forty-nine-year-old Black man, is lynched by three white supremacists in Jasper, Texas.

2005   Hurricane Katrina strikes the mostly Black city of New Orleans, killing hundreds of residents and forcing thousands to flee.

2008   Democrat **Barack Obama** becomes the first Black person to be elected US president.

2011   Donald Trump questions whether Barack Obama was born in the United States.

2012   Unarmed seventeen-year-old **Trayvon Martin** is shot and killed by a twenty-eight-year-old armed neighborhood watchman in Sanford, Florida. Black Lives Matter begins as a social justice movement when Martin's killer is acquitted the following year.

2013   The Supreme Court, in a 5–4 decision, strikes down Section 4 of the Voting Rights Act in *Shelby County v. Holder*.

2014   A community uprising takes place in Ferguson, Missouri, after the police killing of eighteen-year-old **Michael Brown**.

2015   A twenty-one-year-old white supremacist murders nine Black people at the Emanuel AME Church in Charleston, South Carolina.

2016   Donald Trump wins the Republican nomination for president, finally admits President Obama was born in the United States, and wins the Electoral College vote for president.

2017   Republican president Donald Trump claims there were "very fine people on both sides" after a Unite the Right rally turns deadly in Charlottesville, Virginia.

2020   A racial justice protest movement sweeps the country following the police killings of **George Floyd** and **Breonna Taylor** and the murder of **Ahmaud Arbery**. Democrat **Kamala Harris** becomes the first Black woman to be elected vice president of the United States.

2021   In his final days in office, Donald Trump encourages his angry supporters to march to the Capitol to protest his election loss. A violent insurrection follows. Juneteenth becomes a federal holiday.

2022   Democratic president **Joe Biden** signs the Emmett Till Anti-lynching Act. Justice **Ketanji Brown Jackson** becomes the first Black woman on the US Supreme Court.

2023   The US Supreme Court strikes down affirmative action policies that consider race in college admissions.

Introduction

> The function, the very serious function of racism is distraction. It keeps you from doing your work. It keeps you explaining, over and over again, your reason for being. Somebody says you have no language and you spend twenty years proving that you do. Somebody says your head isn't shaped properly so you have scientists working on the fact that it is. Somebody says you have no art, so you dredge that up. Somebody says you have no kingdoms, so you dredge that up. None of that is necessary. There will always be one more thing.
>
> —*Toni Morrison, Portland State University, May 30, 1975*

It was February 2022—my first speaking engagement to a live audience of college students since the beginning of the pandemic, a forty-five-minute Black History Month speech at a public college in upstate New York. At the end, students lined up to ask questions.

The first person in line was a white male student who seemed a bit older than the typical undergrad. "I appreciate your discussion about race," he said into the microphone, "but what about other types of diversity? What about political diversity or geographical diversity?" Why hadn't I spoken about that? he wondered.

My presentation had discussed race, gender, sexual orientation, gender identity, and disability as five common types of diversity, but race was the only part of the conversation that drew his ire, even though my speech had been billed as a Black History Month event. He didn't say it directly, but the question behind his question was clear.

Why does everything have to be about race?

I tried to explain that most colleges and universities already seek ideological and geographical diversity among the students they admit.

If you're a halfway decent student from Alaska applying to college in New York State, for example, you're very likely to be admitted even if you don't meet the school's median test scores, and virtually no one ever complains about that. Colleges routinely reserve spots for athletes, artists, musicians, people with unusual backgrounds, children of alumni, and people from wealthy families, and this rarely gets challenged in court. But simply the mention of race causes concern for many white Americans.

But his question deserved a longer answer—if only because it refuses to go away in the minds of many Americans. This book is that answer.

This book is divided into five parts that correspond to the five main ways people in our nation deflect concerns about white supremacy and anti-Blackness: (1) erasing Black history, (2) centering white victimhood, (3) denying Black oppression, (4) promoting myths of Black inferiority, and (5) rebranding racism.

Within those sections, I answer twenty-five questions (which are actually arguments) in twenty-five relatively brief, sometimes personal, and hopefully informative chapters. Most of the chapters are serious; a couple are both satirical and serious. The book is organized in a way that allows you to read it from cover to cover or to skip around and read various chapters nonsequentially, depending on your time, interests, and needs. Throughout these pages, I have chosen not to edit or abbreviate direct quotations that use the N-word or other profanity as a rude reminder of the raw reality of racism.

The book dives headfirst into the waters of our newest and oldest conversations about race, happening at dinner tables, in break rooms, in college classrooms, and in TV studios across America. But it is not your job to spend your entire life disproving all the racist arguments that surround you. As Toni Morrison reminds us, the function of racism is distraction. Rather, the purpose here is to provide a useful reference guide with an arsenal of information to prevent you from becoming distracted.

Once we know the answers to these arguments that won't go away, then it's up to all of us to create enduring new solutions to build a better world.

PART ONE | ERASING BLACK HISTORY

I n January 2023, Florida officials in the administration of Republican governor Ron DeSantis prohibited any school in the state from offering an Advanced Placement course on African American studies because, they said, it was "inexplicably contrary to Florida law and significantly lack[ed] educational value."

The decision was part of a troubling pattern in which the very people who deny the existence of systemic racism have deployed their power *systemically* to conceal the historical evidence of such racism. As several Black observers noted, the young white people who yelled at Elizabeth Eckford and Ruby Bridges for desegregating their schools in the 1950s and '60s are now trying to prevent their grandchildren from knowing what they were doing.

Some argue that the tragic events of America's racial history belong to the distant past and the country should just move on. Even controversial Black artist Kanye West has objected to government plans to honor the past by placing an image of Harriet Tubman on the twenty-dollar bill, complaining that Black leaders like Tubman,

Malcolm X, and Dr. Martin Luther King Jr. were "too far in the past and not relatable."

But the truth is, the wounds of our history are very recent.

In May 2021, a bearded white man in a baseball cap posted a quick factual video on TikTok under the username @doorbender. He looked directly into a camera and spoke four simple sentences:

> When Harriet Tubman was born, Thomas Jefferson was still alive. And when Harriet Tubman died, Ronald Reagan was alive. Stop saying everything was four hundred years ago. It wasn't.

The point was powerful. The ugliest moments in a history that many Americans would like to forget took place not that long ago. Harriet Tubman, who bravely fought to rescue Black people from enslavement, was born into slavery in Maryland around 1822, four years before former president Thomas Jefferson died. She passed away as a free woman in New York in 1913, two years after future president Ronald Reagan was born.

Tubman was born during the tenure of America's fifth president, the Virginia enslaver James Monroe, and escaped her own enslavement to live through the Monroe Doctrine, the Underground Railroad, the Civil War, Reconstruction, the Ku Klux Klan, the Battle of the Little Big Horn, the Chinese Exclusion Act, *Plessy v. Ferguson*, and the founding of the NAACP, just long enough to see the inauguration of America's twentieth-eighth president, Woodrow Wilson, another problematic Virginian. It was Wilson, a Democrat, who invited guests to the White House for a screening of the racist 1915 movie *The Birth of a Nation*, which depicted the KKK as heroes fighting to protect white people from what the film caricatured as incompetent Black government leaders and lascivious Black rapists.

If all of this seems like ancient history, consider this. When Joe Biden celebrated his eightieth birthday in November 2022 and became the oldest person to serve as president, Carolyn Bryant Donham, the white woman responsible for the lynching of fourteen-year-old Emmett Till in August 1955, was still alive and free. She died in April 2023 at eighty-eight years old.

Just three days after Biden's birthday, the *Washington Post* uncovered a photograph of Dallas Cowboys owner Jerry Jones standing with racist white students in 1957 as they blocked Black students from integrating Little Rock Central High School.

In the same week as Biden's birthday celebration, Ruby Bridges, who had been depicted in a famous Norman Rockwell painting as a six-year-old Black girl escorted by US marshals to integrate a public school in New Orleans, was visiting an elementary school in California to celebrate Ruby Bridges Walk to School Day.

The connection to America's overlooked past is not a faraway memory. In fact, the last living African American known to have been enslaved, Peter Mills, passed away in 1972—in my lifetime. And when Ronald Reagan—the link to Harriet Tubman and Thomas Jefferson—died in 2004, pop stars Billie Eilish, Lil Nas X, and all the members of the Korean boy band BTS were children.

Today, as Americans debate affirmative action, critical race theory, and what to do with old Confederate monuments, we must remember that many of the victims and perpetrators of our country's racist history are still alive.

Part 1 explains why we must resist efforts to erase the truth about Black history and prevent attempts to minimize the significance and relevance of our experience.

1

Barack Obama's election does not compensate for hundreds of years of racism.

ARGUMENT

We've tried to deal with our original sin of slavery by fighting a civil war, by passing landmark civil rights legislation. We've elected an African American president.

—*Senate Republican Leader Mitch McConnell, June 18, 2019*

ANSWER

The legacy of slavery and Jim Crow and discrimination didn't suddenly vanish with the passage of the Civil Rights Act or the Voting Rights Act, or the election of Barack Obama.

—*President Barack Obama, July 9, 2016*

It was 10:45 on a Tuesday evening in November when I got the news. I was the only Black person sitting on set at the CNBC world headquarters in Englewood Cliffs, New Jersey, when a producer spoke into my earpiece. "We're going to make the call at the top of the hour," she said.

The producers wanted me to be ready to give my reaction live on air after the anchors made the announcement. They never told me who won, but the answer was clear. Barack Obama had accumulated 207 electoral votes compared to 142 for his Republican opponent, John McCain. Obama needed 270 votes to win, and polls were about to close in the West, including California, a state with 55 electoral votes that hadn't voted for a Republican in twenty years.

I had been covering the arduous nineteen-month-long presidential campaign since the Democratic primary contest with Hillary Clinton, and now we had arrived at the final moments. In fifteen minutes,

Barack Obama would become the first Black person to be elected president of the United States.

I thought of the ancestors, who had dreamed of a day like this. I thought of Douglass and Tubman, Malcolm and Martin. I remembered the campaigns of Shirley Chisholm and Jesse Jackson, and other Black leaders who had sought the presidency. And I reflected on the white liberal hope that Obama's election might usher in a new postracial America. I knew better, but I allowed myself to dream.

I knew that one Black man's election to a four-year term could not erase the scars of centuries of oppression or the injuries inflicted on millions of Black Americans who would never see the inside of the White House. And although I had spent much of my life studying Black history, I would make new discoveries in the years that followed the election and learn of ancient and recent historical injustices of which I had been unaware.

In the years after 2008, I would learn of the exploitation of Henrietta Lacks, the Black woman whose cancer cells were used for decades for commercial purposes and medical research without her consent. I would learn that the alma mater I shared with Obama, Harvard Law School, had been financed by the sale of enslaved Black people. I would learn the story of Walter Coles, whose white family accumulated two centuries of wealth on the backs of enslaved Black Virginians who now stood to gain none of the windfall from billions of dollars' worth of uranium deposits recently discovered on the land they were forced to work. And from DNA ancestry tests that did not exist when Obama was elected, I would learn the history of my own family, of Black people with the same blood that runs in my veins, who were enslaved, killed, incarcerated, and conscripted to serve their country as they struggled to survive from captivity to Jim Crow and beyond.

For Black people, no single story could capture the totality of the successive devastation of slavery, segregation, and continuing racial injustice of the nation. White America not only took our Black money, Black land, and Black bodies; it controlled nearly every aspect of our Black lives for four centuries. How could one person—even one with the talent, charm, and intellect of Barack Obama—compensate for all that?

Prior to the outbreak of the Civil War, the Census Bureau counted nearly four million enslaved Black people in the United States. Millions more had perished in the previous two centuries of enslavement. The wealth of the young nation rested on the unpaid, coerced labor of enslaved Black Americans and the legacy of their ancestors who had been stolen from Africa. It was an absurd conservative fantasy to suggest that one politician could cure, correct, or compensate for slavery, lynchings, race massacres, sharecropping, peonage, convict leasing, de facto and de jure segregation, police brutality, mass incarceration, and all the iterations of systemic racism through which Black people have suffered.

How could one person in one job for eight years be considered atonement for the beatings of Sojourner Truth, the twelve years of Solomon Northup's enslavement, the scars of Harriet Tubman, the destruction of Wilmington, the burning of Rosewood, the bombing of Tulsa, the lives ruined at Scottsboro, the wrongful execution of George Stinney, the indignity of Claudette Colvin, the pain of Mamie Till, Myrlie Evers, and Coretta Scott King, the shooting of Eleanor Bumpurs, the unjust incarceration of the Exonerated Five, the beating of Rodney King, or the forty-one bullets fired at unarmed Amadou Diallo?

Barack Obama has many talents, but erasing history is not one of them. His life experience is unique. Although he identifies as Black and clearly feels, understands, and resonates with the plight of Black Americans, his mother was white and his father was African. Neither of his parents descended from the enslaved in America. Perhaps this made him more palatable to some white Americans, but it did not deter his critics from hounding and harassing him through two terms of his presidency. They created an entire new political movement called the Tea Party to resist him. They condemned his rare decisions to discuss racism in current events when he expressed concern for Trayvon Martin or Henry Louis Gates Jr. And they tried to erase his legacy by replacing him with an adversary who had challenged his legal right to hold his office.

The argument that Barack Obama's presidency redeemed America from a history of racial oppression underscores a disturbing pattern of prioritizing symbolism over substance in our politics. Even if he had been a direct descendant of Nat Turner, the elevation of one person could never compensate for the suffering of millions of others.

The tendency to focus on personality over policy reflects the same misguided perspective that tells Black people today that we should be happy because Oprah Winfrey, LeBron James, and Beyoncé have become billionaires while millions of others struggle to pay the monthly electricity bill. Individual success stories do not address systemic failures any more than a business rectifies institutional racism by hiring a diversity officer or a college by bringing in a Black History Month speaker. True progress comes by changing policy, not people. It is not produced by empty, episodic gestures but by inclusive, ongoing engagement.

Political analysts and historians can debate President Obama's impact on racial justice given the obstacles and resistance he faced from Congress and white America. No doubt, the lives of millions of Black people were improved during his administration because of the American Recovery and Reinvestment Act, the Affordable Care Act, and other initiatives that moved the nation forward from the Great Recession. But the long-term racial disparities in employment, health care, education, housing, household wealth, criminal justice, and even access to safe drinking water all existed before he took office, and all remained when he left.

It took centuries to construct the infrastructure of systemic racism, and no single person could be expected to unravel it in eight years in the White House.

But perhaps the most duplicitous element of the "Obama as reparations" argument is that the majority of white people did not vote for him in either of his two presidential elections. Obama won the presidency *despite* the white vote, not because of it, both in 2008 and in

2012. You can't take credit for his election without having taken the trouble to secure it, let alone support it. And most white Americans did not vote for the one person who many now argue absolves them of their past and current sins. They did, however, vote twice for his successor, Donald Trump.

2

Critical race theory is not indoctrinating school kids to be "woke."

ARGUMENT

In Florida, we are taking a stand against the state-sanctioned racism that is critical race theory. We won't allow Florida tax dollars to be spent teaching kids to hate our country or to hate each other.

—*Florida governor Ron DeSantis, December 15, 2021*

ANSWER

When the DeSantises of the world say this teaches us to hate America, I say "No, this teaches us to see what America has been, to better understand how we can make America what we want it to be."

—*Professor Kimberlé Crenshaw, critical race theory scholar, August 12, 2021*

When I anxiously opened my admissions letter in 1989, I had no idea that law school would introduce me to three people who would influence American politics more than three decades later.

The first was my schoolmate Barack Obama, who would go on to become president. The second was Bill Clinton, who would speak on campus and inspire me to work on his 1992 presidential campaign and in the White House. The third was Derrick Bell, a Black law professor who would lead a courageous protest for faculty diversity.

Professor Bell was a pioneer of the newly developing critical race theory movement, and his class introduced me to intellectual conversations about previously foreign concepts like interest convergence theory, intersectionality, and the permanence of racism. We read heavily footnoted law review articles and talked about desegregation strategies, antidiscrimination litigation, and other complex legal concepts. And he exposed me to the writings of legal scholars like Kimberlé Crenshaw, Richard Delgado, Mari Matsuda, and Patricia J. Williams.

Unlike many dry law school lecturers, Derrick Bell used creative fiction and historical narrative to illustrate his ideas. The course fascinated me as a law student, but if you weren't a lawyer or an activist, you probably weren't that interested in reading academic writings about race and the law. That's why I was shocked thirty years later when critical race theory suddenly emerged as a major political issue.

I hadn't thought much about the course since 2011, when I spoke at Professor Bell's funeral service at Riverside Church in Manhattan. His obituary in the *New York Times* that year briefly summarized critical race theory as "a body of legal scholarship that explored how racism is embedded in laws and legal institutions." So why did this decades-old academic theory resurface in the middle of a presidential campaign between two old white men, Donald Trump and Joe Biden?

To answer that question, we must look back at history. Since the end of World War II, modern American conservatism has survived by constructing a series of new villains for ordinary people to fear. First it was the communists of the 1950s. Then, the civil rights activists of the '50s and '60s. Next came the radical feminists of the '60s and '70s, the "welfare queens" of the '70s and '80s, and the crack dealers and criminals of the '80s and '90s. They were followed by Muslims after the September 11, 2001, terror attack and LGBTQ couples when gay marriage became legal in Massachusetts in 2004. A new fear of immigrants emerged during the Obama administration, followed by a fear of young transgender students and even adult drag queens in the early 2020s. Now they fear anything "woke."

The little-known scholarship of critical race theory, which dares to interrogate race in the nation's institutions, fit perfectly into this calculus by allowing Republicans to play on white America's longest-held anxiety: fear of Black people.

The background story of how we got here exemplifies the symbiotic relationship between Republican officials and the right-wing media, and shows how the mainstream media is bullied into covering and amplifying their manufactured controversies. Two months before the 2020 presidential election, Fox News host Tucker Carlson interviewed a guest who claimed, in a style reflective of 1950s McCarthyism, that "critical race theory has pervaded every institution in the federal government." I did not see the interview at the time it aired, and if I had I would have laughed out loud at the absurdity of the claim. But one person who did see the interview that night and apparently did not laugh was Donald Trump.

Two days after the Fox News interview, the Trump administration issued a memo ordering federal agencies to "cease and desist" from any trainings involving critical race theory. The memo positioned the forty-year-old academic theory as an imminent threat that was promoting "divisive, false, and demeaning propaganda" that is "contrary to all we stand for as Americans and should have no place in the Federal government." A few weeks later, Trump followed up with an executive order banning federal agencies and contractors from diversity trainings or any instruction that might suggest "the United States is fundamentally racist or sexist." He had mandated a solution for a problem that didn't exist.

Most Americans had probably never heard of critical race theory until then, and I doubt that Donald Trump had either, or that he has since read even a single page written by any critical race scholar. Trump's executive order predictably cited Dr. King's familiar "content of their character" line so beloved (out of context) by Republicans, without any sense of irony that Dr. King's words about the racist origins of America would have been restricted by the same executive order.

The executive order also, astoundingly, accused *antiracist* critical race scholars of trying to "resurrect the discredited notions of the nineteenth century's apologists for slavery." It was classic conservative doublespeak: it attempted to equate the very people working to fix America's race problem with the racists who created it.

Issuing an executive order about a nonexistent threat a few weeks before a major election was a desperate and transparently political attempt to stir up white resentment. But it was not enough to change the election result. During the two-month presidential transition to the Biden administration, which was fraught by the loser's unwillingness to leave office, critical race theory never crossed my mind.

Then, in the first few days of 2021, Georgia elected its first Black senator and first Jewish senator, an angry white mob stormed the US Capitol in an unsuccessful attempt to stop the final certification of the 2020 presidential election, and the newly inaugurated President Biden revoked the absurd executive order, among several others. It was in that dangerous climate that Republicans rediscovered their loathing for critical race theory.

From January 2021 through September 2022, forty-two states introduced bills or took steps to restrict teaching critical race theory or limit how teachers could discuss racism and sexism, *Education Week* reported. During that time, seventeen states enacted bans or restrictions on what they considered critical race theory. By June 2021, a report from Media Matters found that Fox News had mentioned critical race theory more than 1,900 times in the previous three and a half months, rising from 29 mentions in February to 901 in June.

Critical race theory had become a news story solely because of "a well-resourced, highly mobilized coalition of forces," law professor Kimberlé Crenshaw told the *New York Times* in November 2021.

Starting in 2021, the words "critical race theory" or "CRT" began to appear almost everywhere, and it troubled me that it was often presented as some sort of nefarious new tactic invented by the "woke" left to indoctrinate impressionable young public school kids.

Despite all the anguished, nonsensical anxiety, very few of the people involved in the public discussion seemed to have any real idea of what exactly critical race theory was. Some on the right twisted the conversation so that virtually any discussion that did not promote a positive view of America's racial history was relabeled critical race theory. They accused elementary school teachers, business leaders, politicians, and even military generals of promoting it. CRT quickly morphed into a catchall phrase used to condemn all so-called woke policies that promoted diversity, equity, and inclusion or progressive values. A Republican member of Congress blamed a disastrous Ohio train derailment on a railroad company's DEI policies. A Republican senator even blamed a California bank failure on "woke" policies.

Books and teachers and librarians also became targets. Texas governor Greg Abbott signed a bill that banned the teaching of any material from the Pulitzer Prize–winning *1619 Project*, a collection of essays published in 2019 about the four hundredth anniversary of the first African slaves brought to Virginia.

Florida governor Ron DeSantis supported a bill that prohibited teachers from any classroom instruction that would make white people "feel discomfort, guilt" or "anguish" based on their race. In response to the new rules, one textbook maker tried to tell the story of Rosa Parks's refusal to give up her seat on a bus in Alabama in 1955 by deleting any reference to her race, the sole reason she was forced off the bus and arrested.

Conservatives could not contain themselves. Angry parents demanded school boards ban critical race theory in their children's classrooms. One claimed that critical race theory was supporting "anti-Christ indoctrinations of our children," though he never said how an academic theory had accomplished this feat. And the State of Florida even rejected twenty-eight *math textbooks* because they allegedly "included references to Critical Race Theory."

Conservatives went so far overboard in their attacks on CRT that progressive commentators started mocking their arguments with posts of their own. "Critical Race Theory took my guns and give [*sic*] them to the transgenders," writer Michael Harriot tweeted in June 2021. "Critical race theory ate my homework," journalist Josh Marshall added.

Although the conservative arguments were easy to satirize, it was not ever clear what they were talking about when they condemned CRT. Over the course of more than a year of painful news coverage, I do not recall seeing any critic of critical race theory who could accurately define it. But the critics didn't need to: they just needed something to hate. And the less precisely it was defined, the easier it was to imagine that it was, in the words of a popular film, everything everywhere all at once.

It's important to understand that critical race theory is not a single theory but a collection of ideas developed by various scholars over many years. It started in the 1970s in the legal academy with pioneering professors like Derrick Bell, who encouraged his colleagues to think more deeply about the influence of race in American law. In 1981, a group of Harvard Law students, led by Kimberlé Crenshaw, organized an alternative course on race and law. Then, in 1989, law professors Crenshaw and Mari Matsuda organized the first major national conference on critical race theory.

When I graduated from law school in 1992, I don't think anyone I knew had ever heard of critical race theory outside of the legal community, but the scholarship migrated into other academic disciplines in college courses and graduate schools in the years that followed.

In 1995, Crenshaw and three other legal scholars, Neil Gotanda, Gary Peller, and Kendall Thomas, edited and published a groundbreaking book called *Critical Race Theory: The Key Writings That Formed the Movement*. The book featured pieces by several scholars who were widely known in legal academic circles.

The book's introduction explains critical race theory: "Critical Race Theory embraces a movement of left scholars, most of them scholars of color, situated in law schools, whose work challenges the ways in which race and racial power are constructed and represented in American legal culture and, more generally, in American society as a whole."

That's it. That's the definition the critical race scholars use themselves that conservatives never mention. Critical race theory was never about the Antichrist or Marxism or hating white people. It was about examining the role of race in law and society.

So, what did critical race theory stand for that was so controversial?

There is no canonical set of doctrines or methodologies to which we all subscribe. Although Critical Race scholarship differs in object, argument, accent, and emphasis, it is nevertheless unified by two common interests. The first is to understand how a regime of white supremacy and subordination of people of color have been created and maintained in America, and, in particular, to examine the relationship between that social structure and professed ideals, such as "the rule of law" and "equal protection." The second is a desire not merely to understand the vexed bond between law and racial power, but to *change* it.

If it sounds a lot more technical and a lot less menacing than the right would have you believe, that's because it's an *academic* theory that has been politicized and vilified by cynical operatives for their own purposes.

But what about those K–12 school kids? And what about math?

In the spring of 2021, the Association of American Educators surveyed their members and found that 96 percent said their schools did not require them to teach critical race theory. When you look at the actual writings of the critical race scholars mentioned above, it's easy to understand why. Most critical race scholars operate at the college and graduate level and write in language that isn't readily accessible to the average middle-school student.

Yes, many public schools do teach about uncomfortable subjects like the inconsistencies in the Declaration of Independence and the Constitution, slavery, the Civil War, the Ku Klux Klan, Jim Crow segregation, and the struggle for women's rights and LGBTQ rights. But what those K–12 students are learning in the classroom that far too many conservative parents are objecting to is not critical race theory.

It's American history.

3

Dr. King didn't say America should be color-blind.

ARGUMENT

We want a color-blind society, a society, that in the words of Dr. King, judges people "not by the color of their skin, but by the content of their character."

—*President Ronald Reagan, January 18, 1986*

ANSWER

Yes, I'm Black. I'm proud of it. I'm Black and beautiful.

—*Dr. Martin Luther King Jr.*

think if Martin Luther King was alive today, he would . . ."

Those are the only words on the screen in a popular GIF widely used on Black Twitter. At the very moment a pasty, bow-tied man begins to whitesplain what Dr. King would really want, he's hit by a chair and a Black boy runs on screen and punches him.

Many of us immediately recognize the visual from the popular animated TV series *The Boondocks*, created by Aaron McGruder. It's from an episode in which Rev. Martin Luther King Jr. comes back to life and wonders what went wrong. In the episode, the bow-tied man, a conservative TV host, interrogates Dr. King and demands that he profess his love for America. In the GIF, however, the caption indicates that the white TV host is about to quote Dr. King to support an argument that is inconsistent with the civil rights leader's true beliefs.

It's a painfully familiar scenario for Black people, not only on social media but in every part of our lives. White conservatives are constantly telling us what they think Dr. King really believed, and they're constantly quoting the one line from the one speech they seem to know: "I have a dream that my four little children will one day live in a nation where they will not be judged by the color of their skin but by the content of their character."

Contrary to popular belief, Dr. King's "I Have a Dream" speech at the 1963 March on Washington was not a dream about his four Black children playing kickball with white kids. It was about an entirely new vision for America based on the principle of justice, a word he used ten times in the speech that is often derided by today's conservatives, who mock King-like activists as "social justice warriors."

While they quote one line from Dr. King's speech, they ignore another powerful line from the same speech where he accuses America of writing "a bad check" to Black people. His speech condemns "racist" politicians, denounces the "unspeakable horrors of police brutality," objects to discriminatory housing policies, demands full voting rights for African Americans, and threatens the nation with "a rude awakening" and an outright "revolt" if Black people's demands are not met. It's essentially the same message that Black Lives Matter activists are articulating today.

So what did Dr. King mean when he spoke of his children being judged "by the content of their character?" He did not want his kids to be treated *unfairly* because of the color of their skin. He wanted to create a world "where people are not color blind, but color kind," writes author Colin Seale. Dr. King never said he wanted Black children's color to be ignored. In fact, he spoke of "the beauty of diversity" and told Black people to "be proud of our heritage." Throughout his public life, he repeatedly embraced his race and condemned white America for creating negative stereotypes associated with Blackness. In one speech, he said:

> Somebody told a lie one day. They couched it in language. They made everything Black ugly and evil. Look in your dictionaries and see the synonyms of the word "Black." It's always something degrading and low and sinister. Look at the word "white," it's

always something pure, high and clean. Well, I want to get the language right tonight. I want to get the language so right that everyone here will cry out: "Yes, I'm Black, I'm proud of it. I'm Black and I'm beautiful!"

Those are not the words of a man who wanted to create a society so color-blind that it ignored race. That's why Dr. King's "I Have a Dream" speech was meant to uplift Black people, not to erase our existence. His vision about the world he wanted for his children was a statement that recognized that Black children were being racially profiled, singled out, segregated, and denied opportunities in America in 1963. Six decades later, that problem still exists. Although state-sanctioned segregation has been outlawed, Black children were still being racially profiled, singled out, and denied opportunities in America in 2023 because of their skin color.

Unlike the conservatives on today's Supreme Court, King also understood that race must be considered to remedy anti-Black discrimination. In his 1964 book, *Why We Can't Wait*, he criticized white people who claimed to believe in equality but objected to "compensatory or preferential treatment" for Black Americans. "A society that has done something special *against* the Negro for hundreds of years must now do something special *for* the Negro."

King's dream was not for America to stop talking about race. His words expressed a pointed demand for America to stop *using* race *against* Black people. As he explained to the Southern Christian Leadership Conference in 1967, "Let us be dissatisfied until men and women, *however Black they may be*, will be judged on the basis of the content of their character and not on the basis of the color of their skin." King's words remind us that Black people were the focus of his concern here.

If King had only wanted a milquetoast racial utopia without transformational change, he would have been much more popular in his lifetime. But in an August 1966 Gallup poll, after the Civil Rights Act and Voting Rights Act had both been signed into law, 63 percent of Americans held an unfavorable opinion of him. African Americans largely supported King, but white Americans did not. That's because they knew he wanted the kind of change that would disrupt their privilege.

If Dr. King had truly represented the inoffensive modern caricature that white conservatives have now created of him, surely their predecessors would not have fought so hard to avoid honoring him. Future Republican presidential nominee John McCain voted against creating the Martin Luther King Day holiday when it came up for a vote in Congress in 1983. Conservative Alabama Democrat Richard Shelby also voted against the holiday, before switching parties years later to become a Republican.

Former Republican governor of New Hampshire Meldrim Thomson Jr. urged President Reagan to veto the bill establishing the holiday. The president himself opposed the holiday and expressed "reservations" about it, but in October 1983, he was already under attack for firing three members of the United States Civil Rights Commission and failing to reduce Black unemployment, which had reached the highest rate in recorded history, 21 percent, under his watch. Reagan admitted privately to Thomson his concern that King had been a communist, but he concluded he would sign the bill anyway, although he felt "the perception" of Dr. King was "based on an image, not reality." Even then, lawmakers in Arizona resisted the holiday until 1992.

For white conservatives to accept a holiday honoring a controversial, progressive Black civil rights leader, they first had to redefine King in the most innocuous terms possible. They did not want to celebrate his opposition to the Vietnam War, his condemnation of police brutality, his demand for racial compensation for Black people, his support for a national guaranteed income, or his work to create the Poor People's Campaign.

Instead, they settled on something else. They turned their attention to the one sentence from the one speech from his thirteen years as a civil rights leader that they could embrace and then distorted it to use it as a weapon against Dr. King's own beliefs: they cynically elevated "character" over "race."

Many of these white conservatives never shared King's vision of America, as they demonstrated repeatedly in the years after the holiday became official. In March 1988, Reagan became the first president since Andrew Johnson in 1866 to veto a civil rights bill. His successor, Republican president George H. W. Bush, who once condemned the original Civil Rights Act in 1964, vetoed a new Civil Rights Act in 1990.

In those instances when Republicans tried to acknowledge the importance of African American contributions, they often did so by selecting Black people whose work contradicted Dr. King's beliefs, as Bush did when he nominated the relatively inexperienced Black conservative Clarence Thomas to replace the legendary Black progressive Thurgood Marshall on the US Supreme Court: "The fact that he is Black and a minority," said Bush, "has nothing to do with this sense that he is the best qualified at this time."

Few observers believed that Thomas's race was not a factor in his selection, but by elevating him to the Supreme Court, Republicans were able to use a little-known Black judge to dismantle a well-known Black hero's legacy. When the Supreme Court gutted the Voting Rights Act in 2013, it was Thomas who cast the deciding vote to sabotage the very bill that Dr. King had fought so hard to enact.

Nearly a decade later, when Democratic senator Raphael Warnock, the African American pastor of Dr. King's Atlanta church, ran for reelection to the United States Senate, Republicans recruited Herschel Walker, an inexperienced former football player then living in Texas, "mainly because he was the same skin color as his opponent," according to the candidate's own son. It was the ultimate irony. After decades of distorting Dr. King's message to argue that America should be color-blind, Republicans selected a candidate primarily because of his skin color to wage a campaign against the pastor of Dr. King's own church.

4

Republicans are no longer the "party of Lincoln."

ARGUMENT

Who started the KKK? That was the Democrats.

—*Former Republican presidential candidate Ben Carson, November 6, 2016*

ANSWER

I find no constitutional basis for the exercise of Federal regulatory authority in either of these areas.... And so, because I am unalterably opposed to any threats to our great system of government and the loss of our God-given liberties, I shall vote "no" on this bill.

—*1964 Republican presidential nominee Barry Goldwater, announcing his opposition to the Civil Rights Act of 1964, June 18, 1964*

was sitting on set on *CNN Tonight with Don Lemon* in February 2020 when Don showed a video clip from a meeting in the White House that day. I had never seen the video and had no idea what to expect. I saw a group of Black people assembled around Donald Trump. One of the people in the audience who was not visible on-screen spoke up. "Mr. President, I don't mean to interrupt, but I've got to say this because it's Black History Month." He paused and then launched into the most embarrassing six words I've ever heard a Black man say in the presence of a white man: "Man, you the first Black president."

I couldn't believe it. Yes, I remember when Toni Morrison once described Bill Clinton as "our first Black president" in a 1998 essay for the *New Yorker*, but that was a statement by others that she was quoting to illustrate a symbolic sense of shared persecution at a time when the idea of electing an African American to the White House was still a pipe dream. This was different. I couldn't believe that a Black person in a room filled with Black people had the audacity to suggest that Donald Trump, of all people, was the first Black president—after we had already had a first Black president in Barack Obama.

I was so livid that I couldn't hold back when Don asked me for a comment on air. "Trump's been president for almost four years now, and he's never made a single visit to a Black community to attend a Black event," I responded. "The idea that anybody would sit in a room with Donald Trump and call him the first Black president after we had Barack Obama as the president of the United States—it shows just what kind of Uncle Toms were sitting in that room in the first place." Don did not approve of my language, but I did not hold back. I called it "ridiculous," "shocking," "appalling," and "disgusting."

In his four years in office, Donald Trump made a mockery of Black History Month and Black history itself. In his first Black History Month event in February 2017, he seemed not to know who Frederick Douglass was when he cited the long-deceased abolitionist as "an example of somebody who's done an amazing job and is being recognized more and more."

Trump's ignorance of Frederick Douglass was consistent with his lack of knowledge about basic facts from American history, including President Lincoln's political affiliation. "Most people don't even know he was a Republican," Trump told an audience at a GOP fundraising dinner in March 2017. "A lot of people don't know that. We have to build that up a little more," he told the crowd.

Perhaps it should come as no surprise that the leader of a party that is trying to ban books and the teaching of history would assume the public's ignorance about one of America's most famous presidents, but many of us in the African American community have grown tired of ignorant white people thinking they're educating us about things we already know. It reminds me of the Twitter trolls who think they're clever by claiming that the late Democratic senator Robert Byrd was a former grand wizard of the Ku Klux Klan. Although Byrd, who was born in 1917, was once a Klansman, he was never a grand wizard, and he later apologized for his membership and renounced the notoriously racist terrorist network.

The truth is that Republicans have been trying to rewrite their own history for decades, and far too many Black Republicans have been dishonest coconspirators in this long-running campaign.

Yes, Republicans *were* the party of Abraham Lincoln. They passed Reconstruction-era laws and amendments that profoundly changed the nation for the better. They ratified the Thirteenth Amendment, abolishing slavery; the Fourteenth Amendment, giving citizenship to Black people; and the Fifteenth Amendment, guaranteeing Black men the right to vote. They established the Freedmen's Bureau and passed landmark legislation that empowered African Americans after the Civil War.

Because of their early work, Republicans had a hold on Black voters for seventy years after the Civil War. The first Black members of Congress were all Republicans. My great-great-grandfather John Dickerson was a proud Black Republican and chair of the 1912 Republican state convention in Florida. Many other prominent African Americans of the twentieth century were also Republicans, from Jesse Owens to Jackie Robinson.

It's also true that Democrats were the party most associated with racism throughout the nineteenth century and much of the twentieth century. Although they did not start the Ku Klux Klan, as Ben Carson falsely claimed, Democrats carried plenty of racial baggage. The first Democratic president, Andrew Jackson, was a slave owner and notorious "Indian killer." It was Democratic leaders who fled the union to form the Confederacy at the beginning of the Civil War. Democratic president Woodrow Wilson screened the racist film *The Birth of a Nation* at the White House in 1915.

Even twentieth-century Democratic heroes were beholden to their party's racist southerners known as Dixiecrats. Franklin Roosevelt's

New Deal excluded domestic workers and agricultural workers, who were disproportionately Black. And Lyndon Johnson was notorious for his racism long before he became a civil rights champion as vice president and then president.

But Republicans were not exactly saints during this time, either. The period known as Reconstruction lasted only a dozen years after the Civil War because Republicans struck a deal with racist Democrats in 1877 to end federal protection of Black people in the South in exchange for Republican Rutherford B. Hayes becoming president after losing the popular vote.

It was the Republican-dominated US Supreme Court that struck down civil rights legislation, including the Civil Rights Act of 1875; it would take nearly a century for Congress to replace it with the Civil Rights Act of 1964. Republicans failed to pass an antilynching bill in 1922. And Republican president Dwight Eisenhower notably cautioned the US Supreme Court to move slowly on racial integration, warning Chief Justice Earl Warren that southern segregationists were "not bad people" and all they wanted was "to see that their sweet little girls are not required to sit in school alongside some big, overgrown Negroes."

Black voters, understandably, grew disillusioned with Republicans as the twentieth century progressed. Disappointed by the slow pace of progress, the *Chicago Defender*, a prominent Black newspaper, endorsed Democrat Al Smith over Republican Herbert Hoover for president in 1928. Four years later, more Black voters fled the GOP as they disproportionately felt the weight of the Great Depression. In 1936, Franklin Roosevelt became the first Democrat to win the majority of the Black vote in American history. But because of the influence of the Dixiecrats, the Black vote remained competitive for several decades.

"The fact is that both major parties have been hypocritical on the question of civil rights," Dr. King complained in 1960. He accused both parties of "using the Negro as a political football."

That all started to change when Republicans selected Arizona senator Barry Goldwater as their presidential nominee just a few weeks after he voted against the landmark Civil Rights Act of 1964. "I am not going to vote for Mr. Goldwater," Dr. King told a rally in Los Angeles. "I don't think any Negro and white person of goodwill will vote for Mr. Goldwater," he added. Black turnout soared in the November election that year, and a record 94 percent of Black voters opted for Democrat Lyndon Johnson, a dramatic shift from four years earlier, when 32 percent of Black voters supported Republican Richard Nixon.

Southern Republicans used the passage of the civil rights bill to appeal to racist white voters. A young Texas Republican named George Bush, running against Democratic senator Ralph Yarborough, "hit Yarborough on grounds that the civil rights bill which Yarborough voted for will cost white working men their jobs," the *Texas Observer* reported. Bush, who would become president in 1989, told the *Observer* in 1964 why he opposed the Civil Rights Act: "I want to see we don't violate the rights of 86 percent to try to correct the grievances—and legitimate ones, often—of the other 14 percent," he explained.

After signing the civil rights bill, Johnson reportedly told an aide that Democrats had "just delivered the South to the Republican party for a long time to come." Still, he went on to sign the Voting Rights Act of 1965 and the Fair Housing Act of 1968 and appointed Thurgood Marshall as the first Black justice on the US Supreme Court. His prediction for regional realignment didn't come true overnight, but in six of the next fourteen presidential elections after 1964, Democrats failed to carry even a single state in the South.

The *racial* realignment was more abrupt. While Black voters flocked to the Democratic Party, white voters began to leave. As a punishment for Johnson's racial perfidy, no Democratic candidate for president has won the white vote since 1964. Not Jimmy Carter. Not Bill Clinton. And not Barack Obama—in either of his two presidential elections. That's because Black and white voters understood in the 1960s that the two parties were slowly switching roles.

Nixon's presidential campaigns implemented what became known as the "Southern strategy," encouraging Republicans essentially to ignore the needs of Black voters and focus instead on disaffected white voters with "dog whistles" and subtle racial resentment politics. As Republican strategist Lee Atwater explained in a 1981 interview:

You start out in 1954 by saying, "Nigger, nigger, nigger." By 1968 you can't say "nigger"—that hurts you, backfires. So you say stuff like, uh, forced busing, states' rights, and all that stuff, and you're getting so abstract. Now, you're talking about cutting taxes, and all these things you're talking about are totally economic things and a byproduct of them is, blacks get hurt worse than whites. . . . "We want to cut this," is much more abstract than even the busing thing, uh, and a hell of a lot more abstract than "Nigger, nigger."

It's tempting for modern conservative commentators to claim the Democrats have lost touch with their working-class roots. This is far from true. What they mean is that *white* working-class voters have slowly moved away from Democrats; working-class voters of color have not left the party. That's because Democrats still support the same policies that have defined the party since the New Deal.

When Democratic president Harry Truman accepted his party's nomination for president in Philadelphia in July 1948, he called for "an increase in the minimum wage," a national "health program," higher teacher pay, "low-rent housing," support for labor, increased Social Security benefits, and even a "civil rights program," although he admitted, "Some of the members of my own party disagree with me violently on this matter."

"The Democratic Party is the people's party, and the Republican Party is the party of special interest," Truman argued. That fact hasn't changed since the 1930s. What has changed is that since the 1960s, traditional Democratic values and policies have expanded to become more inclusive. White working-class voters happily supported Democratic policies when *both parties* were openly racist and excluded Black Americans and other marginalized groups. But as Democrats slowly began to release their racist history and embrace African Americans, women, immigrants, Muslims, queer people, and other oppressed groups, Republicans found it easier to attract traditionally conservative white voters who only wanted those benefits for their own group.

I've been involved in numerous political campaigns over the course of four decades, and neither party is perfect on race issues. Joe Biden chaired the infamous 1991 Supreme Court confirmation hearings for Clarence Thomas that disregarded Professor Anita Hill's powerful testimony. Bill Clinton signed devastating welfare and crime bills in the 1990s. And Barack Obama failed to push on some critical issues of concern to Black voters.

But even with all their shortcomings, Democrats have been far superior to Republicans on race issues since the 1960s. Democrats support affirmative action. They produced the first Black president, first Black vice president, first Black Supreme Court Justice, and first Black official to lead a political party in Congress. And they've been the only ones in Congress to introduce bills to move forward on reparations. In contrast, Republicans have waged a fifty-year campaign to ban affirmative action and any effort to make amends for America's racial history.

It was Republican president Richard Nixon who launched what became the "war on drugs." And it was Republican president Ronald Reagan who nearly doubled the prison population in eight years, cut funds to Black communities, and refused to impose sanctions on the racist apartheid regime in South Africa. It was Republican George H. W. Bush who used a racist "Willie Horton" campaign ad to scare white voters about Black crime. It was Republican senator Jesse Helms who ran a notorious "white hands" TV ad about "minority" workers stealing jobs from white people. It was Republican mayor Rudy Giuliani who implemented a "broken windows" theory of policing and racially profiled Black men with stop-and-frisk policies. And it was a Republican Supreme Court that gutted the Voting Rights Act in 2013.

Although Democrats have sometimes been unduly cautious in advancing a racial justice agenda, their most notorious recent failures on race have more to do with Republican opposition than Democratic unwillingness. When President Biden tried to provide billions of dollars in aid to Black farmers who had been excluded from previous federal government loan programs, a Republican-appointed federal judge blocked him. When he tried to provide student loan debt relief that would disproportionately help Black borrowers, Republicans sued to stop him. When he tried to pass the John Lewis Voting Rights Act and the George Floyd Justice in Policing Act, Republicans filibustered those proposals in the Senate. And when he appointed the first Black woman to the Supreme Court, all but three Republican senators voted against her.

In contrast, when Kentucky's Black, Republican attorney general, Daniel Cameron, failed to charge the people responsible for the illegal warrant that led to the police killing of Breonna Taylor, Biden's Justice Department stepped in and won the case.

It takes a great deal of dishonesty for Black Republicans to claim that Democrats have done nothing for Black people or that Republicans would somehow do more. It also is the height of hypocrisy for Republicans to complain that Democrats were once the party of slavery when prominent leaders in their own party continue to defend the Confederate flag. It was, after all, a Republican president in 2017 who went out of his way to honor Democratic enslaver Andrew Jackson by placing his portrait in the Oval Office and making a presidential visit to Jackson's Tennessee slave plantation during his first two months in the White House. It was the Obama administration that chose to place Harriet Tubman on the twenty-dollar bill, while it was the Trump administration that stopped the proposal so it could continue to honor Jackson, the nineteenth-century enslaver.

Contrary to conservative stereotypes, most Black people are not delusional about either major political party. In my 2021 book, *Race Against Time*, I argued that "some Black people should join the Republican Party" to try to change it from the inside. That same year, I wrote an op-ed for the *Washington Post* titled "Either Party Can Win the Loyalty of Black Voters Moving Forward." But after those works were published, when I asked former Republican National Committee chairman Michael Steele if he agreed with my argument, he essentially told me it was too late. "I ran the party," Steele told me, and "there's no interest" in the GOP in reaching out to Black voters. Steele was the first Black person to lead the party, but when I asked if his party was now "irredeemable" in its current form, he told me, "Absolutely." Even as recently as 2023, Republican presidential candidates Mike Pence and Ron DeSantis signaled their distance from the party of Lincoln when they proposed to rename the US military base at Fort Liberty after

Braxton Bragg, a nineteenth-century enslaver and Confederate general who fought against US soldiers in the Civil War.

We may not know all the particulars of the Republican Party's history, but most Black voters have some understanding about the general outlines. We know that Democrats are far from perfect and that some Democrats are better than others on race, but we also know that Republicans have been openly hostile to racial progress for the last several decades. That's why Black voters have been the most loyal constituency of the Democratic Party. It's a calculation based on information, not ignorance. They're not "stuck on the Democratic plantation," as Black Republicans insultingly like to argue. Black voters know they can leave the Democratic Party any time they want, but post-1960s Republicans have yet to give them a reason to do so.

5

The Civil War was about slavery, not states' rights.

ARGUMENT

The existence of African servitude was in no wise the cause of the conflict, but only an incident.

—Jefferson Davis, United States senator from Mississippi and president of the Confederate States of America, 1881

ANSWER

Our position is thoroughly identified with the institution of slavery—the greatest material interest of the world.

—"A Declaration of the Immediate Causes Which Induce and Justify the Secession of the State of Mississippi from the Federal Union," January 9, 1861

It started with a car chase. As a thirteen-year-old boy in the Midwest, I was mesmerized by the images of souped-up vehicles racing through dirt roads, soaring over small hills on a country street like Evel Knievel taking flight across a canyon on his motorcycle. The folksy voice of country music star Waylon Jennings, the narrator, introduced the audience to two handsome young men in a Dodge Charger in hot pursuit of a sheriff's car.

It was early 1979, and I was watching the debut of a new action-comedy series called *The Dukes of Hazzard*. I was hooked instantly.

A familiar tune blew from the horn of the Dukes' high-performance muscle car as it recklessly leapt over a hill. It was the first verse of a song I had learned in my junior high school chorus class in Missouri, and I knew all the words by heart. *Oh, I wish I was in the land of cotton. Old times there are not forgotten. Look away! Look away! Look away! Dixie Land.*

My classmates and I had practiced that song many times, never fully appreciating how it glorified the antebellum South. "In Dixie Land, I'll take my stand / To live and die in Dixie," we sang, all the while overlooking the question of why a group of schoolchildren in late twentieth-century Missouri were being taught to sing a song that romanticized a faraway nineteenth-century land.

"Dixie" was part of Americana in the 1970s, taught in classrooms like mine alongside standards like "America the Beautiful." It was as much a part of my youthful midwestern cultural experience as the Friday fish fry at the local Catholic elementary school. I did not flinch when I heard the melody on the prime-time TV show that night. I had no idea that a band had played that same tune at the inauguration of Confederate president Jefferson Davis in 1861.

The music in the TV show didn't bother me. I was more focused on the orange 1969 Dodge Charger zooming through the streets, but it, too, was troubling, adorned with a Confederate battle flag and named after Confederate general Robert E. Lee. I rarely paid attention to the names of long-deceased military leaders in eighth grade, and I surely could not have identified an image of this general in a history book. All I knew was that the vehicle was cool and fast. Not since Speed Racer's Mach Five showed up on my parents' color TV screen had a car stolen my attention so quickly.

The blond-haired young man who drove the General Lee and his dark-haired passenger looked like more attractive versions of the young white men in my suburban Missouri neighborhood. "This is Bo Duke and Luke Duke," the narrator explained. "They're cousins. And they fight the system." Their fit bodies, smiling faces, and perfect teeth blended seamlessly with the strumming banjos of the show's chaotic opening scene to position the "boys" not only as fun-loving young men but as freedom fighters literally chasing the authorities in a video representation of southern defiance of oppressive laws.

Boss Hogg, the county's corpulent commissioner, provided a perfect foil for the Dukes as he schemed with corrupt sheriff Rosco P.

Coltrane to line his pocketbook at the expense of the hardworking residents of Hazzard County. Bo and Luke became the peoples' defenders, battling the crooked authorities in a vehicle not coincidentally named after the South's most famous Confederate hero.

It's complicated to argue that the now-controversial TV series *glorified* the Confederacy when its principal villain was named Jefferson Davis Hogg after the president of the Confederate States of America. Yet the show did *normalize* the Confederacy, by allowing teenage boys like me to become so engrossed in the car stunts and beautiful actors that we could easily ignore the casual nods to the racist rebellion against the Union.

The Dukes were just "good ol' boys," as Jennings reminded us in the show's theme song, fighting the system like a "modern-day Robin Hood," a message that was demonstrated in the very first episode when they stole slot machines from Boss Hogg to help fund an orphanage. The fact that their crew was shown speeding, driving recklessly, stealing police cars, unlawfully removing campaign signs, carjacking a truck, kidnapping a truck driver, assaulting a police officer and grabbing his gun, resisting arrest, and facilitating a jailbreak—all while Bo and Luke Duke were on probation for illegally making moonshine—was completely excusable because they were "never meanin' no harm."

I was too young to understand how this depiction normalized white privilege, but even at thirteen I should have known that no living Black person with an equivalent rap sheet would ever be seen as a lovable figure by white America. *The Dukes of Hazzard* positioned young white Confederate flag–bearing lawbreakers as good-looking, relatable people and contextualized them with sympathetic backstories, a courtesy rarely afforded to similarly situated Black people in real life.

In the show's pilot episode, Luke Duke literally grabs a sheriff's gun that was pointed at him without being shot. In another scene, Daisy Duke kicks the sheriff and steals his car, and lives to tell the story. For Black people, on the other hand, the consequences of even minor weapons and automobile offenses have often proved fatal. Twelve-year-old Tamir Rice was shot and killed by Cleveland police merely for playing with a pellet gun in a park, and twenty-eight-year-old Sandra Bland was arrested in Texas for questioning a police officer who accused her of failing to signal a lane change. Bland died in jail three days after she was arrested.

The Dukes of Hazzard was just art, its defenders respond. John Schneider, the actor who played Bo Duke, complained to Fox News in 2021 that "cancel culture" had forced the removal of the show's reruns from TV. Just a few years earlier, however, Fox News hosts had objected to a musical performance by Kendrick Lamar that began on top of a police car onstage at the 2015 BET Awards. "This is why I say that hip-hop has done more damage to young African Americans than racism in recent years," Geraldo Rivera opined. For Fox News, white characters stealing police cars and assaulting police officers under the banner of the Confederate flag in *The Dukes of Hazzard* could be portrayed as harmless art, but a Black artist rapping about the dangers of police brutality on top of a police car posed a grave threat to society.

As a child, I knew none of this history. I simply enjoyed watching *The Dukes of Hazzard* and tuned in faithfully, never fully appreciating how the seemingly innocuous TV show downplayed the malevolence of the Confederacy and romanticized the "Lost Cause" of America's bloodiest war. By reembodying General Lee as a spectacular stunt car, the show helped to refurbish the image of America's most rehabilitated traitor. Even the presence of tertiary Black characters, mistakenly cited as proof of the show's antiracism, communicated the troubling message that African Americans like me could trust the modern-day white southerners who proudly embraced the Confederate flag as "heritage, not hate." It was almost as if the epic conflict between slavery and freedom had been nothing more than a distant but friendly competition of similar ideas. But it was not.

Nearly 620,000 Americans were killed in the Civil War, a number "equal to the total of American fatalities in the Revolutionary War, the War of 1812, the Mexican War, the Spanish American War, World War I, World War II, and the Korean War, combined," according to historian Drew Gilpin Faust. Two percent of the nation's entire population perished because of the conflict, the equivalent of what would be almost seven million Americans killed in a single war today.

America has never experienced a conflict as brutal as the Civil War. In the Battle of Gettysburg alone, more than fifty thousand men died, equivalent to nearly 90 percent of the total American fatalities from the entire Vietnam War through the 1960s and 1970s—in the span of three days. The commander of the Confederate troops in Gettysburg, who sent nearly thirty thousand of his own men to their graves that week, was a fifty-six-year-old Virginia enslaver named Robert E. Lee.

In a letter to his wife in 1856, Lee observed that "blacks are immeasurably better off here than in Africa" and argued that "the painful discipline they are undergoing is necessary for their instruction as a race." Five years later, after eleven southern states abandoned the union in the wake of the election of President Abraham Lincoln, Lee knew that the cause of their secession was slavery.

Of all the interpretations of the cause for the Civil War, "the states' rights argument is perhaps the weakest," historian James McPherson wrote in 2007. "It fails to ask the question, states' rights for what purpose?" Yes, the South wanted states' rights, but they wanted them so they could maintain the institution of slavery. Yet in July 2015, a Florida gun shop owner named Andy Hallinan, standing in front of a Confederate flag, posted online a disturbing video announcing that his store would become a "Muslim-free zone." Asked about the flag in the 2018 documentary *Rest in Power: The Trayvon Martin Story*, Hallinan cited what he called a "common misconception" that the Civil War was about slavery. "When you study the history, that was *one thing* that the war was about," he said. "People don't go to war for one issue."

When asked to name other issues that caused the war, Hallinan struggled. "Uh, I mean, I'm not a historian," he said. A few moments later, he settled on an answer—the Civil War was about "tyranny," which he defined as "any time a government overreaches, and they control a life too much." The interviewer responded, "Like slavery?" Hallinan stared in silence.

At the time of the war, several secessionist states listed slavery as a principal reason for leaving the union. South Carolina, the first to secede in December 1860, complained of "an increasing hostility on the part of the non-slaveholding States to the institution of slavery."

Virginia, the home of General Lee, cited only one reason for leaving the union in its April 1861 secession ordinance: "the oppression of the Southern Slaveholding States." And Governor Isham Harris of Tennessee, the last state to secede, in June 1861, proposed to leave the union "if the non-slaveholding States refuse to comply" with the demand that the South be "forever slave."

The new Confederate government was organized on the principle of perpetuating slavery and white supremacy. In March 1861, Alexander Stephens, the vice president of the Confederate States of America, openly admitted that "African slavery" was the "immediate cause of the late rupture and present revolution." Even the 1861 Constitution of the Confederate States mentioned slavery ten times and prohibited any law "denying or impairing the right of property in negro slaves."

Yet, a century and a half after the Civil War, a Pew Research Center poll in 2011 found that nearly half of Americans thought the war was mainly about states' rights, while only 38 percent correctly stated it was mainly about slavery. Four years later, a CNN/ORC poll found that 57 percent of Americans saw the Confederate flag "more as a symbol of Southern pride than as a symbol of racism." And in 2018, a report from the Southern Poverty Law Center showed that only 8 percent of high school seniors could correctly identify slavery as the central cause of the Civil War. More than two-thirds of the students surveyed did not even know that it took a constitutional amendment to abolish slavery.

The results were not an accident. After the war ended, organizations like the United Daughters of the Confederacy spent years raising money to build Confederate monuments to obscure the truth about the Civil War. The group successfully promoted public school textbooks that valorized the Ku Klux Klan and demonized the Union for a "war of northern aggression." By the time Donald Trump took office in 2017, Confederate monuments existed in thirty-one states and the District of Columbia, far exceeding the reach of the eleven states in the actual Confederacy. The "150-year-old propaganda campaign," as writer Adam Serwer described it in *The Atlantic*, had tried "to erase slavery" as the cause of the war and "whitewash" the goals of the Confederacy. In so doing, the campaign normalized the most dangerous existential threat in the history of the United States and rebranded the rebels who fought to defend slavery as noble patriots.

It was not just *The Dukes of Hazzard* that created this problem. I saw it when I moved to the Plantation House Apartments in Little Rock, Arkansas, to work for Bill Clinton's 1992 presidential campaign and discovered Confederate flag images used to promote the Democratic ticket. I saw it when a local TV news reporter interviewed parents at Jefferson Davis High School in Montgomery, Alabama, and found little objection even from Black parents to the nearly all-Black school bearing the name of an infamous white enslaver. And I saw it in liberal Hollywood, California, in the annual Christmas Parade in late 2022, when the Dukes' famous orange Dodge Charger proudly rolled its way down Hollywood Boulevard with the Confederate flag on its roof and the sounds of "Dixie" on its horn.

The revisionism has now been normalized, as political leaders like Republican senator Tom Cotton of Arkansas have described slavery as "the necessary evil upon which the union was built." And in 2016, when First Lady Michelle Obama told the Democratic National Convention that "I wake up every morning in a house that was built by slaves," Fox News host Bill O'Reilly protested that the enslaved Black laborers "were well fed and had decent lodgings." The myth of the benevolent enslaver has become so pervasive that a tour guide at a slave plantation in South Carolina told the BBC in 2019 that probably the most frequently heard comment from white tourists was "Slavery was not that bad."

Today's conservatives have helped to minimize the public's perception of the severity of slavery by casually comparing it to any progressive policy they dislike. Dr. Ben Carson, a Black brain surgeon, Republican presidential candidate, and Trump administration official, diminished the evil of slavery and ignored the century of racist Jim Crow segregation policies that followed it when he claimed that Obamacare—which provided health care to more than thirty million Americans—was "the worst thing to happen to the nation since slavery." Black conservative Larry Elder ignored the nineteenth-century enslavers who broke apart and sold families of enslaved Black people when he misleadingly claimed to Fox News that "during slavery, a Black kid was more likely to be born under a roof with his biological mother and biological father than today." Other conservatives simply ignore the violent and disruptive legacy of hundreds of years of slavery, as Supreme Court justice Neil Gorsuch did when he complained that a few months of COVID restrictions may have been "the greatest intrusions on civil liberties in the peacetime history of this country."

In America, slavery defines the Confederacy, but the Confederacy does not define slavery. The sin of enslavement in this land predates both the Confederacy and the founding of the republic. But as long as we continue to deny the truth about slavery and ignore the symbols of its existence all around us, we preserve its legacy in the present.

Black people "need to move on" from bringing up slavery because it happened so long ago, conservative commentator Mark Steyn told Fox News host Tucker Carlson in 2019. Yet millions of white southerners have never moved on from the Civil War, which was fought to preserve what enslaver John C. Calhoun, a former US vice president, euphemistically reduced to a "peculiar institution."

The majority of Confederate monuments in the nation were not erected in the immediate years after the Civil War but were built decades later as symbols of opposition to Black empowerment, according to research by the Southern Poverty Law Center. The largest surge took place in the early 1900s as southern states were enacting Jim Crow laws to disenfranchise Black people, according to the center. A second surge took place during the civil rights movement of the 1950s and '60s, when dozens of schools were named after Confederate leaders. Even after Barack Obama was elected president in 2008, at least half a dozen southern states erected new Confederate monuments for the twenty-first century.

My aunt Susan graduated from Jefferson Davis High School in Montgomery, Alabama, in May 1974. The school was named after the Confederate leader in 1968, the same year that Dr. Martin Luther King Jr. was killed by an assassin's bullet. Rather than honoring King's historic 1955 Montgomery bus boycott, the district chose to name the school after Davis, who had been inaugurated as president of the treasonous Confederate states 107 years earlier. It was all designed to erase the violent, ugly history of the Confederacy and to replace it with a family-friendly image of white supremacy.

So successful was this century-long campaign of erasure that I found myself unknowingly worshiping at the altar of a Confederate monument as an adult. While I was teaching at a public high school in Georgia in 1989, I blithely spent my warm weekends climbing to the summit of Stone Mountain, oblivious to the images of the three Confederate generals carved in the mountain below me.

Ten years after *The Dukes of Hazzard* premiered on national television, I had been successfully programmed to ignore the symbols of hate all around me. That is the danger of normalizing the celebration of an evil past.

6

Black History Month is still needed in a society that denies Black contributions.

ARGUMENT

Why is there no White History Month?

—*Twitter trolls every February*

ANSWER

Every month is White History Month.

—*Comedian Amber Ruffin,*
February 5, 2021

In his ninety-five years on the planet, Johnny Gilbert has seen a lot. He's lived through the Great Depression, World War II, the Kennedy assassination, Vietnam, Watergate, and three presidential impeachments.

Today, the former nightclub singer from Newport News, Virginia, has one of the most familiar voices in the country. If you paid attention to American television in the past four decades, you probably heard him, although you may not recognize his face. He's best known for three words: "This . . . is . . . *Jeopardy.*"

As the announcer for the long-running television game show, Gilbert has seen some of the nation's smartest people answer questions on the nightly TV program on topics ranging from current events to ancient history. But sometimes, even the smartest people can make foolish mistakes. That's the most charitable explanation I can come up with to explain what happened on a November 2022 episode.

In the show, after a contestant selects a category and a monetary amount, the host gives a clue in the form of an answer, and the first of the three contestants to press their buzzer must respond with a matching question. On this episode, host Ken Jennings gave the $1,200 clue: "She's the first Black woman on the Supreme Court and the first justice to have been a federal public defender."

Then there was awkward silence. The three contestants, Amy, Maureen, and Tyler, all white, stood quietly and stared blankly at the board. When the time expired, Jennings gave the answer. "That's Justice Jackson," he said with a smile. "Ketanji Brown Jackson."

Jackson's first name may have been difficult for some to pronounce, and the contestants would have been forgiven if they'd simply answered, "Who is Justice Jackson?" But they said nothing. Not a single contestant even looked like they were struggling to think of the name. This was a judge whose name had been front-page news nearly all year, ever since her historic nomination.

The episode demonstrated just how quickly and easily stories of Black people in American history are forgotten. In 1981, President Reagan mistakenly assumed his only Black cabinet member, Secretary of Housing and Urban Development Samuel Pierce, was a city mayor he was meeting for the day. And, even at a White House event purportedly intended to celebrate Black History Month, Donald Trump seemingly had no clue about the identity of America's most famous Black abolitionist, Frederick Douglass.

Far too many Americans don't know much about the contributions of Black people in the nation's history, but each February, during Black History Month, a small but vocal element of white people, who are apparently upset that they are not getting enough attention the other eleven months of the year, recycle a tired old question: "Why is there no White History Month?"

The question is rooted in the privilege and entitlement that leads some to seek to center whiteness in every conversation. *Why is there a Black Entertainment Television and not a White Entertainment Television? Why are there no historically white colleges? If African American lawmakers can have a Congressional Black Caucus, why can't we have a Congressional White Caucus?*

Although the white interrogators often think these queries are clever and original, not one of these questions is new to Black people. Instead, they reflect the historical ignorance of the white people who ask them, which is one of the many reasons why Black History Month exists in the first place. The reason we have Black Entertainment Television, historically black colleges and universities, and the Congressional Black Caucus is the same reason we had Negro leagues in baseball before Jackie Robinson.

Throughout American history, Black people have been forced to create our own institutions, organizations, celebrations, and events because we have been locked out and excluded from white ones. For hundreds of years, white America created a society that prohibited Black people from their neighborhoods, churches, schools, colleges, restaurants, hotels, businesses, sports teams, and clubs, so we created institutions that supported and reflected ourselves.

The questions that Black people hear from white people each February often reflect a broader heteropatriarchal bias directed at women, people of color, and LGBTQ Americans in other months. Women's History Month doesn't require a Men's History Month, and gay pride parades don't necessitate straight pride celebrations. That's because members of privileged groups are validated in their identities 365 days a year. But is heterosexual cisgender white male identity really so fragile in America that it cannot withstand the momentary recognition of something different?

The truth is, as comedian Amber Ruffin reminds us, every month is White History Month in America—including Black History Month. White history, and specifically the history of straight cis white men, is taught every day. Every school kid knows Christopher Columbus, George Washington, Thomas Jefferson, Abraham Lincoln, FDR, and JFK. And even when America celebrates Presidents' Day *during Black History Month*, the country honors among the nation's leaders the twelve presidents who enslaved Black people.

We are taught to celebrate these and other white men not because they were the only ones who made historically significant contributions to the nation but because they were the ones writing and controlling that history. American history was written from a perspective that purposely excluded or diminished the contributions of women, people of color, and marginalized groups.

Most Black people already know a great deal about what some might call "white history." We must know these things to survive in a white-dominated country. But most white people don't necessarily know a lot about "Black history," or, more accurately, their own history as it relates to Black people. For example, a January 2021 poll by You-GovAmerica found that Black Americans were more likely than white Americans to say they know about Nat Turner's 1831 revolt (57 percent vs. 33 percent or the Montgomery bus boycott (81 percent vs. 65 percent).

Many of Black people's contributions to history and our role in the shaping of America have been whitewashed. That's one reason why writer Nikole Hannah-Jones put together *The 1619 Project*. And it provoked the inevitable backlash. In the final days of the Trump administration, the White House issued *The 1776 Report* to create a more patriotic version of American history, and in the following year, the State of Texas produced *The 1836 Project* to present a sanitized version of the state's history.

James Grossman, the executive director of the American Historical Association, told the *New York Times* that the flawed *1776 Report* used "myths, distortions," and "subtle misreading of evidence" to create a narrative and an argument "that few respectable professional historians, even across a wide interpretive spectrum, would consider plausible." Meanwhile, *The 1836 Project* downplays the desire of Texas's early pioneers to maintain slavery when explaining why Texas bolted from Mexico and all but erases the presence of the Indigenous, Spanish, and Mexican populations as it claims that Texas was "nearly depopulated" before brave American (white) settlers arrived.

While these campaigns replace history with fantasy, the real-life history of Black Americans often goes ignored. But Black history is American history. Our history is more than Martin and Malcolm and Rosa. It's even more than the oppression of enslavement and segregation.

When Kanye West in 2018 claimed that slavery was "a choice," he displayed his own ignorance and dishonored the legacy of the enslaved Africans who rebelled against their oppressors in South Carolina 250 years before the founding of the republic, and the legacy of the hundreds of other revolts in which Black people have fought against their enslavers.

This is precisely the reason why Black historian Carter G. Woodson created Negro History Week in February 1926, a commemoration that has now grown into what we celebrate every year as Black History Month. "If you can control a man's thinking you do not have to worry about his actions," Woodson once wrote. "If you make a man feel that he is inferior, you do not have to compel him to accept an inferior status, for he will seek it himself."

When celebrated actor Morgan Freeman told *60 Minutes* in 2005 that he found the idea of Black History Month to be "ridiculous," he revealed his own magical thinking about race in America by suggesting that racism would somehow disappear if we all simply "stop talking about it." With all due respect, that's what white Americans have been trying to force us to do since they brought our first ancestors to this country's shores hundreds of years ago. They crave the silence not because they seek to end racism but because they hope to maintain white supremacy while absolving themselves of the responsibility for the consequences of their own actions.

On the other hand, I fully understand that some twenty-first-century Black Americans do not like the idea of spending even a month every year rehashing what they perceive to be negative stories about Black suffering from the past. Other progressive African Americans complain that Black History Month is too limited and cannot be properly addressed in one month. I agree. Yes, Black history events need not focus only on the dark past. Yes, we should talk about Black history every month. And, yes, it is ironic that we celebrate this event each year during February, the shortest month of the year.

But whether it lasts twenty-eight days or thirty-one days, and irrespective of the fact that we must honor our history every day of the year, Black History Month still provides an opportunity to focus ourselves and the nation on our struggles, our victories, and our ambitions.

From James McCune Smith, the first African American to earn a medical degree, to Jocelyn Elders, the first Black US surgeon general, we must continue to tell our stories. We can tell the stories of mathematicians like Benjamin Banneker and Katherine Johnson, who helped to power our clocks and our spaceships. And we can share the true tales of warriors like Crispus Attucks, Harriet Tubman, and the Harlem Hellfighters, who fought and sometimes bled for freedom in our country's wars.

Black history is a rich history that can be enjoyed and appreciated by everyone. Intellectuals like Frederick Douglass and Angela Davis have changed the course of the nation's conversations. Activists like Bayard Rustin, Ella Baker, and Fannie Lou Hamer have reshaped our democracy. Elected officials like Joseph Rainey and Shirley Chisholm have pushed the nation to reimagine our vision of leadership. Judges like Constance Baker Motley and Thurgood Marshall have found new wisdom in our laws. Scholars like W. E .B. Du Bois and Claudine Gay have elevated our colleges and universities.

And from Marian Anderson to Tina Turner to Beyoncé, Satchel Paige to Muhammad Ali, Althea Gibson to Serena Williams, Black Americans have performed gracefully on the biggest stages in the world in packed auditoriums, arenas, fields, and stadiums across the continents.

That's a legacy that deserves to be celebrated.

PART TWO | CENTERING WHITE VICTIMHOOD

From 1943 to 1945, Irmgard Furchner served as a stenographer and typist at the Stutthof camp near Gdansk, Poland. At that time, the country was occupied by German forces who had stormed into Poland when Hitler's army invaded in September 1939. Furchner was not involved in the Nazi invasion, and there's no evidence that she committed any physical crimes against any of the people incarcerated in the prison camp. But as a Nazi secretary at the camp, she knew what was happening and served as a critical part of the administrative infrastructure that led to the murder of 10,505 people. That made her complicit.

In 2022, seventy-seven years after the Nazis had been defeated in World War II, Furchner was arrested and put on trial. By December, the ninety-seven-year-old former secretary was convicted for her role in the Holocaust. That same year, a German court sentenced Josef Schütz, a 101-year-old former Nazi, to five years of incarceration for serving as an accessory to murder while working as a prison guard at the Sachsenhausen concentration camp north of Berlin.

Some might consider these crimes ancient history and suggest that modern society should let bygones be bygones. They represent a time that many people would like to forget. And because the surviving perpetrators have aged into the elderly population during the decades since the 1940s, it's tempting to show mercy and sympathy. But the German government has rightly decided that the people responsible for the crimes of the past must be held accountable. There is no statute of limitations for murder.

Compare that to the United States of America. When slavery ended in 1865, no white person was convicted for their role in the brutal institution that often included the murder of innocent Black people. When the Civil War ended, President Andrew Johnson issued "a full pardon and amnesty" for all those involved in the treason and insurrection that resulted in the killing of American soldiers to defend the institution of slavery. And when Congress finally outlawed racial segregation in the Civil Rights Act of 1964, no white person was ever put on trial for their role in perpetuating a savage system that dehumanized and tortured Black people.

In the summer of 2022, a team of researchers discovered a sixty-seven-year-old arrest warrant for Carolyn Bryant Donham, the white woman whose false accusation led to the lynching of fourteen-year-old Emmett Till in August 1955. Her arrest warrant from 1955 had never been served. Its discovery led some to hope that she might finally be brought to justice. But when the case was presented to a Mississippi grand jury, they refused to indict her. She died in 2023, without ever being held legally accountable for her role in America's most notorious lynching.

The grand jury's decision continued a long pattern in American history of sweeping the interests of Black people under the rug to protect the feelings of white people. That's not justice. It's deflection.

Whenever Black people in America demand justice, many white people in America question how it will affect them. But instead of starting with the question of how this action affects white people, we should begin by asking how the (in)action affects the Black victims.

Even when our country has taken steps to protect Black people, the focus on white victimhood has undermined the original intent of those actions. The clear purpose of the Reconstruction amendments of the 1860s was to protect Black people after hundreds of years of enslavement, and the purpose of the civil rights laws of the 1960s was to protect Black people after a century of state-sanctioned segregation. They were not designed to protect white people from racial discrimination because white people were not suffering from such discrimination. But today's "race-neutral" reading of history has allowed white people to hijack historically race-specific remedies to serve white interests. Instead of answering the question of how to make Black people whole, we've moved to the question of how to prevent white people from being hurt.

The chapters that follow in Part 2 of this book focus on how the practice of white centering has turned critical conversations about racial justice for Black people into diversionary debates about white feelings.

7

Affirmative action is not "reverse discrimination."

ARGUMENT

Mr. Hooks favors affirmative action, which involves racial quotas or goals in hiring. It is, by whatever name, reverse discrimination.

—*George Will, in a syndicated column responding to NAACP executive director Benjamin Hooks, November 18, 1976*

ANSWER

Reverse racism is a cogent description of affirmative action only if one considers the cancer of racism to be morally and medically indistinguishable from the therapy we apply to it.

—*Author Stanley Fish, November 1993*

Many years ago, a Black teenager in the small town of Safety Harbor, Florida, had an unlikely dream. The boy shared his dream with his guidance counselor, a middle-aged white man unaccustomed to any lofty ambitions from his students, Black or white, at the local high school. The guidance counselor listened courteously and then revealed a look of concern.

The counselor assumed he knew enough about the boy's history to make an informed recommendation. He knew the boy had been a transfer student from two other high schools. He knew the boy's race, his slightly above-average grades, his below-average test scores, and how involved he was in sports and campus activities. It was not a negative student file, but it did not appear to the counselor to be an impressive record of achievement.

The counselor did not know that the boy was the product of what was once called a "broken home" or that his mother had been an orphan raised in a foster home and his father had abandoned him before birth, but had he known, it would not have changed his advice. Nor did he know that the boy had been born in what was once called "the ghetto," but he may have assumed as much from his experience dealing with the other Black students at the school, many of whom were bused in from the local projects.

Based on what he knew from his years of experience, the guidance counselor informed the boy that his dream to attend an elite college out of state was likely beyond his reach and suggested the teenager pursue a more modest goal somewhere in Florida after high school.

The teenager left the meeting with a sense of disappointment, and the guidance counselor may have assumed that would be the end of the student's pipe dream. But the boy was not completely dissuaded. He applied to several universities and was admitted to some, rejected by others, and waitlisted by one. Sadly, he was not admitted into the dream school he most wanted to attend, but against what seemed to be all odds, one of the schools that did accept him was an Ivy League college in New England.

The teenager "matriculated"—a word he had never heard before college—at the Ivy League school and met with mixed success at first. Like many students, he struggled to identify a major and performed better in some classes than others. But he found a passion in campus activities, joined a sports team as a walk-on athlete, and started working for the student newspaper. Those activities kept him disciplined and engaged in his schoolwork, and things eventually started to click for him.

Then something unexpected happened. At the end of his first year at the elite Ivy League college, the Black student received a letter from the first-year dean informing him that he had won an award as the outstanding freshman man in his class. He thought it was a mistake when he opened the letter and wasn't sure if the school would rescind the award when they realized what they had done. But they never did.

In his next few years on campus, things got better. He competed in the NCAA championships in the very sport in which he had not been recruited, and he served as the editor in chief of the influential daily college newspaper. By the time he graduated, he received another surprising award from the school. It was an all-around achievement award given to "the member of the Senior Class who shows the greatest promise of becoming a factor in the outside world through strength of character and qualities of leadership, record of scholarship and broad achievement, and influence among their fellow students."

After college, he attended Harvard Law School, served in the White House, started a civil rights organization, taught at Columbia University, worked as a political commentator on CNN, and published seven books, including this one. As you've no doubt figured out by now, I was that teenage boy, and the reason I was able to access those opportunities is that the admissions office at Dartmouth College saw potential in me even though my test scores fell well below the college's median. Yes, I was one of those Black students admitted to my college, in part, because of affirmative action.

At first, I was intimidated by my classmates and suffered from impostor syndrome because I did not know that I deserved to be there. Although I had taken Advanced Placement courses at my public high school in Florida, many of my elite college classmates were wealthy prep school grads who were much better prepared for the first year than I was. As I got to know them, however, I realized they were no smarter than I was. But unlike me, they had parents who graduated from college, spoke the Queen's English, enrolled them in the best schools, put them in test prep courses, and gave them a sense of confidence.

I also wrongly assumed my admission meant the college had lowered its standards to allow me to attend. Although I reflexively defended the school's policies from the student critics on my conservative campus, I did not fully grasp the background and history of affirmative action and how it worked.

The term "affirmative action" dates back at least to the New Deal, when President Roosevelt signed the Wagner Act of 1935, requiring employers to take "affirmative action" to correct unfair labor practices. In 1961, Democratic president John F. Kennedy issued the first executive order requiring government contractors to "take affirmative action" in employment practices, to include workers previously excluded based on "race, creed, color, or national origin." Four years later, Democratic president Lyndon B. Johnson issued an executive order prohibiting federal contractors from employment discrimination based on race, color, religion, and national origin. In 1967, he amended his order to include sex as a protected category. And in 1969, Republican president Richard Nixon extended affirmative action with his own executive order.

Since the 1970s, however, affirmative action has been vigorously challenged and criticized by conservative Republicans. In 1978, the US Supreme Court prohibited explicit racial quotas but allowed for "a properly devised admissions program involving the competitive consideration of race and ethnic origin." It was through "the competitive consideration of race" that I was admitted to Dartmouth College in the spring of 1983. Race was not the only component that contributed to my admission, but it was *a factor* that the school, a predominantly white institution, was allowed to consider.

Under pressure from Republicans to abolish affirmative action, Democratic president Bill Clinton spoke in 1995 and urged the nation to "mend it, but don't end it." As the Supreme Court became dominated by Republican appointees, the pro–affirmative action majority narrowed. The court upheld affirmative action in 2003 in a 5–4 decision in *Grutter v. Bollinger* and again in 2016 in a 4–3 decision in *Fisher v. University of Texas*. But when the high court overturned *Roe v. Wade* in the summer of 2022 and heard new affirmative action cases that fall, it was clear affirmative action was doomed.

While much of the debate about the policy has focused on Black people, "the primary beneficiaries of affirmative action have been Euro-American women," Professor Kimberlé Crenshaw explained in an article for the *Michigan Law Review* in 2006. A 1995 report by the US Department of Labor found that affirmative action policies had benefited six million women. Another study the same year in California found that "white women held a majority of managerial jobs (57,250) compared with African Americans (10,500), Latinos (19,000), and Asian Americans (24,600) after the first two decades of affirmative action," according to Vox. But we rarely hear complaints about affirmative action for white women.

Affirmative action helped the nation build a fairer society. The people who fought for civil rights in the 1950s and 1960s understood that the passage of federal civil rights legislation, however critical, would not root out racism in people's hearts or end racial discrimination in their actions.

A year after the Civil Rights Act was passed, President Johnson called on the nation to move to the "next and the more profound stage of the battle for civil rights" when he delivered the commencement address at Howard University in June 1965: "You do not take a person who, for years, has been hobbled by chains and liberate him, bring him up to the starting line of a race, and then say, 'You are free to compete with all the others,' and still justly believe that you have been completely fair."

In Johnson's words, it was "not enough just to open the gates of opportunity" if Black Americans did not "have the ability to walk through those gates." Telling Black people that we were equal under the law without providing the federal resources to implement that equality was meaningless.

White America's resistance to Johnson's more aggressive action has led to the persistence of dramatic racial inequality in employment, access to health care, education, student loan debt, housing, household income, criminal justice, and environmental conditions. By 2019, for example, median household income for Black households was $45,438 compared to $76,057 for non-Hispanic white households, according to the Census Bureau. Even as Black families began to move to middle-class suburbs, they gained the illusion of equality but were never fully equal with their white counterparts whose families maintained a head start because their parents or grandparents were never forced to attend underfunded racially segregated public schools.

By ignoring the historical context that led to racial disparities, the same white Americans who fought against civil rights for Black people suddenly found a way to portray themselves as victims of affirmative action. They called it "reverse discrimination." It was an argument as old as Reconstruction, when Judge Daniel G. Fowle complained as early as 1866, one year after the formal end of slavery, about "unjust discrimination against the white race and in favor of the negro." Then in 1883, as the Ku Klux Klan began to rise in power, the Supreme Court warned that basic civil rights protections for a people who had only recently been liberated from enslavement would somehow make Black Americans "the special favorite of the laws."

I heard similar arguments as a college student when pampered white classmates would complain that Black students like me had taken spots from their peers. It didn't matter that we had classmates who received preferential treatment because they came from wealthy families or were children of alumni, or both. One of my schoolmates, Nelson Rockefeller Jr., had an entire building named after his famous father on campus. But no one ever questioned how those students were admitted or whether they had special advantages from their upbringing that Black students rarely did.

It was the Reagan '80s, and the idea of white victimhood was popular because it promoted the myth that the remedy for centuries of racism was the same as, or worse than, the disease itself. Mediocre white men had been admitted to elite schools for centuries without raising an eyebrow of concern on those campuses, but the presence of intelligent Black and brown students caused a ruckus among white conservatives.

Conservatives promoted myths that colleges and employers were selecting unqualified people. But in my case, I came to learn this was not true. Yes, my test scores were not the best, but I was *differently* qualified. Despite all the obstacles I had faced as a young Black kid in a white society, I had become the president of my student government at a non-Black high school, an award-winning debater, an editor of our school newspaper, a columnist for the local city newspaper, a successful varsity athlete, the chair of the local school board student committee, and a member of the Safety Harbor Parks and Recreation Commission.

I also understood that no one had an absolute right to attend any selective college because admissions decisions are based on the needs of the institution in any given year. If there had been ten other kids like me who applied, I might not have been admitted, but that year I stood out. Years later, when I helped my friend Chris Georges on a book called *100 Successful College Application Essays*, I read binders of boring, predictable essays to find a few gems to include in the book and came to appreciate how important it was for admissions officers to identify students who make a unique impression.

If they wanted to, top schools could probably limit their incoming classes to people with perfect test scores, but they might end up with a student population from privileged backgrounds who all took the same test prep courses and all attended the same prep schools in Connecticut, Massachusetts, New York, and California. But what would this accomplish?

When voters in California passed Proposition 209 in 1996, prohibiting public universities from considering race in admissions, the Black share of the freshman class at UC Berkeley fell by half, to 3 percent, and the Latino share dropped to 7 percent. By 2022, Latinos, who accounted for 55 percent of California's public school students, represented only 19 percent of UC Berkeley undergraduates. How does it help students to navigate their young careers in a diverse state when they graduate from a school without the same diversity as the population into which they enter?

Race and ethnicity should never be the *only* factor determining whether a student is admitted to a college, but neither should it be the only factor that college admissions officers cannot consider. Just like test scores and numerical indicators, race does not tell us everything we need to know about a student, their full story, or their potential, but it does give us one valuable data point to consider.

Many colleges already recognize the limitations and false sense of meritocracy provided by test scores, and some have started to move away from them. Test scores don't measure raw intelligence, artistic or athletic talent, tenacity, honesty, courage, or other nonacademic abilities important for success in life. If universities focused on only one criterion or were forced to ignore an important criterion, they would deprive students of the opportunity to learn from people who look, act, think, and experience the world differently.

For me, the experience of college was enriched by heated debates with conservative intellectual friends, passionate conversations with liberal activist friends, late nights with student newspaper colleagues, and field trips with track-and-field buddies. We were all differently skilled and differently qualified to be there.

Despite the conservative rhetoric to the contrary, affirmative action is not about selecting "unqualified minorities" to fill a quota. It's about selecting among many qualified candidates to provide opportunities to people who have often been overlooked. It's about building a pipeline for *future* qualified candidates. And it's about understanding which qualifications are essential and which reflect preconceived biases not relevant to a candidate's performance or ability.

The great irony here is that for all their complaints about liberal "identity politics," conservative critics of affirmative action in the GOP often engage in the very sin they decry by elevating right-wing women and people of color for prominent positions as a political tactic in response to the diversity they see in the Democratic Party. But the true purpose of affirmative action is not to help any political party make short-term electoral gains. The concept of affirmative action that Kennedy, Johnson, and Nixon articulated was about rebalancing the scales of justice after centuries of weighted favoritism for white men.

So when does it end? Unfortunately, you can't erase the scars of 350 years of slavery and 100 years of state-sponsored racial terrorism with 50 or 60 years of a limited government policy. As President Johnson said in his speech at Howard, we must commit to equality not just "as a right and a theory but equality as a fact and equality as a result." So the work ends when we finally reach equality and eliminate racial disparities. That hasn't happened and isn't likely to happen soon without a major shift in our priorities.

Maybe affirmative action is not the answer for the long-term future. Maybe there's another way to reach "equality as a result." Before we replace it, though, we ought to have an alternative solution, or we'll find ourselves moving backward on race issues instead of forward. Whatever method we choose to reach President Johnson's goal, it will be controversial because the only way to disrupt the inertia of four hundred years is to change the status quo.

Any alternative solution must prove itself to be more effective and less disruptive than affirmative action at reaching the goal of equality.

That's a difficult task because affirmative action benefits everyone. It creates a more just society. It exposes all of us to new people, ideas, and experiences. It makes us more competitive as a nation in a world where most of the inhabitants are people of color. It creates opportunities for historically underrepresented groups. It reduces social tension in marginalized communities. So if we are going to improve on affirmative action, those are the baseline qualities we should expect.

Justice Ketanji Brown Jackson's dissenting opinion in the Supreme Court's 2023 decision striking down affirmative action is worth reading in full. Jackson painstakingly explains the long history of federal government policies that "affirmatively acted" to dole out preferences to white people throughout the 1800s and 1900s and how the race-based gaps that still exist today are echoes from the actions of centuries ago. Requiring colleges to ignore the race-linked opportunity gap "will inevitably widen that gap, not narrow it," she writes. The way to end affirmative action, Jackson argues, is to provide opportunities today so that future generations will compete in a society where race no longer matters. "But deeming race irrelevant in law does not make it so in life," she writes.

It is not easy or quick to root out racial discrimination. We should still be guided by the words of the Reverend Martin Luther King Jr. In a speech at the National Cathedral in Washington, DC, in 1968, Dr. King articulated the need for transformational public policy to confront the centuries-long legacy of racial bias and white supremacy: "We must come to see that the roots of racism are very deep in our country, and there must be something positive and massive in order to get rid of all the effects of racism and the tragedies of racial injustice."

Four days later, he was assassinated in Memphis.

8

Even the poorest white people have white privilege.

ARGUMENT

My neighborhood was poor Black, poor white.... So I didn't feel any white privilege. I know some people had it.... I knew some motherfuckers with sweaters. But I was two tank tops in the winter.

—*Comedian Theo Von,*
August 22, 2017

ANSWER

I have come to see white privilege as an invisible package of unearned assets which I can count on cashing in each day, but about which I was "meant" to remain oblivious. White privilege is like an invisible weightless knapsack of special provisions, maps, passports, codebooks, visas, clothes, tools and blank checks.

—*Author Peggy McIntosh,*
July/August 1989

A few years back, a Black teenager in Chicago named Keshawn had an epiphany. He saw an Instagram post about a Black Lives Matter protest and decided he wanted to be involved. Black people were under attack, he felt, and he wanted to fight on their behalf. Against his mother's wishes, Keshawn dropped out of high school and started getting involved in the movement.

One day he was scrolling through Instagram on his phone and came across a photo of Malcolm X. It was an iconic image that had appeared in *Ebony* magazine in 1964, taken by a Black photographer named Don Hogan Charles. In the photograph, Malcolm X was

WHY DOES EVERYTHING HAVE TO BE ABOUT RACE?

shown pulling back the curtains of a window in his home in Queens, New York, while holding a rifle in his other hand. The prophetic scene represented the threats Malcolm and his family faced just a few months before he was assassinated.

After seeing the image, Keshawn decided he wanted a gun. At seventeen, he was too young to buy one legally, so he asked his sister's nineteen-year-old boyfriend to get an AR-15 rifle and hold it for him.

Not long afterward, the seventeen-year-old was visiting his grandmother when he saw a story on the news about a right-wing rally in nearby Indiana, where a group of conservatives were amassing to defend a controversial Confederate monument. He called his sister's boyfriend to get the gun, put some gas in the tank of his grandmother's car, and jumped on the Dan Ryan Expressway to begin his drive to Indiana.

When he arrived at the scene that night, he joined a group of counterprotesters, openly carrying his AR-15 in the streets to patrol and protect the neighborhood. As the evening passed, he broke off from the group and eventually found himself in the middle of an unfriendly crowd of Confederate defenders. He felt threatened, pointed his gun, and shot one of them. Then he ran from the scene of the crime. The protesters scrambled to flee, but a few pursued him and tried to stop him from getting away.

When he saw them coming, Keshawn turned around and shot again, killing two of them on the street.

He kept running.

The police arrived on the scene in riot gear moments later. One of the white Confederate supporters continued filming Keshawn from a distance as he ran down the street, fully expecting that the police would stop and arrest him.

While still carrying his assault rifle on a strap, Keshawn knew he was about to be in trouble. He raised his hands to surrender to the police. The white man who filmed the scene yelled out to the police that the Black teenager with the gun had just shot two people in the street. But as three armored police vehicles approached Keshawn, they did nothing. They drove right by him. An officer in one vehicle even used his PA system to ask the Black teenage killer for help identifying the victims. "Someone injured straight ahead?" the officer asked.

Even after shooting three people, killing two of them, carrying the murder weapon over his shoulders, offering to surrender to police, and being identified as the killer by a bystander, the police never arrested him.

Keshawn kept walking and returned home. He became a celebrity in Black communities and made appearances on BET and MSNBC. Once he was finally charged with a crime, he raised millions of dollars to buy the best lawyers to defend him in court. A jury of eleven Black people and one other person acquitted him of all charges. A few days later, he met with former president Obama and took a celebratory photograph. Just two Black men who beat the system.

If this all sounds ridiculous, it's because it never happened. Yet this is the mirror image of what did happen with Kyle Rittenhouse, a white seventeen-year-old high school dropout from Antioch, Illinois, who crossed state lines with an illegal gun and shot three people at a Black Lives Matter protest in Kenosha, Wisconsin, in the summer of 2020. He was feted as a hero and acquitted of all charges, and then he flew down to Mar-a-Lago to meet with former president Trump. If there was ever any doubt about the existence of white privilege, there is no more dramatic recent example than the police failing to arrest a visibly armed Kyle Rittenhouse after he had just shot and killed two people. If Kyle had been Keshawn, the outcome very likely would have been different.

Unarmed seventeen-year-old Trayvon Martin couldn't even walk home from a convenience store with a bag of candy and a soft drink without being profiled, followed, assaulted, and killed by a neighborhood watchman. Unarmed twenty-two-year-old Rekia Boyd was just hanging out with friends in a city park when she was shot and killed by an off-duty Chicago police detective. Unarmed twenty-three-year-old Elijah McClain was merely walking down the street in Aurora, Colorado, when police approached him in an encounter that led to his death. All three victims were Black.

For far too many Americans, a white man with a gun appears less threatening than a Black person without one. Implicit bias tests have found that ordinary people are more likely to associate Black people with danger, and even a 2017 report in *Police Quarterly* acknowledged that trained police officers "tend to associate African Americans with threat."

If you're white and you don't worry about everyday experiences turning into deadly confrontations, you can thank your white privilege for that. And thanks to the unique terms and conditions, you don't have to be rich to receive it.

Even poor people have white privilege. That's not to say that low-income white families don't struggle to survive. They do, and America bears a responsibility to help all its citizens. But white privilege is designed to be unacknowledged by its beneficiaries.

White privilege is not based on individual income or economic circumstances. It's based on the cultural currency that comes from whiteness. As white author Liz Gumbinner posted on Twitter in April 2021, "No one looks at your bank account before pulling a gun on you for a traffic violation." That's the privilege of whiteness in an ordinary police stop, and it's replicated in thousands of other spaces and places of everyday life.

To understand this discussion, it's important to recognize that privilege is relative. For example, although I am Black, I still have privilege as a cisgender man, an American, and a person with a college degree. I have more privilege than some and less than others. Nearly everyone has privilege relative to someone else.

If you are an American who has traveled abroad, which itself is a privilege, you may have discovered that a United States passport grants you a certain sort of privilege. Once, when I studied in Spain and took a trip across the Mediterranean to Morocco, I discovered that a classmate from my college's foreign study program could not enter the country because she was Trinidadian and needed a visa, while I could walk right in as American.

In my travels to Cuba, to the Dominican Republic, and throughout Latin America, I've discovered that an American passport can be a useful tool, especially as a Black man. On several occasions, my Black friends who lived in those countries were stopped, detained, and arrested by the police, but my American passport often protected me. On the other hand, if I were to travel to Russia, North Korea, or Iran, I might want to conceal my American identity in some circumstances.

One could also think of privilege as a state driver's license. It enables you to vote, cash a check, or operate a motor vehicle, but it will not work at an ATM. It gives you many benefits in many circumstances but not in others. It could be a get-out-of-jail-free card but not a debit card. But even the ability to move about the world freely without harassment has economic value.

In a frequently cited 1993 article in the *Harvard Law Review*, law professor Cheryl Harris explained how "the law has established and protected an actual property interest in whiteness itself." Citing James Madison's definition of property as "every thing to which a man may attach a value and have a right," Harris showed how white identity confers "tangible and economically viable benefits" that have been "jealously guarded as a valued possession."

Think of it this way. Nathan Connolly and Shani Mott, a Black married couple in Baltimore, had their home appraised for $472,000. They felt the number was low, so they tried something different. A few months later, they removed any signs that Black people lived there and asked a white man to pretend it was his home. This time a second appraiser valued the exact same home at $750,000, a $278,000 gain. It's a process called "whitewashing," and Black homeowners find themselves doing it so they won't be ripped off.

In Seattle, the Clark family had their three-bedroom home appraised at $670,000. After removing African art and family pictures indicating they were Black, a second appraiser valued the home at $929,000, a $259,000 gain. And in Northern California, the Austin family had their beautiful home appraised for $995,000. But when they whitewashed their home and asked a white friend to pretend it was his, the property value skyrocketed to nearly $1.5 million, a gain of nearly half a million dollars.

That's the benefit of white privilege, and most white people are free to live without acknowledging its existence. A study by the Urban Institute in 2020 found that Black *college graduates* had a lower home-ownership rate than white *high school dropouts*. Even beyond home-ownership, a study by Demos in 2015 found that white people who dropped out of high school were wealthier than Black and Hispanic people who graduated from college.

But what about white families who can't afford a home? "Even when the white working class did not collect increased pay as part of white privilege," Harris wrote in her law review article, "there were real advantages, not paid in direct income." She cited a pattern that has existed for centuries, as W. E. B. Du Bois noted in his book *Black Reconstruction in America, 1860–1880*. Whiteness might have "small effect upon the economic situation," said Du Bois, but "great effect on their personal treatment."

There's a famous 1980s *Saturday Night Live* skit where Black cast member Eddie Murphy goes undercover as a white man. After a makeup artist changes his appearance, he dons a suit and a brief-case and moves about the city, finding that store clerks, bus drivers, and even bank loan officers treat him differently. In one scene, a white banker gladly gives him $50,000 in cash when he asks for a loan with no collateral, no credit, and no ID. The skit, called "White Like Me," obviously exaggerates the benefits of whiteness to make a point. The way white privilege works in the real world is somewhat more subtle.

"I have come to see white privilege as an invisible package of unearned assets which I can count on cashing in each day, but about which I was 'meant' to remain oblivious," wrote author Peggy McIntosh in her seminal 1989 piece called "White Privilege: Unpacking the Invisible Knapsack." McIntosh described white privilege as "an invisible weightless knapsack of special provisions, maps, passports, code-books, visas, clothes, tools and blank checks."

It's like raising your arm to get a taxi on the street and not having to worry about your skin color. Or walking into a store and not being followed by security. Or submitting a job application with no concern that your name sounds "too ethnic." It's the ability to live your life normally without the weight of race as a permanent background issue.

If you're broke and white and barely getting by, the idea of white privilege may seem unimaginable in a world with Black billionaires, professional athletes, celebrities, and even a Black president and vice president. How could you possibly have privilege over such successful Black people? Well, from a purely economic perspective, you don't. But from a racial perspective, you still do. If you could trade places with any of those people and become rich and Black, your financial condition would improve dramatically, but it would not insulate you from the issue of race.

Successful Black people have proved the persistence of white privilege when they have found themselves on the wrong side of it: Academy Award–winning actor Forest Whitaker was falsely accused of shoplifting and frisked by an overzealous employee at a Manhattan deli. A store employee told the *New York Daily News* it was just "an honest mistake." Harvard professor Henry Louis Gates was accused of breaking into his own home and wrongly arrested in Cambridge, Massachusetts. America's first Black president was forced to hold a "beer summit" to apologize to the officer after expressing his opinion that the police had "acted stupidly" by arresting the professor. And former professional tennis star James Blake was tackled and handcuffed by police outside a New York hotel as he waited for his car to take him to the US Open. NYPD later claimed it was a case of mistaken identity.

African Americans have been complaining about incidents like these for centuries, but they were rarely documented until the smartphone era brought video cameras to our pockets. Suddenly we could provide proof of what was happening all around us, and the internet exploded with examples. In 2018, CNN prepared a brief list of incidents from just that year when police were called on Black people who were involved in absolutely ordinary activities, including barbecuing at a park, babysitting two white children, moving into an apartment, cashing a paycheck, waiting for a friend at Starbucks, operating a lemonade store, and even golfing too slowly. In 2020, a white woman even called the police on a Black man in New York City's Central Park because he asked her to follow the rules and keep her dog on a leash.

Such incidents have been happening to Black people for years, regardless of their socioeconomic status. In one case, a woman called the police on three Black Airbnb guests because she thought it was suspicious that they didn't wave at her. In another example, a prominent Black law professor once told me he wore a suit every time he left the house because it gave him protection from the police. Even Black Republican senator Tim Scott acknowledged he had been stopped several times by police officers at the US Capitol.

In 2015, Black pollster Cornell Belcher released a report called *Hailing While Black* that showed that two-thirds of African Americans in Chicago felt that taxicab drivers deliberately discriminated against them. It was a truth I experienced numerous times in New York City when taxis would pass me by and pick up white customers instead, and it was for that reason that I welcomed the introduction of new services like Uber and Lyft. Then a 2018 study from UCLA found that Black rideshare customers experienced longer wait times and more cancellations than white, Asian, or Hispanic customers. As the technology evolved, the racism simply morphed into a different form and venue.

Many white Americans don't see, believe, or want to believe that these racist incidents still take place so frequently in this country. That, too, reflects white privilege. Years ago, I heard a law professor explain racism with an analogy about a magnet. Think of the big red-and-silver horseshoe magnets from science class. Now imagine you have to walk around the world with a huge version of this magnet on your neck all day, every day, while most other people do not.

Aside from the weight of carrying the magnet, the first thing you may notice is the omnipresence of metal in the world. Keys, coins, cell phones, even appliances would suddenly get a lot more of your attention as the magnet attracts them. But those without the magnet would continue to remain oblivious to the metallic assault on your body. Racism operates in a similar way on African Americans. We are constantly inundated by the metal of racism while those who do not carry the magnet of Blackness remain oblivious to our experience. All of this is exhausting for many of us who are African American.

In a 1977 episode of the TV series *Little House on the Prairie*, actor Todd Bridges played the role of Solomon, the young son of a Black Mississippi sharecropper whose father has been killed. He goes to the Ingalls family for help, and they take him in. One day, Solomon gets in trouble for something he said in school, and he explains his actions to Michael Landon's character, Charles Ingalls.

"If I was white, my pa would still be alive," Solomon says. "Those days are over," Charles replies assuredly. "You can start a new life now." Solomon doesn't buy it. "Ain't nothing over," he says. "Laws don't change nothing." Then Solomon asks a simple question that stumps Charles. "Would you rather be Black and live to be a hundred or white and live to be fifty?" Charles doesn't respond.

We all know the answer, but some people don't want to say it. That's white privilege.

9

Yes, European immigrants struggled, but they were not slaves.

ARGUMENT

White Irish slaves were treated worse than any other race in the U.S. When is the last time you heard an Irishman bitching and moaning about how the world owes them a living?

—Tea Party meme, 2013

ANSWER

The "Irish slaves" meme is a subset of the "white slavery" contemporary discourse which emphasizes class over race and is fueled by a potent cocktail of bad history, false equivalence, conspiracy theories, and reductionist fallacies.

—Liam Hogan, research librarian at the Limerick City Library, April 19, 2016

When George Wallace lost his 1958 bid to be governor of Alabama as a moderate Democrat, the future infamous segregationist came to a stunningly racist conclusion: "I was out-niggered, and I will never be out-niggered again," he told an aide. Four years later, he ran a blatantly bigoted campaign and won the election.

Half a century after that, Republican Tim James ran for the same post with his own blatantly bigoted message, updated for modern times. In a controversial campaign ad, he asked why the state gave driver's license exams in multiple languages. "This is Alabama. We speak English. If you want to live here, learn it," he said.

Alabama is not known as a hotbed of progressive thinking in America, but the anti-immigrant sentiment James hoped to tap into was never limited to his state. America's history with immigration has been inconsistent at best. On the one hand, we celebrate a Statue of Liberty emblazoned with the words "Give me your tired, your poor, / Your huddled masses yearning to breathe free." On the other hand, we elected a president who gained popularity for claiming that Mexico was sending rapists and drug dealers across the border and promising to ban all Muslims from entering the country.

Americans can swoon at the sound of British and Australian accents at a local bar or pub yet ignore the cries of Haitian immigrants chased by border patrol agents on horseback. Our current debates about immigration reflect not a fear of foreigners but a panic about people of color entering the country.

We like to tell ourselves that we are a nation of immigrants, yet we use this limited fantasy to romanticize our vision of determined European migrants sailing through New York Harbor into Ellis Island. "My grandfather came here with nothing but the clothes on his back, but he worked hard and built a business from the ground up," we hear people say.

The effect of these messages is to center white victimhood from yesterday and erase the concerns of people of color today. This "get over it" form of racism, according to Irish scholar Liam Hogan, is based on a belief that Black people can't move on in life because of their racial inferiority or social pathology. The argument communicates the mistaken idea that modern racism and xenophobia are easily overcome by hard work and assimilation. *My people were oppressed, too, and they got over it, so why can't you?* These stories also promote a "melting pot" myth that the "wholesome" ancestors of the past seamlessly assimilated into American culture. Even Martin Luther King Jr. recalled hearing these stories in the 1960s, as he explained in a speech in March 1968:

> I remember the other day I was on a plane and a man starting talking with me, and he said, "I'm sympathetic toward what you're trying to do, but I just feel that you people don't do enough for yourself," and then he went on to say that "My problem is, my concern is, that I know of other ethnic groups, many of the ethnic groups that came to this country and they had problems just as negroes and yet they

did the job for themselves, they lifted themselves by their own boot-straps. Why is it that negroes can't do that?"

Dr. King looked at the man and told him that he "failed to recognize that no other ethnic group has been enslaved on American soil." King then told the man that "nobody, no ethnic group has completely lifted itself by its own bootstraps."

The problem is that a great deal of the lore of the American immigration story is not true. The first European immigrants to arrive on America's shores did not assimilate into the Indigenous culture; instead, they destroyed it. But even as America created its own identity as a nation of immigrants from various cultures and countries across the world, some groups were more welcome than others.

Within those various communities, some found success, but many did not. "The nostalgic view of immigrants in the past moving quickly from rags to riches does not fit the facts," economic historians Ran Abramitzky and Leah Boustan wrote in their book *Streets of Gold*.

The modern myth suggests that past immigrants immediately learned English and assimilated, but a report from *Family Tree Magazine* challenged that notion: "Immigrants didn't shed their foreign identities the moment they stepped off the boat. Rather, they settled together with their countrymen in ethnic neighborhoods where everyone spoke the native language. That's why today we have New York's Little Italy, Cincinnati's Over-the-Rhine and Chicago's Andersonville. Immigrants brought their foods, music, traditions and activities to their new homes."

A 2008 study by researchers at the University of Wisconsin–Madison of German immigrants confirmed that even "after 50 or more years of living in the United States, many speakers in some communities remained monolingual." In fact, contrary to popular opinion, recent immigrants who arrived between 1980 and 2010, who were largely from Latin America and the Caribbean, were more likely to learn English than those who came to the country from 1900 to 1930, who were mostly from Europe, according to a September 2019 report from the libertarian-leaning Cato Institute.

It's also not true that early immigrants didn't need or were too proud to accept "handouts." Although state-supported "welfare" did not exist at the time, *Family Tree Magazine* noted that immigrant aid societies and charitable organizations, including the YMCA, YWCA, and Salvation Army, provided assistance.

Perhaps modern descendants can be forgiven for idealizing family history into noble tales of victory, but the most dangerous of these myths suggest that European Americans, and particularly Irish Americans, were treated worse than the Black people who were brought here in chains. The Southern Poverty Law Center has warned that this form of revisionism has attracted neo-Nazis, white nationalists, neo-Confederates, and Holocaust deniers.

The most popular of these myths is that Irish Americans were also enslaved. In a post on Medium in September 2015, Irish scholar Liam Hogan methodically sorted through dozens of images on the internet about alleged Irish slaves and demonstrated how none of the photographs showed what those who posted them claimed they did. Yes, some Europeans came to America through indentured servitude, but unlike slaves, "servants were considered legally human," *New York Times* writer Liam Stack noted in March 2017. "Their servitude was based on a contract that limited their service to a finite period of time, usually about seven years, in exchange for passage to the colonies."

For Black people, enslavement was permanent and hereditary, passed on from one generation to the next. The descendants of indentured servants, however, remained free. In response to the Irish slave myth, a group of eighty-two Irish scholars wrote an open letter in 2016 calling it "an obscene rhetorical move" to "equate indentured servitude or penal servitude with racialised perpetual hereditary chattel slavery."

The myth also misunderstands how European immigrants were gradually allowed to assimilate into whiteness. The definition of whiteness has evolved over centuries and across continents. That's because there is no biological basis for the racial categories we use to distinguish ourselves. Race itself is a social construct unknown to humanity for most of human history. Whiteness is an invented concept that has shifted from generation to generation to reach its definition today.

When non-Black indentured servants partnered with enslaved Black people in colonial America, white planters responded by "luring Whiteness away from Blackness," according to author Ibram X. Kendi. Following Bacon's Rebellion in 1676–1677, the planter class created a "racial bribe" to provide "special privileges to poor whites in an effort to drive a wedge between them and Black slaves," wrote legal scholar Michelle Alexander.

The Naturalization Act of 1790 limited United States citizenship to immigrants who were "free white persons" of "good character." But over time, the "racial bribe" expanded to allow other racial and ethnic groups to advance "by becoming 'white,'" according to authors Lani Guinier and Gerald Torres. To accomplish this feat, wrote law professor Cheryl I. Harris, "the amalgamation of various European strains into an American identity was facilitated by an oppositional definition of Black as other."

That's why the Black experience in America is unique and distinguishable from that of white indentured servants and immigrants. In order for the Irish, Italians, Poles, Germans, and other groups to become "white," they had to assimilate into an identity that was defined by its difference from Blackness. Black people, even if we chose to assimilate, were never invited into this identity. As Princeton University history professor Tera Hunter wrote in the *Washington Post* in March 2017, "The descendants of the enslaved call ourselves African Americans, not Ghanaian, or Guinean or Sierra Leonean Americans because of this ancestral rupture and exile."

Still, the mythology persists. Former secretary of housing and urban development Ben Carson ran into trouble in March 2017 when he appeared to rebrand enslaved Black people as "immigrants" who came here "in the bottom of slave ships." At first, he defended himself by retreating to the term "involuntary immigrant." But eventually, even Dr. Carson was forced to admit the truth. "The slave narrative and immigrant narrative are two entirely different experiences," he said in his apology. "The two experiences should never be intertwined, nor forgotten."

Being a Black descendant of enslaved people in America is not the same as being a descendant of white immigrants. That's why the mythology about the early origins of Thanksgiving rings hollow with many African Americans. As Malcolm X explained in his 1964 speech "The Ballot or the Bullet," "Our forefathers weren't the Pilgrims. We didn't land on Plymouth Rock; the rock was landed on us. We were brought here against our will; we were not brought here to be made citizens. We were not brought here to enjoy the constitutional gifts that they speak so beautifully about today."

Because our African ancestors did not come here voluntarily as immigrants, we struggle to trace our history to our native countries and our Black antebellum forebearers. Our families were deliberately broken and consigned to multigenerational deprivation of their basic human liberties. We were denied the right to vote, to marry, to read, to sit in juries, to testify at trials, and to participate in our own governance. We were often identifiable by our skin color, which made it easier to target us. And, yes, we were enslaved.

I do not suggest this to create a hierarchy of oppression that denies the suffering of immigrants from non-African countries. No group of people should be forced to suffer. As Dr. King said, "Injustice anywhere is a threat to justice everywhere." But the experience of that injustice and suffering differs from group to group, and this requires different acknowledgments, approaches, and remedies.

The failure to atone for or acknowledge the benefits of that oppression not only wounds the oppressed but also weakens the soul of the oppressor. As James Baldwin wrote in his 1985 book, *The Price of the Ticket*, "The price the white American paid for his ticket was to become white." Baldwin argues that this "dim-witted ambition has choked many a human being to death here: and this, I contend, is because the white American has never accepted the real reasons for his journey. I know very well that my ancestors had no desire to come to this place: but neither did the ancestors of the people who became white and who require of my captivity a song. They require of me a song less to celebrate my captivity than to justify their own."

10

White Americans still benefit from the legacy of slavery.

ARGUMENT

No one alive today was ever a slave. And no one alive today has ever owned a slave. Politicians calling for reparations in 2020 is one of the most insane things to ever be proposed, and I'm not paying for it.

—*Conservative activist Kaitlin Bennett, February 25, 2020*

ANSWER

We are taught that the history of slavery is something that happened almost like when there were dinosaurs.... This history that we are told was so long ago wasn't, in fact, that long ago at all.

—*Author Clint Smith, June 1, 2021*

There's a well-known joke that comedian Chris Rock told in a 2008 comedy special that immediately resonated with millions of Black people. He spoke about his expensive home in the wealthy enclave of Alpine, New Jersey, where he said there were hundreds of houses but only four Black people: Mary J. Blige, Jay-Z, Eddie Murphy, and himself. After describing the world-renowned accomplishments of the famous Black celebrities who live in the neighborhood, Rock asked a question: "Do you know what the white man that lives next door to me does for a living? He's a fucking dentist."

Rock explained that his neighbor was not the world's best dentist and wasn't in the dental hall of fame. He was just a regular dentist. In contrast, Rock said, he had to host the Oscars just to be able to afford that house, and he still didn't believe it belonged to him. But then he asked the audience a rhetorical question: "Do you know what a Black dentist would have to do to move into my neighborhood? He'd have to invent teeth!"

The story, although apocryphal, reflects the built-in advantages that many ordinary white people enjoy in society. When world heavyweight champion Muhammad Ali tried to buy a six-bedroom home in a well-to-do neighborhood of Pittsburgh in 1971, the white neighbors, according to the *Pittsburgh Post-Gazette*, objected to the sale. It was seven years after the passage of the Civil Rights Act of 1964, and the owner did not accept Ali's $195,000 offer for the home and 1.3 acres of land. The owner eventually sold the home and part of the land for $110,000—to a dentist.

Over the course of my lifetime, I've heard numerous white people tell me that slavery ended long ago and there's nothing we can do about the past. "There is no one alive today in these United States that either owned a Slave, nor was a Slave," Lynn Bryant DeSpain, a conservative critic of reparations, told the Oregon legislature in 2021. Teaching the history of slavery "widen[s] the separation of peoples," DeSpain continued, and provides "excuses for personal failings and shortcomings." Black conservatives have followed suit. "Not one, single Black American alive today, can say they lived in slavery," Republican Herschel Walker told a congressional committee in 2021.

On the surface, this may appear to be a reasonable argument, but it misunderstands both the extensive and brutal nature of hundreds of years of enslavement and the effects of that legacy 150 years later.

First, slavery wasn't just an event that benefited a small percentage of slave owners. It benefited the entire nation. "Cotton grown and picked by enslaved workers was the nation's most valuable export," wrote Princeton professor Matthew Desmond. "The combined value of enslaved people exceeded that of all the railroads and factories in the nation."

Slavery was also an architectural infrastructure built on the premise of universal white supremacy, which has never been dismantled. DeSpain's argument centers white victimhood over Black oppression by deflecting attention from the evils of that racist system and refocusing on the perceived unfairness of making the modern beneficiaries of that system have to think about what their ancestors did to get the privilege they enjoy today.

Second, slavery wasn't that long ago in the broader scheme of American history. "Nearly two average American lifetimes (79 years) have passed since the end of slavery, only two," noted Desmond. The enslavement of Black Africans started well before the founding of the republic and continued for nearly a century after the Declaration of Independence. In the long history of African people in America, whether from 1526 or 1619, Black people were enslaved far longer than they have been free. Harriet Tubman's life spanned the lives of Jefferson and Reagan; the last-known living enslaved person died in my lifetime. History still resonates.

One hidden figure from that history is Elijah Odom, who was born into slavery in 1859 and spent the earliest years of his life "toiling in the Mississippi heat," according to *Smithsonian Magazine*, before he managed to escape, educate himself, and become a doctor in Arkansas. Odom's daughter, Ruth, left the South and moved to Cleveland, where she became active in local politics. Years later, in 2016, after celebrating her ninety-ninth birthday, Ruth Odom Bonner stood on a stage with President Barack Obama and rang the 130-year-old Freedom Bell from a Black church in Virginia to open the National Museum of African American History and Culture. There they stood in Washington, DC, linking the present to the past—the daughter of an enslaved Black man and the first Black president of the United States.

In 2020, *Washington Post* reporter Sydney Trent profiled Dan Smith, the eighty-eight-year-old son of an enslaved Black man. He served in the army in the Korean War, moved to Washington, DC, and became the head usher at the National Cathedral. Smith told Trent a graphic story his father had shared with him about an enslaved Black person forced to stick their tongue on the metal rim of a wagon wheel in the winter until the only way to remove it was to rip off part of their tongue.

The 1870 US census listed Smith's father, Abram Smith, as a "boy laborer," Trent reported. This designation reflects yet another truth about slavery. The masses of enslaved people did not simply wake up and leave when emancipation came. Many had no place to go and few options available to them in a white-dominated society, so they were forced to continue working on plantations as poorly paid laborers or sharecroppers.

When slavery ended, the legal ownership of human beings ceased, but its infrastructure of white supremacy did not. It morphed into other forms: racist law enforcement, convict leasing, lynchings, Ku Klux Klan terrorism, voter disenfranchisement, Jim Crow segregation, public accommodations discrimination, employment discrimination, and denial of access to government assistance programs.

When 1960s civil rights legislation finally outlawed racial discrimination, white supremacy morphed again, this time reinventing itself in politically palatable manifestations such as white flight, racial profiling, mass incarceration, and more sophisticated forms of voter suppression. Instead of forcing Black voters to guess the number of jelly beans in a jar, authorities reduced the number of polling places, created longer lines, and implemented burdensome new restrictions that one federal court said "target African Americans with almost surgical precision."

After creating a criminal justice system that disproportionately criminalized Black people, they used felony disenfranchisement laws to disproportionately block them from voting. Then opportunistic conservative politicians like Governor Ron DeSantis of Florida made a public spectacle of arresting people for minor voting offenses.

None of this is slavery, but all of this is the legacy of slavery.

Millions of white people didn't abandon their racist beliefs because a constitutional amendment was ratified in the 1860s or a law was passed in the 1960s. They simply found other ways to express themselves. A Gallup poll conducted two months after the 1964 Civil Rights Act was passed found that 59 percent of Americans approved of the law and 31 percent disapproved; 10 percent didn't know or wouldn't say. By May 1965, another Gallup poll found that 61 percent of southerners felt the government was moving too quickly on civil rights.

I felt the racial tension when my family lived in Georgia in the 1980s. I remember living down the street from former segregationist governor Lester Maddox, seeing my first KKK march, and eyeing older white customers suspiciously when they approached me at the Gap store where I worked in a mostly white shopping mall. I knew that racism had not disappeared just because Black families like mine were legally allowed to live among white people.

The young people who yelled racial obscenities at Elizabeth Eckford outside Little Rock Central High were adults with children by the 1980s. Ruby Bridges, the Black girl who needed federal protection to walk to elementary school, was just turning thirty and getting married. Carolyn Bryant Donham, the white woman involved in the murder of Emmett Till, had still not been charged with a crime. And Jerry Jones, who had yet to be exposed for his presence with the white students at Little Rock Central High School in 1957, had just bought the Dallas Cowboys.

The same year Jones purchased the Cowboys, the US Supreme Court made it harder for Black people to prove racial discrimination. In a series of notable cases where plaintiffs introduced evidence of disparate impact of employment practices, the high court required plaintiffs instead to prove actual discriminatory intent, something that was becoming increasingly difficult to do because white employers had learned to hide their racist practices behind neutral language.

The pattern of racism and denial persisted for decades, and it would take the election and presidency of Donald Trump to expose the white supremacy that had been hiding underneath the surface all along.

The infrastructure of white supremacy that began during slavery has not been dismantled. At some level, whether we acknowledge it publicly or not, most of us already know this. A June 2019 Pew Research poll found that 63 percent of Americans, including 58 percent of white Americans, believe the legacy of slavery affects the position of Black people today. Every racial group in the poll agreed with this sentiment, but the results differed when it came to political affiliation. The only group in the poll to claim that slavery does not affect the lives of Black people today was Republicans.

If all racial groups in America already understand this concept, then the unique Republican denial may reflect yet another attempt at gaslighting, forcing Black people to distract ourselves, as Toni Morrison would say, by spending time proving the obvious.

This brings us back to Dan Smith, the son of an enslaved man who was interviewed by Sydney Trent for the *Washington Post* in 2020. The former Korean War medic told Trent how he had once come across a young white woman who had fallen into a quarry in 1957 and how he had rushed down to help. Her pulse was still beating, so he moved in to perform mouth-to-mouth resuscitation. But a police officer on the scene did not want this Black man's lips to touch this white woman in distress, and he ordered Smith to back off. Smith complied, and the young woman died.

That was the price of white supremacy. It was then, and remains today, a legacy of slavery that traps all of us. Two years after Smith shared that story with the *Post*, in October 2022, he passed away—one of the last known sons of the enslaved.

11

Being called a "Karen" is not comparable to being called the N-word.

ARGUMENT

Yes. The K-word is stronger than the n-word, at least currently. Misogyny and patriarchy has been around longer than slavery. Just don't use either, ok?

—*@EvaSarnoff (Twitter),*
April 19, 2020

ANSWER

"Nigger" is the all-American trump card, the nuclear bomb of racial epithets.

—*Journalist Farai Chideya,*
1999

In the spring of 2008, as Hillary Clinton and Barack Obama were slugging their way through the final days of the bitter Democratic presidential primary season, political journalists and investigative reporters started digging into an unusual story that threatened to disrupt the entire campaign. It was not about Obama's birth certificate or Clinton's controversial vote for the Iraq War. In fact, the "scandal" did not directly implicate either candidate. It concerned a spouse.

A former CIA operative named Larry C. Johnson began feeding a story to reporters that Michelle Obama, the wife of then-senator Barack Obama, had been caught on tape using a racial slur. By early June, as Obama appeared certain to clinch the nomination at the convention in Denver that year, Republican operative Roger Stone expanded on the accusation. "At least seven news organizations have contacted me, wanting to know how to get their hands on this tape," Stone told Fox News. Stone, whom the DC newspaper *The Hill* described as a "legendary conservative political hit man," claimed the existence of the tape was part of the reason Hillary Clinton was staying in the race.

And what was the dramatic racial slur that caused all the controversy? Johnson and Stone claimed a tape of Mrs. Obama was about to surface showing the Harvard-educated lawyer referring to white people as "whitey."

I nearly spit out my drink when I heard this story. In my entire life, after encountering tens of thousands of Black people, many of whom openly dislike white people, I can't remember hearing anyone I knew personally refer to white people as "whitey." I have heard numerous euphemisms that Black people use to describe white people, often as a secret mechanism to express their frustration with the white people they encounter in their lives, but I have no recollection of *anyone*—with the exception of an old *SNL* skit with Richard Pryor and the fictional character Fred Sanford from the 1970s TV show *Sanford and Son*—using the term "whitey." The very idea that Michelle Obama had allegedly given a public speech referring to white people as "whitey" seemed comical to me. Not surprisingly, the story was eventually debunked and no tape ever emerged.

Eight years later, another political controversy emerged about another racial slur supposedly caught on another secret tape. This time, a white candidate had allegedly been caught using the worst racial slur in American English. (The fact that I don't have to say it for you to know what it is proves the point of this story.)

The speculation came shortly after the candidate had been caught on tape by the TV show *Access Hollywood* using sexually offensive language about women. Mark Burnett, the producer of *The Apprentice*, allegedly was sitting on the tapes and refused to release them. This time the story felt more plausible only because the alleged villain was Donald Trump, who had already developed a history of publicly making racist, sexist, and otherwise offensive comments. But the reason the controversy resonated is that the word he had allegedly used had a longer and more hateful history than any other racial slur: the N-word.

Years later, when former Trump White House aide Omarosa Manigault Newman alleged that the president had used the N-word, it caused yet another controversy. This time, Trump claimed that Burnett called him personally to say that there were no tapes of him using what he called "a terrible and disgusting word." He even tweeted, implausibly, "I don't have that word in my vocabulary, and never have."

Since he became a national political figure, Trump has never been known for his racial sensitivity. But the fact that he went out of his way to deny the allegation indicates that he, too, realized just how damaging the story could become to his reputation. That's because the N-word holds a unique place in the annals of American racism.

Which brings us to the K-word: Karen. I'm not sure if we're being punked when people claim that being called a Karen is as bad as being called the N-word, but a few people have said this, and in an unrelated incident in 2020, Domino's Pizza in New Zealand had to apologize for a giveaway they promoted to "(nice) Karens."

"Karen" was originally a derogatory slang term used to refer to an entitled, sometimes obnoxious white woman who asks to "speak to the manager." Over time, it took on a more overtly racial and political connotation as white women were called Karens for calling the police on Black people who were minding their own business. In 2023, protesters in Philadelphia even coined the term "Klanned Karenhood."

I fully understand why the use of the term "Karen" can be problematic inasmuch as it sweeps a group of disparate people into a single insulting category. But here's where I draw the line. Being called a Karen, no matter how insulting, is not the same as being called the N-word. To illustrate the point, let's broaden the conversation beyond one specific insult to white people and look at a few other words in modern history.

In 1975, comedian Paul Mooney wrote a now-famous *SNL* skit in which his fellow comedians Chevy Chase and Richard Pryor discussed race in America. Chase, the white man, played an employer conducting a job interview, while Pryor, the Black man, played the role of a job applicant. Chase tells Pryor that they need to do one last psychological review, a word association test, before they can hire him. Pryor is asked to say the first word that comes to his mind when he hears a word from Chase.

At first, it's easy. Chase says "dog" and Pryor says "tree." Chase says "fast" and Pryor says "slow." Chase says "rain" and Pryor says "snow."

Then it becomes more complicated. Chase says "white" and Pryor says "black." Chase says "Negro" and Pryor says "whitey." Chase says "colored" and Pryor says "redneck." The words get worse until Chase says "jungle bunny" and Pryor replies with "honkey." Chase then says "spade" and Pryor, running out of words, doubles down with "honkey honkey." When Chase finally utters the N-word, Pryor delivers the coup de grâce: "dead honkey." Chase is visibly flustered as Pryor stares at him angrily with flaring nose and twitching eyes. Needless to say, he gets the job offer.

The point in 1975 was the same as the point today. There is no word more racially offensive than the N-word. It's been awhile since I've heard a Black person use the word "honkey," but the ghost of Richard Pryor could literally read the entire *Roget's Thesaurus* and the online Urban Dictionary and never find a comparable insult with which to attack Chevy Chase. Only when the threat of fatal retaliation emerged did Chase back down.

In this country, racial insults directed at white people have never carried the same weight as the N-word because of our unique power imbalance and historical legacy. Yet, in May 2023, Representative Marjorie Taylor Greene complained that she took "great offense" to being called a white supremacist. "That is like calling a person of color the N-word," she said. The Georgia Republican, who spent years harassing Representative Alexandria Ocasio Cortez and once spoke at a white nationalist conference in Florida, made the comparison as she attacked a Black Democratic colleague for being "aggressive" and claimed that she felt "threatened" by him. This was a white woman who had launched her political career by harassing a person of color in Congress suddenly claiming to be threatened when a Black member of Congress challenged her in public. That's exactly what a "Karen" would do.

The N-word has been used against Black Africans and African Americans in this country for hundreds of years. Enslavers and the overseers they employed hurled the epithet at the Black humans they considered property. Klansmen on horses yelled it at Black people before killing them. And good ol' boys in pickup trucks rolled down their windows to scream it at Black motorists to taunt and terrorize them. Indeed, it is not unreasonable to assume that the last word heard by Emmett Till before he was lynched may have been the N-word.

While white Americans have terrorized Black people with the N-word, there is no comparable history of Black people using derogatory racial language to enslave, segregate, profile, or in any way oppress white people. Black Americans have never possessed the systemic or institutional authority to do so. When Black people do use derogatory terms about white people, it's often a reflection of the *lack of power* we have to do anything but use our words to fight injustice.

But if the N-word is so hurtful, why do Black people use it themselves, and why can't white people repeat the same words they hear from African Americans? Well, Black people are not monolithic, and the use of the N-word remains controversial in some Black communities. Many Black people despise the word, while many others use it religiously. Others object to the word yet don't feel it should be banned. But as Black people, the victims of the word for centuries, we have the right to do so.

African American use of the N-word reflects a broader tradition of reappropriation in which marginalized groups reclaim negative language used against them. In the same way that many LGBTQIA people have chosen to embrace the once-derogatory term "queer," many Black people have come to welcome the N-word, particularly in describing ourselves or one another affectionately with the softer version of the word ending in "a" instead of the hard "er." It is, in some ways, an act of building a shield from the same rough material as the spear used to attack us.

As for those white people who still feel the desire to use the N-word, ostensibly to fit in with Black people rather than insult them, I would ask them a different question. If you care about Black people and know the harmful history behind the N-word, why do you still feel the need to say it?

PART THREE | DENYING BLACK OPPRESSION

TV host Steve Harvey tells an inspirational story about flying first class on an airplane. They close the curtain between the cabins, according to Harvey, because "you ain't gonna believe what's going on up there."

He then goes on to list some of the amenities provided to first-class flyers. "They bringing out hot washcloths so you can wash up. They passing out menus. Everybody get hot nuts. You get all you want to drink. You ain't got to pay for the headsets. You get to watch the movies free. You get a choice of what you want to eat."

Harvey uses the story as a motivational tool to encourage young people to expose themselves to new things. "Once you sit in that first-class seat, you have now been exposed," he says. "The game changes." Being exposed to better treatment, Harvey believes, changes your perspective. "Once you fly first class," he says, "walking past first class gonna be hard."

He's right. Years ago, when I started flying a lot for work, I acquired a significant number of frequent flyer miles and gained platinum status on my favorite airline. Those miles often allowed me to upgrade to first-class seats when I flew that airline. The benefits were exactly as Steve Harvey described them—the hot washcloth; the warm nuts; the menu; the choice of food; the free drinks; the Bose headset; the additional legroom; and my favorite, the warm chocolate chip cookie.

When my work travel slowed and my platinum status disappeared, I found myself back in the familiar and less comfortable coach seats. But the larger part of my experience was the loss of a sense of privilege. In many aspects of American life, some people enjoy first-class experiences while others are crowded into second-class status.

One example is financial status. The typical white family has eight times the wealth, or net worth, of the typical Black family, according to a September 2020 report from the Federal Reserve. The impact is particularly significant among people under thirty-five, according to the data. The median young Black family has almost no net worth ($600) while the median young white family has a net worth of $25,400.

Another example is the criminal justice system. A Black person is five times more likely to be stopped by police without just cause than a white person, according to research from the NAACP. In addition, Black people are imprisoned at a rate that is roughly five times the rate for white Americans, according to an October 2021 report from the Sentencing Project. Although African Americans make up only 13 percent of the population, we account for 47 percent of the cases of people who have been exonerated after being wrongfully convicted.

Black Americans have been relegated to second-class citizenship in this country while white Americans are enjoying a first-class experience. Yet when African Americans attempt to discuss these persistent racial inequities, we're often told that we're disloyal, troublesome, and even unpatriotic.

For some white Americans, I suspect the idea of moving toward full racial equality for Black people feels a bit like leaving the privilege of first class to sit in coach. But relaxing in comfort while an entire group of uncomfortable passengers sits behind you will eventually cause friction. The longer the flight, the more likely the conflict. And eventually, you can't just offer peanuts to the people in second class to satisfy them.

Black people have been forced to remain in the functional equivalent of second-class seats, or worse, since we arrived in this country. Part 3 examines some of the ways in which white society denies the existence of Black oppression and refuses to acknowledge the legitimacy of the grievances of those who have been forced to live in a second-class America. I argue that the way to resolve that oppression is not simply to create opportunities for a chosen few to sit in first class but rather to expand the supply of resources so that they can be more fairly distributed to everyone.

12

Complying with the police does not protect us.

ARGUMENT

All these major headline incidents that we've had in this country involving law enforcement in the last at least five years could have all been prevented if people would just comply with police, would follow orders and not resist arrest.

—*Conservative political commentator Tomi Lahren, October 2021*

ANSWER

When will the American people realize what cellphone videos keep showing them, what body cameras keep recording, what the graveyards of history keep reporting? Black and brown people's defiance is not the problem. Our compliance is not the solution.

—*Antiracist author Ibram X. Kendi, April 19, 2021*

Muhammad Abdul Muhaymin had to use the bathroom—badly. As he approached the restroom door at a local community center, an employee blocked him from entering. Muhaymin was carrying a small Chihuahua named Chiquita, and the staff member warned him that dogs were not permitted.

"It's a public restroom," Muhammad told the man. Moments later, the police arrived, and Muhammad politely turned around to greet them. "How you doing, officer. This is my service dog. I just wanted to use the restroom."

An officer asked for the paperwork for the dog, and Muhammad said it was stolen. He then bent his torso in what looked like an attempt to contract his muscles to prevent himself from having an accidental discharge. "Excuse me, officer. It's a natural thing, a natural function," he said.

The conversation continued calmly until one of the officers on the scene interrupted Muhammad from "ranting and raving" to ask the community center employee a question. "Did he assault you?"

"No," the man responded, "he was trying to get in and I didn't let him in." The officer then told Muhammad that the animal "needs to be on a leash, even if it's a service dog" and escorted him out of the building.

As Muhammad walked out of the front door with his dog, one of the officers ordered him to stop. "Put your hand behind your back," the officer told him. "You got a warrant."

Muhammad, whom the *Arizona Republic* later said was "homeless" and "had schizophrenia," seemed surprised by the arrest and held on to Chiquita. The police tried to get him to put the Chihuahua down, but the dog, which had been silent throughout the entire ordeal, suddenly barked.

The bodycam footage of the incident, released by the Phoenix Police Department, then skips to a struggle in a different location at some point later. In the new scene, Muhammad shrieked as several police officers pulled him to the ground and held him face down with their knees on his neck and his head. "I cannot breathe. I can't breathe. I cannot breathe," he screamed.

One officer pulled Muhammad's hair from behind, holding his dreadlocks to control him as he lay on the ground handcuffed. Muhammad continued panting loudly, as though struggling for air, and then stopped. A thin brown broth of Muhammad's recent meals hurled from his mouth and onto the concrete. Only at that point did the officers respond to his medical distress. They radioed the fire department and appeared to loosen one of the handcuffs, but Muhammad's condition deteriorated rapidly. Just a few seconds later, it was over. "I don't feel a pulse," one officer announced. "He's dead," said another.

The story of Muhammad Muhaymin was one of several incidents that caused me to worry about one of my neighbors in New York City. A young man who lived on my block in Harlem had occasional episodes of what appeared to be mental health crises. On most days, he seemed fine and friendly. But some days, he would stand on the corner and talk to himself or yell at people who weren't there.

Nothing about his behavior seemed threatening to me, but I worried that the new neighbors in my gentrifying community might not see it that way. I could imagine a scenario in which someone would call the police during one of his episodes and the responding officers would perceive a young Black man screaming on the street as a threat—and kill him. It later occurred to me that one of my new neighbors could be a perpetrator of such an action. The thought came to me after a white twenty-four-year-old ex-marine named Daniel Penny killed a thirty-year-old homeless Black man named Jordan Neely after Neely was allegedly loud and aggressive on a New York subway train. "We keep criminalizing people with mental illness," the Reverend Al Sharpton observed at Neely's Harlem funeral. "They don't need abuse," he said. "They need help."

The fear of an overly aggressive law enforcement response to a mental crisis is not unprecedented. In one of the most famous cases, Eleanor Bumpurs, an elderly Black woman with a history of mental illness, was shot and killed by NYPD officers in 1984 while she was being evicted for falling four months behind on her monthly rent of $98.65. In 2014, Ezell Ford, a twenty-five-year-old Black man who had been diagnosed with schizophrenia and bipolar disorder, was shot and killed by police in Los Angeles. In 2019, a New York City police officer shot and killed a thirty-two-year-old Black gay man named Kawaski Trawick, who was experiencing a mental health crisis in his own home. And in 2020, Daniel Prude, a forty-one-year-old Black man suffering a mental health crisis, died in police custody in Rochester, New York, after officers encountered him naked in the street and placed a hood over his head as he was handcuffed on the ground.

Police treatment of Black people has been a continuing problem, but almost every time a Black person is killed by police, a chorus of conservative law enforcement defenders race to social media and right-wing television programs to justify and contextualize what happened. If these people had only complied, they would be alive, the argument goes.

Sadly, even when we do comply, we're still abused. In May 2018, a Miami police officer kicked a handcuffed suspect while he was restrained on the ground. That same month, a police officer near Columbus, Ohio, was caught on video kicking another handcuffed suspect. In March 2020, a Black man with his hands visibly raised over his head was violently kicked by a sheriff's deputy in Sacramento, California. In September 2021, an Indianapolis police sergeant calmly lifted his boot and stomped a Black man in the face as he lay handcuffed on the ground. These are just a few of the numerous incidents in which police have abused Black suspects in custody. A quick search of the internet turns up many more, and even those are just the ones that were reported or caught on video.

In some cases, the situation turns deadly. Eric Garner was already subdued and had no ability to resist arrest on a New York City sidewalk in 2014 when undercover officers ignored his pleas for help. "I can't breathe," he said, before they choked him to death. Laquan McDonald was walking and skipping through the street when Chicago police shot and killed him in 2014. Philando Castile was shot and killed while attempting to comply with police orders during a traffic stop in Minnesota in 2016.

The internet is also filled with videos of white people resisting arrest, disrespecting police officers, stealing police vehicles, fighting police, and even chasing officers, all without being killed. Black people often cite these videos as proof that complying with the police does not protect us.

The problem with relying on these anecdotal tit-for-tat discussions is that for every ten videos that Black activists present, someone will find one video where a white person is shot, or a Black person is not, and use that information as evidence to contradict the racial disparity. Conservatives also tend to focus on hyperspecific details to distinguish any one case from another while ignoring the larger trend that Black and brown people are disproportionately victimized.

Complying with the police does not protect us.

The "just comply" rhetoric also obscures the reality that Black people often have good reason not to comply with police. The "foundation for modern policing" was the "slave patrol," according to scholars Leslie Alexander and Michelle Alexander. The eighteenth-century patrollers were "required to hunt fugitives and rebellious enslaved people and to visit every plantation at least once a month," they write.

The Black intergenerational trauma with law enforcement reaches back to our parents and grandparents, who watched as police stood by and did nothing, or even participated, when African American people were strung up and lynched by lawless mobs in the twentieth century. The distrust is also born from our own lived experience, as we watch police in the twenty-first century racially profile and target Black communities.

When I lived in New York City, at the height of the "stop-and-frisk" era, police stopped 685,724 people in 2011. Of that number, 87 percent were Black or Latino and 88 percent (605,328 people) "were innocent," according to data from the New York Civil Liberties Union. This took place at a time when Black people accounted for only 22.8 percent and Hispanic residents 28.6 percent of the city's population.

Research conducted on a national level has found similar racial disparities in criminal justice. A 2019 study published in the *Proceedings of the National Academies of Sciences* found that Black men face the "highest levels of inequality in mortality risk" and are about 2.5 times more likely to be killed by police than are white men. The study also found that "young men of color face exceptionally high risk of being killed by police." Similarly, research from Campaign Zero's Mapping Police Violence project found that Black people were nearly three times more likely to be killed by police than were white people from 2013 to 2022.

Given our history, it's not surprising that a Pew Research poll in September 2016 found only 14 percent of Black people said they had "a lot of confidence in their local police" compared to 42 percent of white people who expressed that sentiment. From my experiences living in mostly Black communities, mostly white communities, and mixed-race communities, white people tend to see the police as a service to *protect* them while Black people often see the police as an occupying force to *control* them.

Police officers who do not live in Black communities, who do not know our people, and who do not understand our culture will often bark commands to people in our neighborhoods and exhibit a casual and callous disregard for our lives and our homes. I rarely see police behaving the same way in the white communities where I've lived.

The Fort Worth police officer who killed Atatiana Jefferson in 2019 felt it was okay to stand outside her home and shoot through her bedroom window while the twenty-eight-year-old Black woman was playing video games with her eight-year-old nephew. Similarly, police officers in Louisville, Kentucky, felt it was appropriate in March 2020 to storm into the home of Breonna Taylor, a twenty-six-year-old medical worker, on a late-night drug raid following a crime in which she was not involved.

Many African Americans also understand that police lie to protect themselves and their colleagues. Police are trained to use evasive language that obscures the brutality of their conduct. Think of the phrases "officer-involved shooting," "arrest-related death," "shots fired," "feared for his life," "suspect refused to comply," and "discharged his duty weapon."

This is how the Minneapolis police department described the death of George Floyd in a news release on May 25, 2020: "Two officers arrived and located the suspect, a male believed to be in his 40s, in his car. He was ordered to step from his car. After he got out, he physically resisted officers. Officers were able to get the suspect into handcuffs and noted he appeared to be suffering medical distress. Officers called for an ambulance. He was transported to Hennepin County Medical Center by ambulance where he died a short time later." There's no mention of the nine minutes and twenty-nine seconds in which an officer pressed his knees into George Floyd's neck and back.

Similarly, the initial police report on the death of Breonna Taylor provided very few details about the incident, and police checked the "no" box under "forced entry," even though they broke into her apartment with a battering ram. And the initial February 2020 police report for the death of Ahmaud Arbery in Georgia merely repeated the narrative of the white men who killed him.

For decades, white America largely ignored Black complaints of police abuse. James Baldwin called the police "a very real menace to every Black cat alive in this country" in an interview with Dick Cavett in 1969. Marvin Gaye complained about trigger-happy police officers in his 1971 song "Inner City Blues (Make Me Wanna Holler)." The rap group N.W.A recorded a song called "Fuck tha Police" in 1988. But few white people took those complaints seriously until the video era produced what some thought would be irrefutable evidence, beginning with the police beating of Rodney King in 1991 and accelerating with the advent of smartphones.

Many of us know that police make fatal mistakes, often based on their sense of fear around Black people. In 2014, unarmed twenty-eight-year-old Akai Gurley was shot and killed by a New York police officer who accidentally discharged his gun while patrolling the stairway of a housing project. In 2018, twenty-six-year-old Botham Jean was shot and killed in his own Dallas apartment when a police officer who lived in the complex opened the wrong door and was startled to see a Black man in the unit. In 2021, twenty-year-old Daunte Wright was shot by a police officer in Minnesota who claimed that she thought she was grabbing her Taser instead of her gun.

That's why we have The Talk with our children. I remember having an unexpected conversation with one of my godsons years ago when he jokingly ran down the street in Miami when he saw a police car. I had to inform him that Black boys get killed for pranks like that. On the other hand, I knew from my childhood in a Missouri suburb that my young white male neighbors enjoyed the freedom to live their lives without concern for the presence of the police. They openly carried BB guns on the street, practiced shooting at a local farmer's tractor in a nearby cornfield, and got away with it all because they were "just being boys."

In contrast, I have been wrongly stopped by the police many times and forced to show my papers to prove my right to be there. Once, an elderly Black woman who had seen me on CNN had to interrupt the white police officer wrongly trying to arrest me for subway fare evasion to vouch for my standing in the community. I appreciated her assistance, but the incident reflected a troubling class bias because I was able to end my harassment by virtue of my perceived status. In a just society, no one should be harassed or abused by police, regardless of their socioeconomic status.

Police misconduct should compel us to reexamine the expansive powers we grant to law enforcement, but far too often, our conversations deviate into needless debates about the sainthood of the victim rather than the policies that empower the police to kill. Instead of asking whether the victim was perfect or complied with police orders, we should ask why we allow *any* officials to kill in relation to crimes that don't threaten the safety of the public. Why should police have the authority to kill *anyone* merely for having a broken taillight or failing to comply with their orders?

When conservative police defenders predictably dig into victims' backgrounds and discover some offense from the past that they feel justifies a detainee's execution, they avoid acknowledging the many ways in which Blackness itself is criminalized by racially selective enforcement of the law. He was "no angel," they argue, but they decline to interrogate the system of police bias and prosecutorial discretion that leads to outcomes in which Black people are disproportionately likely to be arrested and prosecuted.

Many of the crimes that initiate police contact in Black and brown communities are minor offenses. Eric Garner was stopped for selling loose cigarettes. George Floyd was arrested for allegedly using a counterfeit twenty-dollar bill. Arrests for crimes like jaywalking or riding a bike on a sidewalk, although facially neutral, are disproportionately deployed against Black and brown people.

Some offenses are enforced differently from block to block, a point I discussed years ago with my students at Columbia University, who would almost never be arrested for a crime like marijuana possession. Meanwhile, just a few minutes down the hill in Harlem, the young people in that community were still being targeted. Yes, rules are rules, as conservatives argue, but the rule enforcers get to decide when they're applied.

Many conservatives also engage in cynical double standards in their law-and-order rhetoric, attacking young people of color for failing to comply with the police but celebrating rich white guys who openly defy the law and fail to comply. When young Black kids committed a simple misdemeanor in New York City, they had to be prosecuted, according to former mayor Rudy Giuliani, but when a powerful white president violated the laws and the Constitution years later, he deserved sympathy and compassion. That's why a group of Black kids protesting police brutality in Chicago is described as "criminal" but a thousand white men storming the US Capitol in a violent insurrection becomes "legitimate political discourse." It's inconceivable that police would allow hundreds of angry Black people to survive an attempt to storm the nation's seat of government in an angry, violent effort to stop our democracy.

Ordinary Black people are rarely afforded the same grace given to white Americans in the criminal justice system. Just think back to the case of Muhammad Muhaymin, the man whom police killed after he tried to enter a restroom with his dog. The apparent reason why the incident escalated to an arrest is that Muhammad had an outstanding warrant for failure to appear in court in a misdemeanor drug paraphernalia case. What was that case? He had a marijuana pipe in his bag one day while he walked down the street. And how did police come to discover this pipe? They found it when they searched his bag after stopping him for jaywalking.

One minor jaywalking citation led to a minor marijuana charge, which then led to a misdemeanor warrant, which then led to an unnecessary arrest, which then led to the death of a Black man—who just wanted to use the bathroom.

13

No, we're not going back to Africa.

<table>
<tr><th>ARGUMENT</th><th>ANSWER</th></tr>
<tr><td>She's telling us how to run our country. How did you do where you came from?

—*President Donald Trump, criticizing Rep. Ilhan Omar, who was born in Somalia, September 22, 2020*</td><td>Firstly, this is my country & I am a member of the House that impeached you. Secondly, I fled civil war when I was 8. An 8-year-old doesn't run a country even though you run our country like one.

—*Minnesota congresswoman Ilhan Omar, responding to President Trump, September 22, 2020*</td></tr>
</table>

Amílcar Cabral was approaching the end of a busy week.

On Sunday, he received an honorary degree from Lincoln University in Pennsylvania and spoke about leaders who choose to "return to the source" of their people after they have the opportunity to escape the oppression of their communities.

On Monday, the West African leader delivered an address at the United Nations in New York, "determined to make whatever sacrifices are necessary in order to liberate the Cape Verde archipelago from Portuguese domination."

By Friday, the forty-eight-year-old Cabral was ready to sit down with Black Americans to talk about connecting the struggles between their two peoples.

It was October 20, 1972, just weeks before the presidential election that would reelect Republican Richard Nixon, and more than 120 people from various Black organizations came to the meeting in New

York City. Cabral, a charming, soft-spoken intellectual, flattered the audience: "Each day I realize that if I did not have to do what I have to do in my country, maybe I would come here to join you," he told them.

For more than a decade, Cabral had served as the leader of the African Party for the Independence of New Guinea and the Cape Verde Islands as they fought for freedom. When Portuguese authorities killed fifty striking dock workers in August 1959, Cabral's organization transitioned to armed conflict to take back the country. That day in 1972, he reminded the Black people in the room which countries had enabled and supported his people's oppression.

Cabral described Portugal as "an underdeveloped country" and "the most backward" in Western Europe. "Portugal would never be able to launch three colonial wars in Africa without the help of NATO, the weapons of NATO, the planes of NATO, the bombs of NATO," he said. Then he connected the dots. "NATO is the creation of the United States," said Cabral. As he described it, Portuguese colonial rule over Black people in Africa was essentially an extension of US imperialism.

A few months after Cabral returned home, Richard Nixon and his wife, Pat, stood at a podium at the US Capitol on a cloudy Saturday in January. She held the family Bibles below her fur-trimmed coat as her husband placed his hand on them and took the oath of office for his second time. It was still two years before the last US helicopters would airlift Americans from the rooftops in Saigon, but Nixon chose to place his hand on a page in the Bible with a familiar passage from Isaiah 2:4: "Nation shall not lift up sword against nation, neither shall they learn war any more." His inaugural address that day echoed the biblical sentiment, promising Americans "a new era of peace in the world." That same day, four thousand miles away, Amílcar Cabral was assassinated outside his home in Conakry.

I didn't hear of Cabral until twenty-four years later, when I flew to Cape Verde. As our military plane completed its final descent and approached the runway, I looked out the window and saw a vast empty stretch of reddish-brown land.

We touched down at Amílcar Cabral International Airport. It was the first of several stops in Africa I would make as part of a delegation appointed by President Clinton to attend a summit in Zimbabwe. At each stop along the way to our final destination in Harare, we met with government officials in various countries, and in each location, I wondered the same thing: Were these my people?

Between my life in America and my ancestors' lives in West Africa lies a vast chasm of uncertainty. I have followed family history and government records to trace my heritage back several centuries, but the same obstructions always appear. At some point, I, like millions of other African Americans, run into the roadblock of slavery. It was a time of cultural genocide when white supremacy ripped Black families apart, gave white men unfettered access to Black bodies for sexual exploitation, and tore mothers from their children to turn them into property. It was a time when my ancestors were not allowed to read or write, use their native tongues, or record their own history.

So when I hear racist white Americans today tell me that if I do not love this country, I should go back to Africa, I want to ask them: Where would I go? Where is my homeland? Where are my people? You cannot kidnap 12.5 million people over the course of centuries, enslave their children and grandchildren, rob them of their histories, demand that they build you a country, and then expel them to "return" to a place where they have never lived.

But such was the attack directed at Democratic representative Ilhan Omar, a former Somali refugee, who was told to "go back and help fix" Somalia before "telling the people of the United States . . . how our government is to be run."

"Go back to Africa" is one of the oldest racist tropes in America, but the notion of sending Black people back to the continent became a serious policy objective for a number of nineteenth-century elected officials. For some, it offered what appeared to be an ideal solution for a complex problem. Yet it was rooted in our nation's moral failure to end slavery and dismantle white supremacy.

The American Colonization Society hoped to send Black people back to Africa in the early 1800s and sent thousands to a colony in West Africa in what is now Liberia. During the Civil War, Lincoln also contemplated the idea of helping Black people voluntarily relocate to other countries. "Your race suffer very greatly, many of them by living among us, while ours suffer from your presence," he told a group of Black people in 1862. "It is better for us both, therefore, to be separated."

Some Black people in America shared this desire to leave the racism of the United States and return to the motherland. In the early 1900s, Pan-Africanist leader Marcus Garvey moved to Harlem and created the Universal Negro Improvement Association, which supported the Back to Africa movement. Garvey founded the Black Star Line shipping company to transport passengers across the seas, but his movement floundered after he was targeted by the FBI, labeled a "Negro agitator" and prosecuted.

W. E. B. Du Bois, one of the founders of the NAACP in 1909, also embraced Pan-Africanism, and when Ghanaian prime minister Kwame Nkrumah became the first president of Ghana, Du Bois left the United States to become a citizen of that country, where he lived until he died.

Black America's relationship with Africa has been complicated. Most of the Black people I've encountered in my life are not enamored with the United States, but they also feel disconnected from any ancestral homeland.

Black people also recognize the hypocrisy of the "go back to Africa" rhetoric and the selective application of the "America, love it or leave it" message from white conservatives. When Jews complain about antisemitism in America, white people don't tell them to go back to Israel. When Italian Americans complain about offensive mafia stereotypes, they're not told to go back to Italy. And when the descendants of immigrants from other white European countries complain about what they dislike in America, they're not told to go home to some country across the Atlantic. Instead, people in positions of power address their concerns, just as they should address the concerns of African Americans.

Whether we love it here or not, this is our country. We're going to keep saying what we like and what we don't like. And we ain't going nowhere—unless we want to.

14

Black people don't have to prove our patriotism.

ARGUMENT	ANSWER
I wish some of these players who get on one knee during the national anthem would get on both knees and thank God they live in the United States of America. *—Former Arkansas governor Mike Huckabee, September 25, 2017*	As far as I'm concerned, they could burn this bitch to the ground. And it still wouldn't be enough. And they are lucky that what Black people are looking for is equality and not revenge. *—Author Kimberly Latrice Jones, June 6, 2020*

Colin Kaepernick wore a red sweatshirt, red headphones, and a red-and-white pom-pom beanie when he sat at a table and leaned into a microphone. The twenty-five-year-old quarterback had just arrived in New Orleans for his first-ever Super Bowl, and he was ready to take questions from journalists.

A reporter tossed a softball question to get started. Did he have a message for the US service members who would be watching the game in Afghanistan? "Shout-out to all the troops overseas," Kaepernick said. "Appreciate everything you do so we can come out and play football on Sundays."

Did he ever think he would be the starting quarterback in the Super Bowl? "At the start of the season, I was just hoping to get on the field someway, somehow," he answered.

What did he think about his team? "It's really like a family," he said. "We're around each other more than we're around anybody else."

It was January 2013, and the humble young man with a short fresh haircut was on top of the world. Just four years later, he would be the subject of the biggest controversy in sports, attacked by the new president of the United States, branded unpatriotic by former fans, criticized by fellow players, and effectively banned for life from the sport that made him famous.

What happened during those four years is not only the tale of one man's football career but the story of how America itself came to be more divided than any time since the 1960s civil rights movement.

It began five months after the Baltimore Ravens defeated the 49ers in the Super Bowl that year. In July 2013, a nearly all-white jury in Florida acquitted George Zimmerman for the murder of unarmed seventeen-year-old Trayvon Martin. Immediately after the conviction, the hashtag #BlackLivesMatter began trending online, and three Black women organizers—Alicia Garza, Patrisse Cullors, and Ayọ Tometi—created an organization to support the movement.

The movement drew the engagement of well-known lawmakers, entertainers, celebrities, and professional athletes, but their activism rarely threatened any of their careers until the spring and summer of 2016. That's when a string of news stories about police shootings of Black people collided with the election cycle.

On May 11, North Charleston, South Carolina, police officer Michael Slager was indicted after he was caught on video killing unarmed fifty-year-old Walter Scott by shooting him in the back as he ran away from the officer.

On July 5, police in Baton Rouge, Louisiana, were caught on video killing thirty-seven-year-old Alton Sterling in the parking lot of a convenience store.

The very next day, police in Minnesota killed thirty-two-year-old Philando Castile in his own car while his girlfriend livestreamed the video on Facebook.

On July 18, police in North Miami, Florida, shot an unarmed mental health therapist named Charles Kinsey as he tried to rescue a patient who had run away from a group home.

Three days later, while activists protested the shootings in various cities, the Republican National Convention nominated a presidential candidate who had attacked demonstrators for "threatening the peace on our streets and the safety of our police" but never expressed sympathy for the Black people who had been shot by the cops.

A few days after that, on July 27, the state's attorney in Baltimore dropped all charges against the police officers involved in the death of Freddie Gray, a twenty-five-year-old Black man who died after suffering spinal cord injuries in the back of a police transport wagon.

By August, the country was on edge, and Black leaders were frustrated and upset. It was in that climate that Colin Kaepernick decided to remain on the bench during the national anthem at a preseason game. It was a quiet, one-man protest and nothing happened. He did it again the following week, and again no one noticed or paid attention. Then on August 26, he remained seated in a preseason game against the Green Bay Packers. It was his first time sitting while wearing his uniform. He did not issue a press release, post a selfie on social media, or draw attention to himself. He just sat on the bench.

An NFL Media reporter noticed him and asked why. "I am not going to stand up to show pride in a flag for a country that oppresses Black people and people of color," he said. "To me, this is bigger than football and it would be selfish on my part to look the other way. There are bodies in the street and people getting paid leave and getting away with murder."

The reaction was swift. President Obama, a former constitutional law professor in his final months in office, defended Kaepernick's First Amendment "right to make a statement," but Donald Trump, the new Republican presidential nominee, sensing a political issue, announced that Kaepernick should "try another country."

Kaepernick did not back down. At the suggestion of a service member who thought it would be more appropriate to kneel instead of sitting on the bench, he amended the protest in the following week, joined by his teammate Eric Reid. But Trump continued to raise the issue. In a campaign speech in Alabama, he called on the mostly white billionaire team owners to terminate Kaepernick's contract. "Wouldn't you love to see one of these NFL owners, when somebody disrespects our flag, to say, 'Get that son of a bitch off the field right now. Out! He's fired. He's fired!'"

Following Trump's victory in the election that November, Kaepernick's fortunes were doomed. He became a free agent at the end of the season and was never signed to another team.

That four-year span from Super Bowl quarterback to presidential target represented a dramatic shift not just for Kaepernick but for the country, which was forced to move beyond the postracial fantasy of the Obama era into the racist reality of a new administration.

The president's attempts to bully his critics into empty, symbolic gestures of patriotism exposed his grotesque distortion of revered constitutional principles. As Supreme Court justice Robert Jackson wrote in the 1943 *West Virginia State Board of Education v. Barnette* opinion, "To believe that patriotism will not flourish if patriotic ceremonies are voluntary and spontaneous, instead of a compulsory routine, is to make an unflattering estimate of the appeal of our institutions to free minds." In that case, decided in the middle of America's involvement in World War II, the court struck down a requirement that public-school students salute the flag. "Freedom to differ is not limited to things that do not matter much," Jackson wrote. "That would be a mere shadow of freedom."

As for the idea that a president of the United States would attempt to punish a US citizen for expressing an unpopular opinion, nothing could be more un-American. In the Supreme Court's words: "If there is any fixed star in our constitutional constellation, it is that no official, high or petty, can prescribe what shall be orthodox in politics, nationalism, religion, or other matters of opinion, or force citizens to confess by word or act their faith therein. If there are any circumstances which permit an exception, they do not now occur to us."

Attacks by conservatives on Colin Kaepernick and other Black public figures they deemed disloyal reflected the continuing hypocrisy of their vision of patriotism. In Kaepernick's case, they mischaracterized his principled stand against police brutality as an attack on the flag and the national anthem. Even if it had been, he had every right to make such an attack; but his was actually an attack on injustice, in the same way that Dr. King called on the nation to "rise up and live out the true meaning of its creed."

The conservatives who defended and amplified the attacks on Kaepernick's free speech had no such criticism when President Trump equated Russian president Vladimir Putin's brutality with America's own. In an interview with Fox News host Bill O'Reilly, Trump acknowledged that Putin was a killer, but "we got a lot of killers," he said. "You think our country's so innocent?" I can't disagree with Trump's critique. Our country is far from innocent. But if I had said that or Barack Obama had said that, white conservatives would have attacked us as unpatriotic. Trevor Noah, the host of *The Daily Show* in 2017, described it this way: "When a white billionaire spends a year screaming that America is a disaster, he's 'in touch with the country.' But when a Black man kneels quietly, 'he should be grateful for the successes America has allowed him to have.'"

Ironically, the national anthem itself reflects the hypocrisy of American patriotism. Written by a white supremacist enslaver named Francis Scott Key, the third verse of the anthem threatens revenge against enslaved Black people who joined the British in the War of 1812 in exchange for the promise of freedom. "No refuge could save the hireling and slave / From the terror of flight or the gloom of the grave," wrote Key. In Key's vision, the white colonists who fought against their oppressors in the American Revolution were *patriots*, but the Black enslaved soldiers who fought for their freedom in the War of 1812 were *traitors*.

James Baldwin exposed the double standard of America's view of race and freedom in an interview on *The Dick Cavett Show* in 1969: "When the Israelis pick up guns, or the Poles, or the Irish, or any white man in the world says 'Give me liberty or give me death,' the entire white world applauds. When a Black man says exactly the same thing, word for word, he is judged a criminal and treated like one, and everything possible is done to make an example of this bad nigger, so there won't be any more like him."

The white conservative construction of patriotism in America defines white rebellion as honorable but Black resistance as disloyal. Following the Civil War, Confederate soldiers were rewarded with amnesty after they had committed treason against the union and killed hundreds of thousands of their countrymen. Even today, white men are permitted to construct Confederate monuments to those traitors, and the white people who attacked the US Capitol in the January 6 insurrection are lauded as heroes in some conservative circles. But Black people have been accused of being unpatriotic for the peaceful acts of merely raising their fists at the 1968 Olympics or taking a knee during a football game in 2016.

African Americans have served in all the nation's wars, even as they were unfairly treated. They fought for their own freedom with the British and for the freedom of white men alongside Revolutionary colonists who claimed to believe that "all men are created equal." An estimated two hundred thousand Black men, 78 percent of the free Black population of the North, fought to preserve the union in the Civil War even though they were not paid the same wages as their white counterparts. Black soldiers also fought against tyranny and fascism in the twentieth century while they were forced to serve in racially segregated units until 1948. And African Americans continue to serve in the twenty-first century.

We have demonstrated our loyalty to the country and its founding principles, yet we are condemned when we demand the country return its loyalty to us. When legendary musician Stevie Wonder took a knee during a concert in 2017, former Republican congressman Joe Walsh slammed him as "another ungrateful black multi millionaire." And when basketball icon LeBron James spoke about the country's increasingly hostile racial climate in 2018, Fox News host Laura Ingraham told him to "shut up and dribble."

Yet when Kanye West became a Trump supporter, Republicans openly embraced the Black entertainer. And when former football player Herschel Walker ran an underwhelming campaign for the United States Senate, they never told him to shut up. White conservatives have embraced African American public figures only when those

African Americans endorse positions inconsistent with the preferences of the majority of the Black community. This allows the white conservatives to put a Black face on white supremacy.

What these conservatives refuse to acknowledge is that criticism is an essential element of patriotism. The American tradition, from the Boston Tea Party to the abolitionist movement, from women's suffragists to Freedom Riders, from antiwar protesters to queer activists, is a legacy of protest. The attempt to coerce patriotism from Black people dishonors that history.

For all its promise, America remains a deeply flawed country with a troubling past and an uncertain future. We need not construct a sanitized history of the nation to appreciate its value and potential.

Most Black people I have encountered know very well that America is imperfect. We have been the victims of that imperfection for generations. And we have no reason to genuflect to demonstrate our gratitude. In fact, America should express its gratitude for our presence.

"The principal product that will elevate us from poverty is cotton," wrote future Texas founder Stephen F. Austin in 1824, "and we cannot do this without the help of slaves." Black Americans provided the uncompensated labor that helped Texas and the rest of the nation generate its wealth. That coerced Black labor enabled a backwater collection of fledgling state alliances to develop into a thriving international economy. Black activists fought to establish the true democracy that the white framers of the republic resisted. And Black people and Black artists created a rich culture that gave the nation its unique soul.

For all that we have contributed to America, we have the right to enjoy the fruits of our labor. And for all that we have suffered in America, we have the right to demand justice. Perhaps some white Americans fear that Black people will eventually do to them what has been done to us, but that has never been a goal for Black leaders. In the words of author Kimberly Latrice Jones, "They are lucky that what Black people are looking for is equality and not revenge."

15

We will never reach equality without reparations.

ARGUMENT

I don't think reparations for something that happened 150 years ago, for whom none of us currently living are responsible, is a good idea.

—*Senate Republican Leader Mitch McConnell, June 18, 2019*

ANSWER

Indeed, in America there is a strange and powerful belief that if you stab a black person 10 times, the bleeding stops and the healing begins the moment the assailant drops the knife. We believe white dominance to be a fact of the inert past, a delinquent debt that can be made to disappear if only we don't look.

—*Author Ta-Nehisi Coates, June 2014*

As the sun rose on Christmas morning in 1857, all was not well for William and Matilda Bowie of Prince Georges County, Maryland. Their family had just been torn apart by the whims of the enslavers who held them captive, and things were about to get worse.

Some members of the family were scheduled to be released in the new year, while others would have to remain enslaved in perpetuity at the forced labor camp known as the McGregor Plantation. One of those assigned to remain at the camp was William and Matilda's twenty-one-year-old son, Jack. While his parents and four of his siblings would soon be free, Jack would remain enslaved.

Much of the true story that follows derives from a history of the McGregor and Bowie families by author James L. Bacon; from historical records posted online by researcher Susan Tichy on the Magruder's Landing website; and from a February 16, 1864, report titled *Emancipation in the District of Columbia* produced by the US Treasury Department.

When Roderick McGregor died in September 1857, his will instructed the executor of his estate to manumit six of the enslaved people he held in captivity: "William Bowie and his wife Matilda and their children Thomas, Nathaniel, Margaret and Boston." The six chosen members of the Bowie family were designated to be taken to the District of Columbia and "hired out for twelve months" and then to be "free at the expiration of one year from my death." There was no mention of Jack Bowie in McGregor's will.

Jack had spent his entire life enslaved, but four days after Christmas, he decided it was time for him to execute a plan for departure. In so doing, he followed the tradition of prominent African Americans before him. Maryland was the birthplace of two of the nation's most famous formerly enslaved people: Frederick Douglass and Harriet Tubman. Born in different parts of the state four years apart, both escaped to freedom. Jack also followed in the footsteps of his mother, Matilda, who had escaped from captivity years earlier but was caught and brought back to enslavement. But on Tuesday, December 29, 1857, Jack made his move and escaped as well.

A few days later, in early January 1858, the executor of the estate posted an ad in the *Baltimore Sun* offering a $100 reward (roughly the equivalent of $3,000 in 2023) for the return of Jack Bowie. It described Jack as a "negro man" between five feet eight and five feet ten inches tall, with a dark mulatto complexion, "rather long face and voice effeminate." Nathaniel McGregor, the brother of the deceased enslaver, who posted the ad, suspected that Jack might have fled to the District of Columbia and indicated that he had "relations and acquaintances in Washington city."

His suspicion proved correct, as Jack was soon captured and then incarcerated in the District of Columbia. Fearing that Jack might be "sold south" after his attempted escape, Matilda came up with a resourceful plan to get him out of jail. She found a rich white family in Washington, DC, to buy her son.

"Boy Jack," as he was described in the bill of sale, was sold out of the Washington jail for $1,000 (about $30,000 in 2023) on February 2, 1858. The sale was reportedly "ordered by the Orphans Court," and the two men who purchased Jack were brothers, Joseph Clapp Willard and Henry Augustus Willard, owners of a popular hotel at 14th Street and Pennsylvania Avenue. Henry Willard was hired in 1847 as the manager of what was then the struggling City Hotel, but the entrepreneurial twenty-five-year-old soon took over, remodeled the building, and changed the name to Willard's City Hotel.

The hotel's proximity to the White House helped to position it as a place of power and influence in the nation's capital. It was there in 1861 that former president John Tyler held a peace convention to try to prevent the nation from plunging into civil war. And the man who prosecuted that war for the union, Abraham Lincoln, also stayed at the hotel in the days before his March 1861 inauguration.

A year after the Civil War began, well before the Emancipation Proclamation, President Lincoln signed a law that formally abolished slavery in the District of Columbia. The word spread quickly, according to historian C. R. Gibbs. One Black resident described the reaction when he delivered the news to two female friends, one of whom had an enslaved son: "When I entered they perceived that something was ahead and emmediately [sic] asked me 'What's the news?' The District's free says I pulling out the 'National Republic' and reading its editorial. When I had finished the chambermaid had left the room sobbing for joy. The slave women clapped her hands and shouted, left the house saying, 'let me go and tell my husband that Jesus has done all things well.'"

It was called the District of Columbia Compensated Emancipation Act, and it included three primary features.

- First, it immediately emancipated Black people who were enslaved in the District.

- Second, it authorized compensation to enslavers of up to $300 for each person they claimed to own.
- And third, it allowed Black people to receive up to $100 in compensation if they agreed to leave the country.

The three-man commission that reviewed the petitions from enslavers created an elaborate administrative architecture to decide the claims. They published a notice in local papers announcing they would meet every day except Saturdays in City Hall. They brought in a slave dealer from Baltimore to help value the lost "property." They created a formula that depreciated the value of the enslaved people because of their lost marketability due to the war. They required petitioners to submit proof and documentation of their claims. And because many Black people left their enslavers immediately after emancipation, some enslavers had to bring witnesses to testify to the "age, size, complexion, health and qualifications" of "absent servants."

In May 1862, Joseph and Henry Willard petitioned for compensation for the people they had enslaved. One of the names on their list was Jack Bowie, now twenty-seven years old and described as "generally healthy, but not so strong & stout as the others." Although the law initially limited payments to $300 per person, federal records indicate that the Willards received $547.50 for the loss of Jack Bowie and $1,883.40 for four other enslaved people who had been freed by the act.

When it was all over, the new law granted freedom to 2,989 formerly enslaved Black people and paid claims to more than 900 other people, like the Willards, to compensate them for the injury they suffered. It was the first major example of reparations for slavery in American history, and the people who were compensated were the enslavers themselves.

Just the mention of the word "reparations" in a casual conversation today elicits a visceral reaction and a litany of questions from some listeners. *Why are you bringing this up now? Why should I be punished for something that happened hundreds of years ago? How much is that going to cost? Who's going to pay for it? How would you determine whom to pay? How is a check going to solve anything? And why don't we focus on a "race-neutral" approach instead?* Black people have been demanding reparations since the nineteenth century, but nearly all those pleas have been ignored.

On November 15, 1864, Union general William Tecumseh Sherman burned the Confederate city of Atlanta and led his sixty thousand soldiers on a 285-mile-long March to the Sea to Savannah. After meeting with Black leaders, General Sherman issued Field Order Number 15 on January 16, 1865. It ordered confiscated land from Charleston to Jacksonville be used "for the settlement of the negroes now made free."

Within those settlements, Sherman designated that "each family shall have a plot of not more than (40) forty acres of tillable ground." Later, he agreed to loan the settlers mules from the Union army. This became the origin of the phrase "forty acres and a mule," which Black people were led to believe they would receive when slavery ended.

By June 1865, the Civil War was over, Lincoln was dead, and forty thousand formerly enslaved Black people had been resettled on four hundred thousand acres of Atlantic coastal land. The future seemed to be promising for Black people, but Lincoln's successor, Democratic president Andrew Johnson of Tennessee, had other ideas. Johnson, who sympathized with the southern states, issued a proclamation granting amnesty to former Confederates. Then, on September 12, 1865, he revoked Sherman's field order, evicting African Americans from the land they had just been given. Instead of compensating the people who had been most injured by slavery, the federal government once again compensated the enslavers, and this time it rewarded the very people who caused the war and fought against the Union.

Twenty-five years later, in 1890, Republican representative William Connell of Nebraska introduced an unsuccessful reparations bill (H.R. 11119) that would have provided pensions to formerly enslaved people. At the suggestion of a Democrat, Connell considered rebranding the plan as a "Southern-tax relief" bill because it would boost the ailing southern economy by providing an influx of capital.

Then, in 1915, an organization representing formerly enslaved Black people filed an unsuccessful class action lawsuit seeking $68 million in reparations from the US Treasury, which had collected tax revenue from cotton produced by the "involuntary servitude" of the plaintiffs and their ancestors.

In 1969, a group of Black leaders assembled at the National Black Economic Development Conference and issued the Black Manifesto, demanding that white churches and synagogues pay $500 million for a "southern land bank," a research skills center, four TV networks, and other projects. The group estimated the cost represented only "fifteen dollars for every Black brother and sister in the United States" as "a beginning of the reparations due us." Separately, Muhammad Kenyatta, the vice chair of the organization, argued that Black Americans were owed "back pay" by the nation's institutions because "slave labor" had been a source of capital for the development of America and "Black people after slavery were further exploited economically."

In 1989, Representative John Conyers of Michigan introduced a bill to create a federal commission to study the impact of slavery.

In 2000, Randall Robinson, the founder of TransAfrica, an international human rights organization, argued the case for reparations in his bestselling book *The Debt: What America Owes to Blacks*. And in 2014, author Ta-Nehisi Coates published "The Case for Reparations" in *The Atlantic*.

There are several precedents for the idea of paying reparations. Not only did the federal government provide reparations to enslavers in 1862, but it has also provided compensation to various groups of people who have been wronged throughout history.

In 1892, the United States paid reparations to the families of Italian Americans who had been the victims of a lynching in New Orleans in 1891. In 1980, the Supreme Court ordered the federal government to pay more than $100 million to the Sioux Nation because in 1877 the United States had reneged on an 1868 treaty that granted them the Black Hills of South Dakota by taking back the land. Eight years later, Congress passed the Civil Liberties Act of 1988, authorizing the payment of reparations to Japanese Americans who had been incarcerated in prison camps during World War II.

One of the main reasons why reparations are still needed is that our nation has never dismantled the infrastructure of white supremacy on which slavery was built. The vast racial disparities in America today trace their roots directly to the hundreds of years in which Black people were systemically dehumanized, enslaved, deprived of basic civil liberties and human rights, and coerced to work for the social and economic benefit of white people.

Once slavery was abolished in 1865, the government engaged in an ambitious but halting twelve-year effort to make things right called Reconstruction. But that ended in 1877 as the nation retreated from its commitment and left Black people in virtually the same condition they were in before, except for the physical shackles.

After Reconstruction, the nation moved into a ninety-year period of Jim Crow segregation and racial terrorism against Black Americans. No substantive and enduring steps were taken to repair the breach left by slavery. Far too many white Americans hope to overlook this history and pretend we're all equal. But as Malcolm X said, "If you stick a knife in my back nine inches and pull it out six inches, there's no progress. If you pull it all the way out, that's not progress. The progress is healing the wound that the blow made. And they haven't even begun to pull the knife out, much less heal the wound. They won't even admit the knife is there."

Ta-Nehisi Coates continues Malcolm's knife analogy in his writings. "Indeed, in America there is a strange and powerful belief that if you stab a black person 10 times, the bleeding stops and the healing begins the moment the assailant drops the knife. We believe white dominance to be a fact of the inert past, a delinquent debt that can be made to disappear if only we don't look."

For those who argue that reparations will divide the country, look around. America is already divided, as Coates argued: "American prosperity was ill-gotten and selective in its distribution," he wrote in *The Atlantic*. "What is needed is an airing of family secrets, a settling with old ghosts. What is needed is a healing of the American psyche and the banishment of white guilt."

The idea of making amends for racial justice is not just a pipe dream of Black intellectuals and nationalists; it's a basic principle of social justice as articulated by one of the Black people whom white

Americans love to misquote. Dr. King expressed his support for a "multibillion-dollar program" to help Black people and endorsed "a policy of preferential treatment to rehabilitate the traditionally disadvantaged Negro." King explained that "for two centuries the Negro was enslaved, and robbed of any wages—potential accrued wealth which would have been the legacy of his descendants." He also compared the proposed investment in Black communities to the Marshall Plan to rebuild Europe after World War II: "If America can afford to underwrite its allies and ex-enemies, it can certainly afford—and has a much greater obligation, as I see it—to do at least as well by its own no-less-needy countrymen."

Reparations are not solely about what happened years ago. They're about what's happening now. White America is still benefiting from the interest accumulated on the stolen capital of Black bodies. Yet, Senate Republican Leader Mitch McConnell has objected to "reparations for something that happened 150 years ago" because "none of us currently living are responsible." Yes, no one is responsible for the theft committed by their ancestors, but they are responsible for how they benefit from that theft, and in Mitch McConnell's case, two of his great-great-grandfathers, James McConnell and Richard Daley, owned at least fourteen enslaved people in Limestone County, Alabama.

In fact, numerous families, colleges, businesses, and other institutions that exist today benefited from the institution of slavery. Most importantly, our federal and state governments benefited from tax revenue of wealthy white families that was generated by the labor of uncompensated enslaved Black people.

Some argue that it's too late to ask for reparations for the descendants of the enslaved, but part of the reason why it remains necessary is that the Black people who lived through slavery failed in their attempts to collect comprehensive reparations for the debt owed to them while they were enslaved. One of the first examples took place on February 14, 1783, when an elderly woman named Belinda Sutton filed a petition in Massachusetts describing how she had been abducted in Africa by "an armed band of white men," shipped to America, and forced into slavery. She lived long enough to seek reparations, or "an allowance" from the estate of her enslaver, whose family enslaved more people than any other household in Massachusetts. "The face of your Petitioner, is now marked with the furrows of time, and her frame feebly bending under the oppression of years, while she, by the Laws of the Land, is denied the enjoyment of one morsel of that immense wealth, apart whereof hath been accumilated [sic] by her own industry, and the whole augmented by her servitude," her petition read.

The name of Belinda's enslaver was Isaac Royall Jr., and the institution I attended two centuries later, Harvard Law School, was created in part by a gift from Royall, who accumulated wealth from the labor of Belinda Sutton and other uncompensated Black people. The college where I taught, Columbia University, received donations "from prominent New York families with slave plantations in the West Indies," according to the *New York Times*, and allowed enslavers to borrow money at below-market interest rates, according to historian Eric Foner. And the building where I once worked, the White House, "was built by slaves," as former first lady Michelle Obama observed in her 2016 Democratic convention speech. "Starting with Jefferson's administration, the majority of the White House staff from 1800 through the Civil War consisted of slaves," according to Jesse Holland's book about the construction of the Capitol.

The banking industry also benefited, as Jamie Dimon of JPMorgan Chase acknowledged in an apology in 2005. Slavery was "a tragic time" in the company's history, he said in a statement.

Even America's most beloved whiskey benefited from those who had been enslaved. It was an enslaved master distiller named Nathan "Nearest" Green who taught Jack Daniel the distilling process in the 1800s, and it took until 2017 for someone to honor that legacy, when Fawn Weaver created a company called Uncle Nearest Premium Whisky.

"The past is never dead," wrote William Faulkner. "It's not even past."

Reparations act as restorative justice for a people who continue to suffer today because of the uncorrected evils of the past. White America stole our treasure, our lives, our families, our history, and our precious labor and used those resources to build a country that still dispropor-tionately benefits white people. Since we can't repossess the numerous intangible things that were stolen from us, we deserve compensation for the lost value of those things.

That's a debt that's still owed.

In many conversations about reparations, people often ask how much they would cost to implement. The truth is no one knows. It all depends on what those reparations look like and how they function. That's one of the issues that could be studied if Congress passes H.R. 40, a bill to create a commission about slavery and reparations.

Not paying reparations is already costing America. We're paying for it with persistent race-based social and economic inequality. We're paying for it with growing distrust of our democracy. We're paying for it with the billions of dollars spent on the criminal justice system and the prison industrial complex because our society refuses to deal with the causes of crime and the inequities in law enforcement.

As most of us have seen in court cases where wrongfully incarcer-ated people are freed or the families of wrongfully killed people are compensated, it's impossible to put a specific dollar figure on a human life. It's even more difficult when you're dealing with millions of lives. But that's all the more reason to begin the process. Millions of peo-ple walking around with unresolved complaints about the fairness of the country their ancestors helped to build is a formula for permanent social unrest and disruptive upheaval.

"Perhaps no number can fully capture the multi-century plunder of black people in America," wrote Ta-Nehisi Coates in *The Atlantic*. "Perhaps the number is so large that it can't be imagined, let alone cal-culated and dispensed. But I believe that wrestling publicly with these questions matters as much as—if not more than—the specific answers that might be produced."

I don't think of reparations as a one-time dollar figure payment to Black people but rather as a continuing investment in a more just soci-ety. That means setting a long-term goal of racial equality and creating short- and medium-term targets to measure the achievement of that goal until the underlying racial disparities in employment, health care, schools, housing, income, criminal justice, environmental quality, and overall quality of life are eliminated.

As Coates put it, "More important than any single check cut to any African American, the payment of reparations would represent America's maturation out of the childhood myth of its innocence into a wisdom worthy of its founders."

In other words, reparations are not about writing a check; they're about righting a wrong.

In every Congress from 1989 to 2019, Representative John Conyers introduced a bill on reparations. When Conyers died, Representative Sheila Jackson Lee took up the task, along with other House members. The modest bill, usually titled as H.R. 40 to represent General Sherman's promise of forty acres and a mule, would establish a fifteen-member commission to study the effects of slavery and discriminatory policies on African Americans and recommend appropriate remedies, including reparations.

The bill was voted out of committee for the first time in 2022, but it has never passed in Congress. The point of the commission would be to determine appropriate mechanisms to make reparations work, but many thoughtful scholars and thinkers have come up with suggestions.

Rashawn Ray and Andre M. Perry, two senior fellows at the Brookings Institution, have proposed the Harriet Tubman Community Investment Act, which includes, among other things, individual payments to descendants of enslaved Black Americans, college tuition and student loan forgiveness for descendants of enslaved Black Americans, business grants for start-ups, and down-payment grants to be used toward housing revitalization.

There's no one-size-fits-all solution for racial inequality, and I think many African Americans would welcome the opportunity to think collectively about which solutions work best.

Reparations should also include ancestral research grants so Black people can learn more about their family histories, not so much to determine who might be eligible for reparations but rather to rebuild the bonds that were torn apart by centuries of racist government policies.

Although much of the criticism of reparations comes from conservatives, there is a progressive objection that some have raised to the idea, based on the notion that race-neutral policies might be better suited to address inequality. These arguments suggest an elegant solution to a complex political problem, but they fundamentally misunderstand the purpose of reparations.

The purpose of reparations is not simply to eliminate *income inequality*, although reparations would surely move toward that admirable goal because of the correlation between racial and economic disparities. But the purpose is to eliminate *racial inequality*. Race-neutral progressive policies play an important role in creating a fairer society, but they do not eliminate racial disparities. If low-income white people have ten dollars and low-income black people have five dollars, a plan that gives everyone ten additional dollars will help both, but it won't eliminate the racial disparity.

Many times, the disparities aren't even based on economics but on the intangible benefits accumulated from the "property right in whiteness." Even if Black and white people are given access to the same economic resources, such economic equality means little in a world where Black people are still denied racial equality in freedom of movement, criminal justice enforcement, and incarceration.

We must dismantle all the vestiges of a racist system built to benefit white people at the expense of others. This work must continue not just until a commission is appointed, a law is passed, a check is written, or a specific number of years has lapsed. The work must go on until Black people are equal in result, not just word.

The infrastructure of white supremacy has constructed innumerable tools to perpetuate racial disparities in employment, health care, education, homeownership, household income, arrest rates, proximity to toxic waste sites, and community access to clean water, banks, grocery stores, and more. That means we'll need to use a variety of different tools and government policies to achieve that goal. And we'll need to commit ourselves for the long run to make it work.

We've got a lot to do, even in generating broad-based public support. A poll published by the Pew Research Center in November 2022 found that 77 percent of Black Americans support reparations for the descendants of people enslaved in the United States, while only 18 percent of white Americans agree. It sounds daunting, but I've seen public opinion shift in my lifetime on other controversial issues, including legalizing marijuana and same-sex marriage. Americans opened their minds on those issues because of relentless pressure from activists to move the conversations forward. It will take the same pressure to move the issue of reparations.

If you just want to pacify a few Black people, you can pass modest laws and celebrate personal achievements and pretend that it represents change. But comprehensive and enduring change must be substantive, not just symbolic. There's no way for America to reach true racial equality without reparations. Not just a check, but a change. Many of us in the Black community already know that. Many in the white community understand this as well, but not enough of them will say it.

PART FOUR | MYTHS OF BLACK INFERIORITY

The Auburn Tigers held a sixteen-point lead over Virginia Tech with seven minutes to play in the fourth quarter of the last game of their season. It was one of the undefeated team's lowest-scoring games after regular-season blowout victories of 52–7 against Louisiana Tech and 42–10 against Kentucky. But this was no ordinary game. This was the 2005 Sugar Bowl.

Quarterback Jason Campbell had just led the Auburn Tigers in their only touchdown drive of the game after a fifty-three-yard pass to wide receiver Anthony Mix and a short touchdown pass to Devin Aromashodu. Then Virginia Tech fired back as its quarterback, Bryan Randall, connected to Josh Morgan for a twenty-nine-yard touchdown pass and an eighty-yard follow-up touchdown to close the gap to 16–13 with two minutes to play.

But Virginia Tech could not catch up. Auburn's Jason Campbell took the last snap, ending the game, completing his college career as the Sugar Bowl MVP, and leading the Tigers to their first undefeated season in the modern history of Auburn football. The crowd in the Superdome in New Orleans roared.

Auburn's head football coach, Tommy Tuberville, humbly walked onto the field in his orange jacket to shake hands with opposing coach Frank Beamer. The two white men would earn millions of dollars for coaching their teams, a success built with the help of African American players, including both teams' quarterbacks and the wide receivers who scored the only touchdowns in the bowl game.

Years later, a very different Tommy Tuberville emerged. Following a scandal involving inflated grades for football players and a dismal 5–7 record, the man known as "Coach Tubs" was forced to resign with a comfortable $5 million payout. Tuberville coached for a few years at Texas Tech, where he was caught on television physically assaulting an assistant coach for a botched play, and at the University of Cincinnati, where he ran into trouble for yelling at a fan "Go to hell!" after his team suffered an embarrassing loss.

Then he moved to politics, running for United States Senate as an ill-informed Republican who misidentified the three branches of government as "the House, the Senate, and the executive" and mistakenly claimed that his father had fought in World War II "to free Europe of socialism."

In deep-red Alabama, Tuberville won his 2020 Senate race with 60 percent of the vote against Democratic incumbent Doug Jones, but it was a racist remark two years later that revealed what he really believed. Democrats, according to Tuberville, "want crime," he said, "because they want to take over what you got." Speaking to a nearly all-white audience at a rally, Tuberville claimed that Democrats "want reparations because they think the people that do the crime are owed that."

The year was 2022, and a sixty-eight-year-old white man from Alabama, a former college football coach who had built his fortune on the backs of the uncompensated labor of Black bodies, was loudly telling white people that Black people are undeserving criminals.

The Black criminality narrative that Tuberville declaimed is one of the oldest racist tropes in American history, perpetuated by white society through the criminalization of Blackness itself, which allowed the mere presence of African Americans in unwelcome white spaces to become prima facie evidence of suspicious behavior.

If you truly believe that all people are created equal, as our founding document suggests, then you cannot also believe that one race of people is more disposed than another to crime, welfare, dishonesty, family dysfunction, or civil incompetence. To assert that one group of people is inherently more inclined than another to engage in antisocial behavior is the very definition of racism.

Part 4 examines some of the many ways in which white society continues to promote dangerous myths of Black inferiority. Often these arguments are cloaked by a disingenuous paternalism that suggests that Black people would be better off if they focused on their own alleged moral failures instead of addressing the larger societal issues that contribute to their condition.

Black Americans are already well aware of the unique challenges we face in our communities, and our thinkers, activists, and leaders have been working on these issues for years, usually without resources or support from the people who now claim we should turn our attention to them.

16

There are more white people than Black people on welfare.

ARGUMENT

I don't want to make black people's lives better by giving them somebody else's money. I want to give them the opportunity to go out and earn the money.

—*Republican presidential candidate Rick Santorum, January 3, 2012*

ANSWER

My guess is that many still think of these as programs mainly for inner-city Black people (and maybe immigrants), and are unaware that a majority of food stamp recipients are white, and that many are in rural states.

—*Nobel Prize–winning economist Paul Krugman, May 23, 2023*

This is a story of two people. The first is an anthropologist from Kansas named Stanley. The second is a woman in Chicago named Linda. That's only half a dozen words per person to describe them, but those six words communicate volumes about our perception of race, class, and values in America.

When Americans hear the words "anthropologist," "Kansas," and "Stanley," our minds have been conditioned from media, culture, and experience to create a rough sketch of the individual in question. "Anthropologist" is a cue for intelligent, college-educated, and perhaps hardworking. "Kansas" tells us the person is midwestern, perhaps plainspoken, and maybe down to earth. "Stanley" suggests the person identifies as male. The three terms together suggest the person is probably white. These white midwesterners are the people we're told by the media to think of as the "salt of the earth" and "the real Americans."

In contrast, when we hear the words "woman," "Chicago," and "Linda," we get a different impression from our mental conditioning, especially when the words are put together. The word "woman" suggests a gender stereotype. And the word "Chicago" suggests the person may be Black. "Chicago" has been used by conservatives to conjure up "urban" images of the so-called inner city, and it's often associated with corruption and, of course, cold. Depending on your age, you might associate the word with Harold Washington, Oprah Winfrey, Michael Jordan, Barack Obama, Lori Lightfoot, or Brandon Johnson, all prominent African Americans from the Windy City. In recent years, "Chicago" has also become right-wing shorthand for "crime," but this, too, is racialized and politicized. Finally, the name "Linda" is sufficiently versatile not to designate a particular race, but combined with the word "Chicago," it suggests the person identifies as a woman and may be Hispanic.

All those assumptions come from just six words.

When we consider those two individuals in the context of a specific discussion about welfare, we tend to generate even more assumptions. Many of us have been conditioned to associate welfare with race and gender, and because of the assumptions we've already made in analyzing the basic information we had about their identities, we might be able to extrapolate from those assumptions to determine which person we believe is more likely to have received welfare.

The two people described by those dozen words are Stanley Ann Dunham and Linda Taylor. Stanley, who dropped her first name after college, is best known as the mother of former president Barack Obama. Linda, who reportedly had several other aliases, is best known as the subject of Ronald Reagan's infamous "welfare queen" story.

Stanley Ann Dunham was described "first as 'a white anthropologist from Kansas' and then as 'a single mother on food stamps' and 'the woman who died of cancer while fighting with her insurance company at the end of her life,'" according to an NPR *Fresh Air* interview of author Janny Scott, who wrote the book *A Singular Woman: The Untold Story of Barack Obama's Mother*. Scott's book explains how Ann Dunham was more than any of those brief character sketches could ever explain, yet popular narratives inform our perception of her. Because we know she was a white woman from Kansas, that she died of cancer, and that her son became president of the United States, we're conditioned to feel empathy toward her.

Linda Taylor came to fame as the unnamed welfare recipient in a story that Ronald Reagan told during his unsuccessful 1976 campaign for president. "There's a woman in Chicago," Reagan began. The former actor and California governor omitted her name and used only five words to communicate all the racial assumptions I discussed above. In 1976, the CBS comedy *Good Times* was a popular prime-time television show depicting a fictional Black family living in a public housing project in Chicago. When Reagan described the details of his "woman in Chicago," the racial assumptions became clearer.

"She has eighty names, thirty addresses, twelve Social Security cards and is collecting veterans' benefits on four nonexisting deceased husbands," Reagan said. "Her tax-free cash income alone is over $150,000." The story, according to the *New York Times*, was a wildly exaggerated account of a Chicago woman who did not have eighty aliases and did not make $150,000 a year, but the real-life version of Linda Taylor did become the subject of a less dramatic one-woman welfare scandal in the 1970s. But was she Black? The *Washington Post* described her as a "mixed-race woman who often told authorities she was white, Mexican or Hawaiian," citing author Josh Levin, who wrote the book *The Queen: The Forgotten Life Behind an American Myth.*

The stories of Stanley Ann and Linda represent two competing visions of welfare in America. Most Americans would be inclined to believe that Linda more accurately represents the average welfare recipient. Nearly two-thirds of Americans believe that most welfare recipients are Black or that there are as many Black Americans as white Americans receiving benefits, according to a January 2018 HuffPost/YouGov poll.

Asked about six government programs, the poll respondents were more likely to associate Black people with welfare, food stamps, public housing, and Head Start. In contrast, Americans were more likely to associate white people with Social Security and unemployment insurance. The difference, of course, is that virtually all working Americans contribute part of their income to Social Security and unemployment insurance programs, making them more acceptable forms of government aid than the other programs.

One of the challenges with these debates is our misunderstanding of the terminology. There is no line item in the federal budget called "welfare." The Census Bureau defines public assistance as "programs that provide either cash assistance or in-kind benefits to individuals and families from any governmental entity." Among those, the bureau distinguishes between social welfare programs and social insurance programs.

Some of the widely known social welfare programs include these:

- Supplemental Security Income (SSI)
- Supplemental Nutrition Assistance Program (SNAP)
- Program for Women, Infants, and Children (WIC)
- Temporary Assistance for Needy Families (TANF)

Some of the widely known social insurance programs include these:

- Social Security
- Veterans' benefits
- Unemployment insurance compensation
- Workers' compensation

The social welfare programs tend to be more racialized and less popular than the social insurance programs, but all these programs provide public assistance. The difference is that the beneficiaries of the insurance programs are often considered more deserving because they did something (paid taxes, served their country, worked, or were injured while working) that we think entitles them to the benefits.

Many of the conservative arguments against welfare gained popularity in the 1960s and '70s as a backlash to the civil rights movement, which enabled Black people to move into integrated workforces and public schools. The 1970s TV series *All in the Family* began each show with the two lead characters sitting at a piano playing a theme song that romanticized a time in the past when Americans did not need a "welfare state" because everyone "pulled his weight."

The real history of welfare in America is a bit more complicated. The preamble to the US Constitution lists one of the purposes of the document as to "promote the general Welfare," but the term used in that context appears to refer to the overall well-being and prosperity of the people. But at least since the nineteenth century, the nation has been essentially giving things away to certain people.

The Homestead Act of 1862 gave away 270 million acres of land, about 10 percent of the area of the United States, in one of the most generous acts of public charity in American history. Most of the land went to wealthy speculators, cattle owners, miners, loggers, and rail-road owners, according to the National Archives, and most of those people were white.

Franklin Roosevelt's New Deal introduced a series of new federal government services during the Great Depression, but the state and local governments that administered those programs in the South often restricted Black people from accessing them. As the Center on Budget and Policy Priorities explained in an August 2021 report, states' control over the 1935 program that we now know as Aid to Families with Dependent Children "enabled them to exclude many Black and brown people."

The Social Security Act of 1935, signed during the Great Depression, gave much-needed financial support to elderly retirees, but the law originally excluded domestic and agricultural workers, who were disproportionately Black.

The GI Bill of 1944 provided funding for World War II veterans to go to college or buy a home, but this also disproportionately benefited white Americans because Black veterans were not allowed to attend many white colleges or move into white neighborhoods that were developing in the nation's new suburbs.

The National Interstate and Defense Highways Act of 1956 enabled the government to carve through urban communities and historic Black neighborhoods to build highways that could safely transport white people out of the cities to newly developed, racially segregated suburbs.

Then, after a century of government giveaways to white people, antigovernment conservatism grew in the 1960s. That inconsistency was not lost on African American observers, who called out the continuing hypocrisy of a nation that had reneged on its promise of forty acres of land to Black people in the South after the Civil War while giving away land to white people in the West during that same war. As Dr. King said: "At the very same time that America refused to give the Negro any land, through an act of Congress, our government was giving away millions of acres of land in the West and the Midwest, which meant that it was willing to undergird its white peasants from Europe with an economic floor."

King explained how the government not only gave out free land but also built land grant colleges with government money to teach white people how to farm and gave them low interest rates they could use to finance the automation of those farms. "Today, many of these people are receiving millions of dollars in federal subsidies not to farm," King said, "and they are the very people telling the Black man that he ought to lift himself by his own bootstraps."

Decades after Reagan's 1976 "welfare queen" story, these racial perceptions of public assistance continued to be weaponized in American politics with coded language and political dog whistles that any sentient human could hear.

In 1995, Wisconsin's Republican governor, Tommy Thompson, complained about people moving from nearby Chicago to Milwaukee when he announced that Wisconsinites "are just fed up" with "people comin' in from other states, not working." Unlike those other states, "people in Wisconsin expect people to work," Thompson said, adding, "Maybe it's the old Germanic heritage, the old European heritage."

In 2011, Republican former Speaker of the House Newt Gingrich described Barack Obama as a "food stamp president."

In 2012, Republican former senator Rick Santorum added his complaints about welfare. "I don't want to make Black people's lives better by giving them somebody else's money," he said. "I want to give them the opportunity to go out and earn the money." Santorum, then a candidate for president, implausibly claimed that he said "blah people" instead of "Black people" when he spoke those words to a nearly all-white audience in Sioux City, Iowa. The problem is that the specific B-word he chose didn't matter. Welfare has become so deeply racialized in American public opinion that the word "Black" is virtually redundant when referring to the program.

Two years later, Representative Paul Ryan found himself embroiled in controversy when he complained about a "tailspin of culture in our inner cities," of "generations of men not even thinking about working or learning the value and the culture of work." When African Americans criticized the Wisconsin Republican, he claimed "there was nothing whatsoever about race in my comments at all—it had nothing to do with race."

Then, in March 2017, a member of the Congressional Black Caucus told Republican president Donald Trump that welfare cuts would hurt her constituents, "not all of whom are Black." The president reportedly replied, "Really? Then what are they?"

While it is not true that most people on welfare are Black, African Americans are *disproportionately* represented in many of these programs. This inequity, however, is not a flaw of Black people. It's an indictment of an unfair system. Before Black people had equal access to government assistance, white Americans received government resources for decades to help them buy land, purchase a home, go to college, establish stability, build wealth, retire comfortably, and pass money on to their heirs. Then, shortly after Black people gained equal access to government aid in the 1960s and '70s, the government began cutting those resources in the 1980s and '90s.

The truth is that white people comprise the largest group of welfare recipients in America. This fact would not shock any outside observer who casually glanced at US Census Bureau data. Non-Hispanic white people accounted for 59 percent of the total population in 2021. Black people accounted for only 13.6 percent of the population. However, because Blackness has become so connected to perceptions of welfare, we've been programmed to believe that the majority of welfare recipients are Black.

The racial programming helps explains why only 21 percent of respondents in the HuffPost/YouGov poll correctly said there are more white than Black food stamp recipients. As the US Department of Agriculture reported in June 2022, non-Hispanic white people were the largest racial or ethnic group to receive benefits from the Supplemental Nutrition Assistance Program.

Like so many other elements of American society, racial programming about welfare traces its roots to stereotypes that have been passed down for generations. "Slavery and Jim Crow laid the foundation for the economic, reproductive, and behavioral control policies that have permeated later cash assistance programs," according to an August 2021 report from the Center on Budget and Policy Priorities. "Labeling Black people as biologically inferior to white people and inherently lazy, promiscuous, irrational, and resilient to pain, white enslavers employed forced reproduction and labor to exploit, control, and punish enslaved Black women while maximizing their economic returns," the report added.

The racial history connected to welfare helps us understand why conservative policy makers continue to search for new and more punitive terms and conditions to apply to welfare applicants. Now that Black people can receive assistance, the existence of welfare is constructed as a moral failure that requires personal behavior change to resolve rather than a structural problem that requires serious policy solutions.

Poverty and welfare are more common than we like to acknowledge. Four out of five Americans will encounter poverty, near poverty, welfare use, or unemployment during their lives, meaning "poverty is a mainstream event experienced by a majority of Americans," according to Mark R. Rank, a professor of social welfare at Washington University. More surprisingly, 54 percent of all Americans will spend a year in poverty or near poverty, and nearly 40 percent of those between the ages of twenty-five and sixty will experience at least one year *below* the official poverty line, Rank explained.

There are more white people than Black people on welfare.

Despite the tendency to associate poverty and welfare with cities like Chicago, "only approximately 10 percent of those in poverty live in extremely poor urban neighborhoods," Rank wrote. Households in poverty "can be found throughout a variety of urban and suburban landscapes, as well as in small towns and communities across rural America," he added.

Yet a 2018 study by researchers Rachel Wetts and Robb Willer found that white attitudes about welfare are driven by racial resentment. "When whites perceive threats to their relative advantage in the racial status hierarchy, their resentment of minorities increases," according to a paper Wetts and Willer published in the journal *Social Forces*. In addition, "they increase opposition to programs intended to benefit poorer members of all racial groups."

These beliefs lead to funding cuts, stricter work requirements, and other onerous proposals often mislabeled as "welfare reform." Even Democrats, including Bill Clinton in 1996, have supported some of these conservative measures.

There's nothing wrong with the government providing, and people receiving, public assistance. The problem is that white Americans willingly accepted such public aid for a century while excluding Black recipients. But now that modern civil rights laws require federal, state, and local governments to distribute those resources more equitably, white conservatives have constructed racist stereotypes associated with that assistance.

After giving this country 250 years of free labor and then toiling through 100 years of sharecropping, low-wage employment, and second-class citizenship, Black people are the last group of people that white people should be calling lazy and dependent.

17

"Black-on-Black crime" is an outdated media trope.

ARGUMENT

Black-on-Black crime. Why doesn't anyone march about that? Why is it always the limited, the few incidents where cops are involved? Why is there such outrage, and then total ignoring of the majority of cases?

—*Fox News host Sean Hannity, August 27, 2015*

ANSWER

Black-On-Black crime is literally just crime. Oftentimes when people bring up Black-On-Black crime, they are implying that Black people are more violent towards each other than any other race. This is wrong because nearly every race is likely to be killed by their own due to proximity.

—*Journalist Zariah Taylor, September 8, 2020*

It was well past midnight on a Saturday when a burglar alarm rang inside a two-story brick home in St. Louis, Missouri. The homeowner was in distress. Police were dispatched to an address in the 3000 block of Vine Grove in the North St. Louis community known as the Ville. What they discovered was a grisly scene.

The officers found the owner, a thirty-four-year-old Black man, in a doorway, his unclothed body slumped near the burglar alarm button. The man's throat had been slashed, and he had been shot twice in the head and once in the left arm. He was transported to City Hospital, six miles away on Lafayette Avenue, where he was pronounced dead a few hours later. The victim was identified as Michael Holmes, and I knew him. He was my uncle.

The murder of my uncle took place in May 1980, when I was fourteen years old. As far as I know, no one was ever arrested or charged in connection with his murder, and the mystery of his death still bothers me today.

The police don't solve as many crimes as I once believed from watching old episodes of *Columbo*, and part of it may have to do with geography. "There are certain neighborhoods where the police just don't solve murders," crime analyst Jeff Asher told *The Atlantic*'s Derek Thompson in 2022. "In New Orleans, 90 percent of murders in the French Quarter are going to be solved," said Asher, a former analyst with the New Orleans Police Department. "A mile away in the Seventh Ward, maybe 15 percent of those cases are being solved."

Meanwhile, Black people are being disproportionately killed in America. Although we account for just over 13 percent of the US population, we make up nearly half of all homicide victims. Many of these victims, like my uncle, have long been considered disposable by the criminal justice system that is supposed to protect them. Most often, their killers are Black.

In May 1992, just days after an all-white jury acquitted the officers in the videotaped beating of Rodney King, Afro-American studies professor Sylvia Wynter published an open letter about a previously little-known acronym used by Los Angeles police officers and judicial officials to refer to cases where young Black males killed each other. The acronym was NHI, and it stood for "no humans involved."

Perhaps it was a form of the dehumanizing attitude of NHI that allowed police officers in Milwaukee to ignore the victims of serial killer Jeffrey Dahmer, who murdered seventeen men, most of them Black, from 1978 to 1991. This could also explain why police in St. Louis never seem to have apprehended the person who killed my uncle, who was a Black gay man. And it gives us more understanding of why so many murder cases involving Black trans women have gone unsolved. In these cases, and many others, police don't seem to treat Black lives very seriously.

It's precisely because of that sense that law enforcement neglects Black crime victims that activists have tried for years to focus public attention on crime in our communities. But it's not just the police we have to worry about. Mainstream media also contribute to the problem by failing to report on the crime stories that affect us or our community efforts to fight that crime.

In 2004, Black journalist Gwen Ifill spoke about the media's tendency to highlight stories of sympathetic white women who have disappeared while ignoring similar stories of Black women. Ifill called it "missing white woman syndrome." Years later, in response to the dearth of media coverage, journalist Erika Marie Rivers created a website called Our Black Girls, which reports on those stories that "go under-reported in the media—if they're reported at all."

In part because of the neglect they've seen from white America, for decades Black organizations have engaged in local activism to draw attention to the problem of violence in our communities. The Reverend Jesse Jackson has led protests in Chicago and other cities. The Reverend Al Sharpton has led antiviolence marches in New York and several other cities. But it's not just the highest-profile Black leaders who've been engaged. Others, like the Bishop Larry D. Camel, have led marches to "take back the streets." A community march led by Camel in Saginaw, Michigan, honored the memory of nine-year-old Devin Elliott and other victims of violence. "We're not going to tolerate kids getting killed in our streets any longer," he declared.

Despite all that activity, Fox News political analyst Juan Williams, a Black man, published an article in the *Wall Street Journal* in March 2012 asking why Black leaders marched for Trayvon Martin but not for other young Black murder victims. "Nationally, nearly half of all murder victims are black," wrote Williams. "And the overwhelming majority of those black people are killed by other black people. Where is the march for them?" Author Ta-Nehisi Coates responded in *The Atlantic* by posting a list of some of the many protests in which Black people led against violence in Black communities in the preceding years.

The following year, Reverend Jackson led a march to draw attention to the murder of fifteen-year-old Hadiya Pendleton, a Black girl in Chicago who was shot and killed just eight days after she performed at President Obama's second inauguration. Obama mentioned her in his State of the Union address that year, noting that "she was shot and killed in a Chicago park after school, just a mile away from my house."

In 2022 alone, there were numerous other examples of Black leaders marching against violence in Black communities. A group in Watts led their nineteenth annual Stop the Violence march in the historically Black Los Angeles community. A Harlem group held a Stop Shooting/Start Living march in the famous New York city neighborhood. A group in Stone Mountain, Georgia, held a Stop the Madness rally in that city. Not far away, teenagers took part in a Protect the Kids, Stop the Violence march at Atlanta City Hall. Black church leaders in Detroit organized a Stop the Violence march in that city. And Black leaders in Philadelphia led a March for Our Lives rally.

To suggest that Black leaders have been neglecting crime in Black communities is to erase or deny decades of community engagement. White ignorance, or willful blindness, of Black activism is no excuse for perpetuating false information. But white conservative commentators and political actors, and their enablers, make these arguments primarily to serve two purposes: first, to promote stereotypes of Black inferiority, and second, to deflect attention from Black complaints about police brutality and racist attacks on Black people. "Why are you protesting about George Floyd or Breonna Taylor when you should be doing something about crime in your own communities?" they ask. The truth is, Black America has been doing both. White America just wasn't paying attention.

But Black leaders often face white-imposed barriers in their ability to create policy solutions to crime in their communities. When Black mayors and city councils pass effective gun safety laws to hold firearms manufacturers accountable or restrict access to deadly weapons in their communities, white state legislatures block those laws and prohibit their implementation. Black people aren't making the guns that are being used in Atlanta, Birmingham, Cleveland, Houston, New Orleans, or other cities to commit crimes. Those weapons are made by mostly white-run companies with ties to white Republican lawmakers, all of whom share a financial interest in the proliferation of those guns.

Focusing public attention away from the problems of gun violence and state violence against Black bodies allows conservatives to reframe Black crime as a unique moral failure of African American communities, implying that similar problems do not exist elsewhere. In reality, members of every racial group engage in criminal activity. But by associating stereotypes of criminality with Blackness, white rhetoric imposes a burden of group representation on African Americans not shared by others.

When white people engage in crime, only the individual actor is held responsible. When Black people do so, we're told it reflects badly on the entire race. Similarly, crime in white communities is often presented as an aberration while crime in Black communities becomes normative. Ultimately, the existence of crime itself in our communities becomes evidence of moral corruption deserving punitive criminal justice measures directed at Black people, but the prevalence of crime in the white population becomes a basis for evolving public policy. The glaring disparity between the forceful criminal justice response to the "crack epidemic" of the Reagan era and the sympathetic public health approach to the opioid epidemic of the 2010s exemplifies the problem.

The use of the popular media trope "Black-on-Black crime" exacerbates the racial disparity. No one disputes the fact that most Black crime victims are targeted by people of the same race. Most crime in America is *intraracial*, not interracial. That's partly an indicator of continuing racial segregation in our society, but it's also a reflection of the reality that people usually target people close to them. In 2019, 89 percent of Black homicide victims were killed by other Black people, according to FBI data. But in the same year, 79 percent of white people were killed by other white people. Despite the similarity in statistics, media outlets rarely publish stories about "white-on-white crime." It's just crime.

The "Black-on-Black crime" trope fits a racist narrative that claims African Americans are inherently predisposed to crime in ways that white people are not. This allows white policy makers to elude their own responsibility to examine the root causes of crime in Black communities—the persistent racial disparities in employment, education, health care, housing, and criminal justice.

Although Black people do not commit the majority of crime in the United States, it is true we are disproportionately overrepresented in the criminal justice system. This requires us to interrogate the causes of that disparity. First, Blackness itself is suspect in America, ensnaring thousands of innocent Black people a year in a racially targeted "law and order" dragnet. The overpolicing of Black communities leads to racial disparities in arrests for minor offenses, especially for Black youth. Those offenses, no matter how minor, limit Black people's opportunities for socioeconomic mobility in employment, housing, and education and become the basis of justification for more overpolicing.

If white communities experienced the same current social conditions that Black communities experience, along with the racial stigma of hundreds of years of slavery, segregation, and the persistence of a racist social structure and criminal justice system directed against them, white Americans would also be disproportionately represented.

African American leaders have spent decades using their limited tools—including local legislation, moral suasion, and appeals to community pride—to address the problem of crime in our communities, but we do not control the federal and state governmental levers of power needed to change the structural issues that lead to crime.

No one wants to resolve the issue of crime in Black communities more than Black people. We live through it, and we've talked about it endlessly among ourselves. Many of us would welcome a serious substantive engagement by governmental leaders to address the problem we've been fighting on our own for years, but let's not sabotage the process by stigmatizing Black people for a problem that white America helped to create.

18

Black families are not broken.

ARGUMENT

I want you guys in the Black Lives Matter movement to join me, all right? Instead of directing your ire toward the large societal problem of African Americans, let's get into the family fabric first, try to solve that and then go back to the other thing.

—*Fox News anchor Bill O'Reilly, August 20, 2015*

ANSWER

But you can't overlook the vicious legacy of white supremacy, Brother Bill.

—*Dr. Cornel West, August 20, 2015*

Aime and George, a Black couple from South Carolina, raised their young son in a small sawmill village called Alcolu, about eighty miles north of Charleston. George, a former sharecropper, worked at the local lumber mill. Aime, like many Black women, also worked. She was employed as a cook at a local school for Black children.

As the family grew over time, the six of them shared what Charleston's *Post and Courier* newspaper called "a humble three-room company house" near the railroad tracks in a part of town reserved for Black people. By all accounts, they were an ordinary working-class Black family. Then the events of 1944 ripped them apart. Much of the story that follows comes from the extensive reporting done by the *Post and Courier* in a 2018 series and from other original newspaper accounts of George and Aime's son.

On Friday, March 24, 1944, two white girls, eleven-year-old Betty June Binnicker and seven-year-old Mary Emma Thames, went searching for wildflowers after school in Alcolu, South Carolina.

The two girls came across George Jr. and his sister Aime, who bore the same names as their parents. The two Black children were taking their family cow out to graze when the white girls asked them where to find wildflowers. The Black children did not know, so the girls continued looking.

Later that day, the girls were reported missing.

When news of the disappearance spread, fourteen-year-old George Jr. told his parents that he and his sister had seen the girls that day. George then "left with his father to join the search parties," the *Post and Courier* reported.

After the girls' bodies were discovered in a ditch, "there were no signs of a struggle when Dr. Asbury Cecil Bozard examined the bodies," according to the *Post and Courier*.

But speculation quickly turned to young George. Not long afterward, a group of white men drove up to young George's house, walked in while his parents were away, put him and his brother Johnny in handcuffs, and took them away. Johnny was later released, but George remained in custody. A local deputy sheriff claimed that George confessed to the murders within forty minutes of his arrest. The boy's father was fired from his job at the mill the same day, and the family quickly fled the town for safety at a relative's home in nearby Pinewood.

On Monday, April 24, exactly one month after his arrest, the fourteen-year-old boy was put on trial. "Fifteen hundred people swelled into the courtroom," the *Post and Courier* reported. George's parents, afraid of the crowd, were not among them.

The murder trial began at 2:30 p.m. and ended two hours later that same afternoon. Despite the absence of physical evidence or a written confession, George's attorney called "few or no witnesses" to mount a defense and conducted "little or no cross-examination" of the prosecution's arguments, according to a judge who reviewed the case years later.

The jury of twelve white men walked into a room and came back ten minutes later with a guilty verdict. The judge immediately sentenced George to death by electrocution. Despite the nearly unprecedented decision to execute a fourteen-year-old boy, George's attorney did not bother to file an appeal.

George "was tried in an atmosphere of hostility," Greenville resident James Richardson wrote to South Carolina governor Olin Johnston. Local ministers and community leaders also pleaded for clemency. Two weeks before George's scheduled execution, a sixteen-year-old white teenager named Ernest Feltwell Jr. was sentenced to twenty years in prison for murdering an eight-year-old girl. Despite the similarities in the crimes and the different sentences, Governor Johnston refused requests to commute George's sentence to life imprisonment.

Just two months after his conviction, young George walked into the death chamber wearing a striped prison uniform and carrying a Bible under his arm. Another George, a twenty-one-year-old Black man from Savannah, waited to be executed next. The guards had difficulty securing the straps on George's five-foot, one-hundred-pound body as he sat in the wooden chair. He made no final comment. The switch was pulled. And fourteen-year-old George Stinney Jr. was electrocuted eighty-four days after he was arrested.

Seventy years later, on December 14, 2014, a judge in South Carolina vacated his conviction.

It may not be obvious at first, but the wrongful execution of George Stinney Jr. is not just a cautionary tale about the racist influence in America's criminal justice system. It's also a story about Black families.

The dominant narrative about our communities since the mid-twentieth century is that Black families are broken and that this failure explains many, if not all, of the social ills that have fallen on African Americans. This narrative presents a convenient explanation for Black inequality and excuses the larger society of any duty for self-examination or policy change.

I strongly disagree with this "broken family" narrative. Black American families face enormous obstacles in society, as they have since the first Black people arrived on these shores in chains. Our families are far from perfect, and many of them suffer from serious dysfunction, but we must not ignore two other facts. First, Black families were intentionally broken by racist white systems that refused to recognize our marriages, respect the integrity of our familial relationships, or protect our safety. Second, many white families are also dysfunctional in America, despite the relative socioeconomic advantages they enjoy from generations of racial privilege.

The tragic story of George Stinney Jr. helps us contextualize the broken family narrative, as his family unit contradicts many of the racial stereotypes associated with Blackness. Young George had two parents at home. Both his parents were gainfully employed. They were self-reliant people who "grew vegetables in the garden and drank fresh cow's milk in the morning," according to the *Post and Courier*. And they were also religious people who "walked to church with the rest of Alcolu's black families" at nearby Greenhill Missionary Baptist Church, a small white clapboard building next to a cotton field.

The Stinney family did exactly what this country says it expects of Black people, especially given the limitations of what they could do in the South in 1944. And despite all that, their compliance with America's demands for respectability did nothing to protect their family from white supremacy and state-sanctioned racial terrorism.

In 1944, Aime and George Stinney Sr., like so many others before and after them, experienced the loss of their Black child. That was before white retaliation for the civil rights movement would turn Coretta Scott King and Myrlie Evers into widows. It was before the Black Lives Matter movement would create a group that women like Aime never sought to join. Today, we call them the Mothers of the Movement, and we know the names of too many whose hearts were broken: Mamie Till, the mother of Emmett Till; Sybrina Fulton, the mother of Trayvon Martin; Lucy McBath, the mother of Jordan Davis; Gwen Carr, the mother of Eric Garner; and Geneva Reed-Veal, the mother of Sandra Bland.

The problem is not that Black families are broken; it's that generations of Black families have been under attack since the beginning of the colonial experience on this continent. They were ripped apart by their enslavers and deprived of the recognition of their family units. Black mothers were raped by white men who claimed to own their Black bodies as property. Black fathers were punished for defending their wives and their children. Black kids were robbed of their childhood and taken away from their parents too young.

Eight decades after the end of slavery, the Stinney family faced violent white retaliation if they dared to protect their fourteen-year-old child from mob justice in South Carolina. A decade later, Moses Wright would face similar threats for testifying against the white men who abducted fourteen-year-old Emmett Till from his home and lynched him in Mississippi. And not even a decade after that, the God-fearing Black parents of fourteen-year-olds Addie Mae Collins, Cynthia Wesley, and Carole Robertson and eleven-year-old Denise McNair could not protect them from a racist's church bomb in Birmingham.

Conservatives, both Black and white, ignore that history in lecturing Black families about stability. "I want you guys in the Black Lives Matter movement to join me," said Fox News anchor Bill O'Reilly. "Instead of directing your ire toward the large societal problem of African Americans, let's get into the family fabric first. Try to solve that and then go back to the other thing."

The "real challenge" is that Black fathers don't remain with their families, said Woody Johnson, the billionaire owner of the New York Jets and former US ambassador to the United Kingdom.

"If you wanted to reduce crime," said former secretary of education Bill Bennett, "you could abort every Black baby in this country." He went on to clarify that such a solution would be "an impossible, ridiculous and morally reprehensible thing to do, but your crime rate would go down."

It's not just white people who make these arguments. Black conservatives often lead the charge. "Fatherless families are one of the primary root causes of Black Americans' current socioeconomic challenges as a demographic bloc," wrote Curtis Hill in 2020 for Fox News. If that were true, what was the cause of the Black socioeconomic challenges before this "current" trend? What explained the glaring racial disparities in household income, poverty, unemployment, health care, education, housing, and criminal justice before the "absent Black father" narrative was to blame? To ask or answer that question would compel us to address the real root causes, which are connected to racism and white supremacy.

The origin of the "broken Black families" argument dates at least as far back as 1965, the year I was born, when Daniel Patrick Moynihan released a controversial government report called *The Negro Family: The Case for National Action*. The Moynihan Report, as it came to be known, properly acknowledged that a "racist virus in the American blood stream still afflicts us" and that the socioeconomic condition of Black Americans in recent years "has probably been getting worse." The report recognized that "slavery vitiated family life" and that the racial segregation that followed slavery demanded a "destructive" form of racial "submissiveness." The report even spoke of Black resilience in the face of these structural obstacles. "That the Negro American has survived at all is extraordinary—a lesser people might simply have died out."

But the Moynihan Report then veered off and blamed the Black family structure for creating a "tangle of pathology." Careful to assess partial culpability to white people, the report argued that "destroying the Negro family" during slavery "broke the will of the Negro people," but this argument promoted white liberal stereotypes of racial inferiority by suggesting that Black people had given up.

The truth is that Black families are not monolithic. Some Black children are raised by opposite-sex parents, others by same-sex parents. Two-parent, single-parent, and coparent households all exist, while other Black kids are raised by several parents, grandparents, adoptive parents, foster parents, or godparents. Some Black family units do not revolve around raising children at all. I have seen all these various family structures in my extended family, and each has advantages and disadvantages. What's most important in any family unit is the presence of love, and this can exist, or not exist, in any family structure.

Much of the lore about Black families is based on a perception that they were stable and intact in the past but are unstable and divided in modern times. People who make this argument cite numerous causes for this alleged shift: some on the Left blame racial integration and mass incarceration while some on the Right blame feminism and the welfare state. I would argue that Black families have *always* been under attack in America and that there was no time in the past when our families did not face serious challenges.

Part of the issue is how we evaluate Black families today. To do this, we must understand the intended purpose of the unit, and this varies among families. Many parents feel their objective is to raise children who will go to college and pursue successful careers. Some measure success by the ability to transfer wealth or property to each succeeding generation. Others feel their goal is to give their children the freedom to grow and evolve as they choose. There is no universal indicator of Black family health or stability.

The durability of a family unit and the presence of specific members are often used as indicators to evaluate our families, as observers cite statistics of divorce and single-parent households as proof that Black families are broken. But divorce or parental separation does not necessarily indicate the failure of a family. It can also indicate healthy boundaries, which can teach children about the consequences of violating agreements, respect for personal autonomy, and the right to evolve. Similarly, the existence or proliferation of single-parent households does not prove that families are broken; it indicates that families are different. To devalue the worthiness of single-parent or coparent households is to stigmatize the children who are the products of those families.

But perhaps the biggest criticism of Black families is the suggestion that Black men have abandoned their children. The argument is especially important to me because I have two fathers, one biological and one adoptive. My adoptive father's name, Boykin, appears on my birth certificate, and for the first twelve to fifteen years of my life, I believed he was my biological father. That was what my parents wanted for me as a child, but when I grew older, I sought out my biological father, whose last name is Dickerson. Then as an adult, I helped to raise two children who are not my biological children but are still my sons.

What I learned from my experience as both a child and a parent in nonbiological family units is that family is not just about blood; it's also about bonding. This is one of the reasons why the "absent father" narrative troubles me. I believe parents should take care of their children, not just financially but in other ways as well. But I also recognize that some parents are incapable or unwilling to fulfill this responsibility. While the government has an obligation to try to compel financial support from absent parents, society has a broader obligation to provide moral support for the parents *who are present* and for the children of absent parents. Stigmatizing single-parent families does not serve either purpose.

As a parent, I've also learned that "nonresidential parent" does not mean "uninvolved parent." I have never lived with either of my two nonbiological sons, but I have been involved in their lives since they were born, and I remain involved today as an adult. I'm not alone. Two-thirds (67 percent) of Black "non-co-residential fathers" see their children at least once a month, compared to 59 percent of white non-co-residential fathers, according to a June 2011 survey by the Pew Research Center.

Contrary to popular stereotypes, research has shown that Black fathers are more engaged with their children then we're led to believe. For example, a December 2013 report from the Centers for Disease Control and Prevention found that Black men were more likely than white men to eat meals with their children every day. Black fathers were also more likely than white or Hispanic men to bathe, dress, or diaper their children or help their children use the toilet every day. Unfortunately, these "positive depictions of black fatherhood are often ignored or dismissed as atypical by many," according to Louis Harrison and Anthony L. Brown, founders of the Black Male Education Research Collection website.

While it is true that some Black fathers have failed to provide for their children or be present in their children's lives, this does not describe the majority of Black fathers. "Most Black fathers live with their children," author Josh Levs explains.

Still, some statistics we use to talk about Black fathers require more context. "Black biological fathers are far less likely than white biological fathers to be married to the mother of their children," according to the June 2011 Pew Research Center survey, but this fact reflects racial inequities in education: fathers with more education are far less likely to have a child out of marriage than their less-educated counterparts, the Pew survey found.

"It has always seemed to me that embedded in the 'If only black men would marry the women they have babies with . . .' rhetoric was a more insidious suggestion," wrote *New York Times* columnist Charles Blow in June 2015. Blow argued that the rhetoric was based on the assumption "that there is something fundamental, and intrinsic about black men that is flawed, that black fathers are pathologically prone to desertion of their offspring and therefore largely responsible for black community 'dysfunction.'" Blow also noted that the statistics showing 72 percent of Black children are born to single mothers ignored the fact that many parents live together but don't marry. "Those mothers are still single, even though the child's father may be in the home," he writes.

The final irony is that the white people lecturing us about the Black family are the descendants of the people who tried to destroy it. "The splitting of Black families was not peripheral to the practice of slavery; it was central," wrote Clint Smith in his book *How the Word Is Passed*. Smith quoted historian Walter Johnson, who explained in *Soul by Soul* that 25 percent of interstate sales of Black enslaved people "involved the destruction of a first marriage" and 50 percent "destroyed a nuclear family." Smith went on to quote historian Edward Bonekemper, who estimated that about one million enslaved people were separated from their families during the existence of chattel slavery in America.

You cannot spend centuries sabotaging an institution that people rely on and then pathologize the people who have struggled to fix it. To do so is to blame the victim of your own abuse.

Most of the Black people I've encountered in life agree with the idea that strong families matter, and we believe that good parents and positive adult role models are important to childhood development. I've been hearing that message from Black church leaders and community activists since I was a child. But unlike today's conservatives, those Black community leaders don't use that message to deflect attention from the need to implement important policy solutions.

This is not to suggest that Black families are perfect or that they don't face significant challenges and problems. Clearly they do, just as white families do. But the central problem that explains our racial disparities is the unresolved legacy of white supremacy. Many Black families are struggling and in distress, but after all we've experienced, that does not mean the Black family unit is broken. It means it's resilient.

19

Black cities struggle because of decisions by white policy makers.

ARGUMENT

A lot of people are looking at what's happening to these Democrat-run cities, and they're disgusted.

—*Donald Trump,*
September 1, 2020

ANSWER

Mayors are constrained in their ability to execute ideological agendas. Cities can't run deficits. States limit their authority to raise taxes and enact laws on many issues. And cities lack the power the federal government has to shape labor laws, or immigration policies that can affect their population growth.

—New York Times *reporter Emily Badger, September 2, 2020*

The address printed on the death certificate for my maternal grandfather is 3012 Vine Grove in St. Louis, Missouri. It's the same address where his son would later be murdered. It's also the address on my birth certificate.

Michael C. Holmes was a janitor who moved from Tennessee to Missouri during the era of the Great Migration. He settled in the Ville area of St. Louis and bought a home near the corner of Vine Grove and Labadie. A draft card from World War I shows his family members living in the house as early as 1917, one year after St. Louis voters approved a ballot measure prohibiting Black people from moving into any block with 75 percent white residents.

When the US Supreme Court struck down that racist housing law in St. Louis and other cities in 1917, white residents found clever new ways to ban Black people from their neighborhoods. They relied on private contracts, known as racially restrictive covenants, which obliged white property owners not to sell their homes to potential Black buyers.

In the next decade, the Black population in the Ville neighborhood swelled from 8 percent in 1920 to 86 percent in 1930 as the refugees of the Great Migration from the South settled in the area. The proud Black community, with its own high school and hospital, produced legends including rock star Chuck Berry and world heavyweight boxing champion Sonny Liston.

Three decades after my grandfather settled into his home, racially restrictive covenants were still being used in St. Louis to block Black families from living where they wanted. One of those families was the Shelleys: J. D. Shelley; his wife, Ethel Lee Shelley; and their children. On September 11, 1945, they moved into a home at 4600 Labadie Avenue, just three blocks from my grandfather's house. The young Black couple paid $5,700 for the modest two-story brick house and planned to continue renting out the top floor to a white tenant. But the same day they moved in, they were served with court papers demanding that they move out.

White neighbors cited a 1911 racially restrictive covenant that said that "no part of said property" shall be "occupied by any person not of the Caucasian race." The Missouri Supreme Court agreed with the white neighbors and ordered the title to the property be stripped from the Black family.

The Shelleys appealed to the US Supreme Court and won. On May 3, 1948, the court found no constitutional problem with private racially restrictive covenants, but it ruled that state enforcement of those contracts violates the equal protection clause of the Fourteenth Amendment. The case, *Shelley v. Kraemer*, is still taught in law schools across the country as an example of the state action doctrine.

That was the world in which my grandfather purchased his family home in the 1920s. He was allowed to own a home, but only in the racially segregated Black neighborhood of St. Louis. For sixty years, that home in a thriving Black middle-class community with Black homeowners and business owners was the anchor of my mom's family. It's where my grandparents took my mom when they went home from the hospital after she was born in 1944. It's where she lived when she gave birth to me in 1965. It's where my grandmother lived when she passed away in February 1980, and it's where my uncle was murdered almost exactly four months later.

It was there on Vine Grove that I spent summer days eating jelly sandwiches in the kitchen and playing with my cousins in the backyard and summer nights sitting on the living room floor watching black-and-white Dracula movies with my grandmother. Although I was born in the neighborhood that was the subject of the landmark Supreme Court case, I was never taught about it in the public schools in Missouri. I first learned about the case in 1990 in my constitutional law class at Harvard Law School.

Even before the 1990s, that neighborhood was undergoing dramatic change as older homeowners passed away and younger generations moved to the suburbs. Young Black couples like my parents, who were newly protected by the Fair Housing Act of 1968, sought to escape the problems of city life and found homes in St. Louis County. Meanwhile, white buyers were reluctant to buy houses in Black neighborhoods, leaving a shrinking market for the owners of those middle-class city homes and diminishing their property values. The result was a downward spiral.

Now, in 2024, the once-vibrant community where I was born has become a distant memory. Our family home at 3012 Vine Grove still remains intact, with the "M. C. Holmes" name tag on the brick wall where it has stood for decades, but the building has become an orphan. Both homes on either side of our house have vanished, and all the homes across the street have disappeared as well. All that is left are empty lots of yellow grass. I don't know if the other homes in the area were burned down or destroyed, but the block where I played as a child now looks like a ghost town.

Six blocks down, the home where Chuck Berry lived at 3137 Whittier Street now sits on a block dotted with empty lots and vacant homes.

And three blocks from my grandfather's home, a plaque stands on the front lawn of the former home of the Shelley family, recognizing the history behind the house that changed American law, but it's hard to believe that white people once fought all the way to the Supreme Court for the right to control this building that now stands next to multiple empty lots on a forgotten strip of land.

What happened to my neighborhood in St. Louis is similar to what happened to numerous other Black communities in recent decades. After my family left St. Louis in the summer of 1980, we returned many times to visit relatives, and with each homecoming, the old family neighborhood seemed to be in worse condition. It was a gradual deterioration, but a series of policy choices helped to encourage the decline.

For me, it started on August 17, 1979, when the city closed Homer G. Phillips Hospital, the place where I and thousands of other Black babies were born. It was the beginning of the end for the Black community of my childhood. But as my family moved out of town the next summer, I could still root for the St. Louis Cardinals baseball and football teams from a distance. I could brag that my hometown was headquarters to international businesses like Ralston Purina, the pet food company; McDonnell Douglas, the aerospace company where my uncle worked; and Anheuser-Busch, the beer company whose name appeared on the downtown sports stadium. But eventually the football team moved to Arizona, the aerospace company merged with Boeing, and the pet food company was acquired by Nestlé.

Some, like reporter Brian S. Feldman, explain St. Louis's decline by pointing the finger at changes to antitrust laws beginning in the 1980s, "which enabled the same kind of predatory corporate behavior that took the Rams away from St. Louis." Writing in a March 2016 report in *Washington Monthly*, Feldman argues those changes "robbed the metro area of a vibrant economy, and of hundreds of locally based companies." When my family left St. Louis in 1980, the city headquartered twenty-three Fortune 500 companies, according to Feldman, but by 2016, the number had dropped to nine.

Others point to decisions by President Ronald Reagan in the 1980s to cut billions of dollars in funding to America's cities. The Reagan administration justified the cuts with predictable, racially coded regional warfare: "There is no reason for someone in Sioux Falls to pay federal taxes so that someone in Los Angeles can get to work on time by public transportation."

The argument conveniently ignored the fact that California generates hundreds of billions of dollars a year in tax revenue that fund services for states like South Dakota, yet the racial positioning in the choice of cities was difficult to miss. Sioux Falls represented the conservative white middle-class midwestern ideal of America, while the multicultural metropolis of Los Angeles was then governed by a Black mayor named Tom Bradley.

Many factors explain the decline of some of America's cities over the past few decades, but that decline did not happen by accident. Much of it was a result of policy choices driven by conservative Republicans engaged in racial wedge politics designed to transfer wealth, power, and government services from predominantly Black cities to predominantly white suburbs.

Part of the problem is also attributable to public and private policies that encouraged the inequitable distribution of resources. Here's how a report from the Urban Institute described the evolution: "America's separate and unequal neighborhoods did not evolve naturally or result from unfettered market forces. Rather, they resulted from plans, policies, and practices of racial exclusion and disinvestment that primarily targeted Black people and laid the foundation for the segregation of other people of color."

While Trump and Republicans have attacked what they call "Democrat cities" in recent years, the leaders of those cities don't have much power. It's the Republican-dominated state legislatures that control the purse strings, even in distributing federal funds.

"Mayors are constrained in their ability to execute ideological agendas," urban policy writer Emily Badger explained in a September 2020 *New York Times* article. "Cities can't run deficits. States limit their authority to raise taxes and enact laws on many issues. And cities lack the power the federal government has to shape labor laws, or immigration policies that can affect their population growth."

We saw this pattern during the height of the COVID pandemic, when white Republican governors blocked Democratic mayors who tried to impose social distancing, testing, and mask requirements in their cities. We've also seen it in places like Jackson, Mississippi, where the white Republican state legislature rejected the city's plans to raise money to fix its aging water system until it became a nationally publicized crisis. And in Florida, Republican governor Ron DeSantis stripped control from Democratic-leaning local school boards to suit his political agenda.

We've seen similar efforts from Republicans in other states trying to roll back local ordinances on the minimum wage, immigration, gun control, abortion, voting rights, police funding, paid sick leave, transgender rights, Airbnb rentals, inclusive zoning, regulations for Uber drivers, and even the use of plastic bags. When local governments in urban areas attempt to address the problems their constituents face related to crime, schools, affordable housing, pollution, human rights, or quality of life issues, white Republican state legislators from more conservative rural districts exercise the state's veto power to overrule them. This allows conservatives to blame the cities for their problems while denying them the power to fix them. All of this comes from a party that purports to champion the principle of local control but aggressively uses state power to block the decisions of local governments.

It's called state preemption, and it's increasingly being used as a tool for white rural legislators to sabotage Black- and brown-dominated Democratic cities. Most of America's biggest cities, even in conservative red states, have become identified with Democrats and people of color. In Missouri, for example, all the members of the state's federal congressional delegation in 2023 were white Republicans except for the two Black Democrats who represented St. Louis and Kansas City. This rural-urban divide in American politics is not just about geography or political affiliation; it's about race.

When conservative states sabotage Black Democratic cities by cutting their resources and restricting their ability to govern, it creates a self-fulfilling prophecy of failure, which the Republican leaders then use to blame the Black cities and their Black leaders for the problems caused by white Republican state policies. In many cases, Republican legislatures are cutting state funding to cities at the same time they're restricting what the cities can raise on their own through local taxes.

The irony is that the cities have been the drivers of many of the states' economies. "In virtually all of the states experiencing widespread preemption, metro areas are driving most of the statewide increase not only in jobs, but also in population," political analyst Ronald Brownstein explained in a June 2021 CNN article.

This is the part of the story that doesn't get told. White Republicans love to blame Black Democratic cities for their failures, but they rarely credit them for their successes, particularly in the areas of stimulating state economies and reducing crime.

"Leave Democrat cities. Let them rot!"

It's hard to imagine that any serious national political leader would say such a thing, but those were the words of a post retweeted by a Republican president of the United States to his eighty-five million followers in August 2020. Aside from the obvious point that presidents are expected to represent all communities, the idea that the nation's top leader would endorse a comment calling for American cities to "rot" reflects the level of dysfunction associated with Republican regional warfare.

It has become acceptable in conservative quarters for Republican elected officials to attack their own states' constituents and communities in multiracial urban areas while exalting the "hardworking" values of the people in mostly white rural communities that they consider the "real America." And while GOP leaders complain that Democrats dismiss Middle America as a collection of "flyover states," Democratic elected officials rarely engage in Republican-style regional warfare against rural communities. Instead, Democrats tend to acknowledge that white rural Republicans are a part of "the real America," just as the Black and brown urban communities are.

The larger story is that many of America's cities are surviving and thriving, despite the obstacles they face. As urban living has become more desirable, property values have increased in many cities and some crime rates have fallen. Although crime rates fluctuate from year to year, the changes sometimes mirror broader social conditions. The number of homicides in my hometown of St. Louis rose 36 percent from 194 in 2019 to 263 when COVID hit in 2020. But by 2021 and 2022, the number dropped back down to 200.

In New York City, where I lived for twenty years, the number of homicides rose 47 percent during the onset of the COVID pandemic, from 319 in 2019 to 468 in 2020, but that dramatic number fails to provide historical context. When Rudy Giuliani, the popular Republican mayor, left office at the end of 2001, the city had experienced 649 homicides that year. In 2017, under unpopular Democratic mayor Bill de Blasio, that number had dropped to 292 homicides, a 55 percent decrease.

The drop in murder and other crimes took place even after the NYPD ended its racist and unconstitutional stop-and-frisk policy, which at its height ensnared more than six hundred thousand people, mostly Black and brown, each year.

But dropping crime rates don't mesh with the sensationalism of local media coverage, which tends to highlight dramatic footage of crimes caught on video, or with national coverage, which focuses on perpetuating familiar media narratives. It seems hard to believe, with all the news stories about the dangers of big cities, but a June 2022 analysis by Justin Fox of Bloomberg found that the risk of death from external causes was "three times higher in rural and small-town America" than in New York City.

This is not to suggest that all urban areas in America are doing better than their suburban and rural counterparts. Quite the opposite. Each community is different. Some cities are thriving while others are struggling. But the white conservative war on America's cities does a disservice to the urban areas that are engines of growth and creativity fueling much of our nation's productivity. It's a cynical and divisive political game that deprives cities of the resources they need and then attacks them when they fail.

PART FIVE | REBRANDING RACISM

There's a song in a hit Broadway musical that elicits conflicting emotions in me. The show is called *Avenue Q*, and it's a 2003 parody of the long-running TV series *Sesame Street*. Unlike on *Sesame Street*, the actors appear onstage holding the puppet characters, who do the "talking." Also unlike *Sesame Street*, the topics are aimed at adults, not children.

The song is called "Everyone's a Little Bit Racist." On the surface, it reflects my own belief that racism is a pervasive problem that deserves our continued attention. The song also confirms my beliefs that no one is color-blind, that taxicab drivers don't pick up Black people, and that people should be honest in admitting their racism.

But then it veers off into a critique of political correctness and suggests that racist beliefs don't necessarily lead to hate crimes. Relax, the song suggests. We should all just laugh at each other's offensive jokes and admit we're racist for doing so. There is an alluring appeal to the notion that the world might be a better place if we could all admit our biases, but we must be careful not to equate the power of white peoples' anti-Blackness with Black peoples' antiracism.

As I listened to the song, I was reminded of an element of law professor Derrick Bell's famous interest convergence theory from a 1980 *Harvard Law Review* article. "The interests of blacks in achieving racial equality will be accommodated only when it converges with the interests of whites," Bell wrote. This means that when white institutions—schools, churches, businesses, governments, entertainment industries, and others—choose to address diversity, equity, and inclusion, it's generally because they have determined that it is in their own interest to do so. Many white Americans would never admit to their own racism unless Black Americans also admitted to their biases, thus dramatically diminishing the differing impact of the two expressions of prejudice.

To say that racism exists universally cannot be the end of the discussion; it must be the beginning. The acknowledgment of racism demands not just recognition but accountability. It requires us to take action and do something to change it.

That is why the subject of rebranding racism is the final topic of this book. Before the civil rights movement, racism was so widely acceptable that it was rarely necessary to hide it. For five decades after that era, public expression of racism became unfashionable. But in the current era, overt expressions of public racism have reemerged.

The difference, I believe, is that today's racist speakers seek to deny the existence of their racism through consistent gaslighting. If caught in a racist situation, they accuse Black people of "playing the race card," claim they "don't have a racist bone" in their bodies, pretend they "don't see color," and disguise their racist beliefs behind transparently false neutral statements like "All lives matter."

It is white unwillingness to be accountable that perpetuates the racism that we all know exists. That is why everything in America is about race. Because white society created this reality, and white society has yet to acknowledge, admit, and be accountable for it.

20

There is no "race card."

ARGUMENT

Mr. President, in honor of Martin Luther King, Jr. and all who commit to ending any racial divide, no more playing the race card.

—Failed Republican vice presidential candidate Sarah Palin, in a Facebook post addressed to President Obama on MLK Jr. Day, January 20, 2014

ANSWER

People who accuse others—without a shred of evidence—of "playing the race card," claiming that the accusations of racism are so exaggerated as to dull the meaning of the term, are themselves playing a card. It is a privileged attempt at dismissal. They seek to do the very thing they condemn: shut down the debate with a scalding-hot charge.

—New York Times columnist Charles Blow, March 19, 2015

When white people tell me to "stop playing the race card," I'm always confused.

What exactly is this race card?

Is it a plastic-coated wild card I can use like a joker in a spades game? Or perhaps a get-out-of-jail-free note printed on yellow card stock as in a Monopoly game? Is it like a souvenir baseball card to be traded among collectors? Or could it be one of those dreaded red cards used by soccer officials to eject a player from a game? Maybe it's more like a stainless steel American Express platinum card I can fling down on a table to demand respect at will. Or a black card. That would be appropriate. Membership has its privileges, right?

I'm constantly told by white people that I have it, but I've searched my wallet, my backpack, the drawers in my apartment, and all the manila folders stacked on my desk, and I just can't seem to find my card. Maybe it's embedded in my phone like Apple Pay. That way I don't have to walk around burdened by the chore of carrying such a powerful tool in my pocket. Or maybe it's actually invisible. That would be cool.

All this time, I thought the "race card" was just a deflection tactic for conservatives to shut down a losing conversation. But it turns out they may have been on to something. As they love to remind me, racism is *never* an issue in almost *any* controversy in America—unless it's a controversy in which white people are the victims, in which case it's okay to talk about race. For the most part, race only becomes an issue when divisive people like me show up with our meddlesome race cards. We have a lot of nerve!

Why do we have to bring race into the conversation? they ask, as if the issue of race never exists unless one of us whips out that powerful card. I imagine the unlucky Black people without this unique card must be forced to sit around all day quoting that one Dr. King line about judging people by the content of their character. They don't realize what they're missing. The real action is in race cards. That's where the money is.

I can't remember the first time I heard the phrase "race card," but I don't recall hearing it in my youth or early adulthood. I think white people used different terminology back then when they wanted to whine about all the Black privilege that African Americans enjoyed in this country where nearly all our nation's presidents, top CEOs, and leading media figures have always been Black.

I do remember Donald Trump saying back in 1989 that a "well-educated Black" had an actual advantage over a well-educated white. Maybe he was speaking about the "race card" that Black people got to use back then before it got its catchy name.

In any case, since this card has such magical properties, I suppose it's very hard to get your hands on one. That's the only explanation I can come up with for why Black people didn't use their magical race cards to stop white people from engaging in hundreds of years of slavery and segregation and lynchings and mass incarceration. Surely the good white folks of America would have treated us better if enough of us had carried those cards in our dungarees. Didn't Kanye say that slavery was "a choice"?

But if there was a race card back then, it didn't help Nat Turner, Frederick Douglass, Harriet Tubman, or Sojourner Truth in their decades-long battles to get white people to stop buying, selling, and owning Black people as their property.

Nor did it help the nearly four thousand Black people who were brutally and lawlessly lynched in America after the Civil War and Reconstruction period ended.

The race card didn't save the Scottsboro Boys from being wrongly convicted in 1931. It didn't save Emmett Till from being lynched in 1955 or the Exonerated Five from being wrongly accused in 1989. The race card didn't save the lives of Trayvon Martin in 2012 or George Floyd or Breonna Taylor in 2020.

The race card hasn't helped Black people break out of the endless cycle in which white people are consistently paid more than us.

And it hasn't broken the six-decade cycle of Black people experiencing elevated rates of unemployment compared to white people.

The race card also hasn't helped Black people buy a house at the same interest rate as white people or sell a home without having to hide our identity from appraisers.

And the race card hasn't stopped police from profiling, harassing, or arresting me throughout my life. Nor has it made taxi drivers any more willing to pick me up on the streets of New York City. But my card may be defective.

I imagine conservatives think this race card has helped me to win difficult arguments on TV and Twitter because those seem to be the places where I'm most often accused of using my card, but if I did win those arguments, they never seemed to admit it when it happened. They just blamed me for using that card again.

But what am I supposed to do? If I do own one of these impressive cards, am I not supposed to use it? And if so, what's the value of the race card?

If this race card has some other benefit to Black people, I must not be using mine right, because it only seems to bring more negative attention to me from white people.

I guess there's a value in that, too, though. I mean, white conservatives are always accusing me of playing this card, so apparently it's having some effect, even though it's not changing their behavior or ending the racism I experience as a Black man.

You know what? I'm starting to believe there is no race card. Or if there is, I must be doing something completely wrong. Maybe my chip is malfunctioning or my card has expired.

But if all these other Black people are getting something out of their cards, as white people claim they are, then I want it too. And if not, whoever issued this magical card needs to give me my money back. Because my card is not working.

21

Black friends do not immunize people from racism.

ARGUMENT

Here he is with Muhammad Ali and Rosa Parks receiving a civil rights award. Now isn't that amazing? A guy who was with Rosa Parks, they're going to say is a racist?

—*Newsmax host Greg Kelly, showing a photo of Donald Trump with Black people to prove he's not racist, May 23, 2022*

ANSWER

Your personal relationships with Black people don't magically opt you out from having racist tendencies, nor do they end the systematic racism your Black friends face.

—*Writer Leenika Belfield-Martin, June 8, 2020*

There's a powerful scene in the film *One Night in Miami . . .* where Black football legend Jim Brown drives his Cadillac convertible up a tree-lined driveway to the home of a white family friend in St. Simons Island, Georgia, in 1964. A young white woman greets him tentatively when he rings the doorbell.

"Yes, may I help you?" she asks.

"Yes, ma'am, I'm here to see Mr. Carlton. Would you tell him that Jim Brown is—"

"Jim Brown!" The woman is so overcome with excitement that she cuts him off. "Oh, God, from the NFL," she screams. She unlocks the screen door, welcomes him onto the covered porch, shakes his hand, and calls her grandpa to come out.

When Mr. Carlton arrives, he's excited to see his old friend. He asks his granddaughter to bring some lemonade, and the two men shake hands and sit on the porch. "No man who has run 1,860 yards in a season needs to be so humble," Carlton tells him. They chat about football for a few minutes, and Carlton heaps praise on Brown. "Your record is going to be remembered forever," Carlton says.

At first blush, the interaction appears to be a model for positive interracial relationships in 1960s Georgia. "Jimmy, I just want to let you know, if there's ever anything I can do for you, you should never hesitate to reach out," Carlton says, reminding Brown that their two families go way back.

While the two men reminisce, the white woman returns with lemonade and reminds her grandfather that he promised to help move some furniture. Mr. Carlton gets up to help, and Jim Brown rises to offer his assistance. "Ah, that's so considerate of you, Jimmy," Carlton says, "but you know we don't allow niggers in the house."

A stunned Jim Brown stands alone on the porch as Carlton turns and walks inside.

There's no evidence that this scene happened in real life as depicted in the movie, but the characters are based on real people, and the events illustrate the disconnect between affinity and bigotry. Racism, according to the dictionary, is a belief that race is a fundamental determinant of human traits and capacities and that racial differences produce an inherent superiority of a particular race. It is not, as commonly misunderstood, an unwillingness to associate with that particular race.

When people say "Some of my best friends are Black" or "My wife is Black" or "I have Black children and grandchildren," they're expressing a desire not to be judged racist. These remarks often come after someone has just said or done something outlandishly racist, and they're used to disprove that racism by associating the white offender with any random Black person. But the argument is not only tiresome to Black people; it's historically inaccurate.

From the earliest day of slavery to the ugliest nights of Jim Crow segregation, Black and white people in America have associated with one another, even when those white people openly believed that Black people were inferior or deserved to be enslaved, segregated, or treated as second-class citizens.

In his 1785 book *Notes on the State of Virginia*, Thomas Jefferson claimed that Black people "secrete less by the kidneys, and more by the glands of the skin, which gives them a very strong and disagreeable odor." Jefferson, who enslaved hundreds of people at his home in Monticello, argued that Black people "seem to require less sleep," even "after hard labor through the day." And he concluded that African Americans "are inferior to the whites" in both "body and mind."

Despite his alleged disdain for the Black body, mind, and odor, Jefferson repeatedly raped a Black teenage girl named Sally Hemings, who was his late wife's half sister. The author of the Declaration of Independence fathered six children with this enslaved girl while he held her captive at his forced labor camp in Virginia. Jefferson's white supremacist views did nothing to stop him from interacting with this Black woman, or with the six hundred other Black people he enslaved over the course of his lifetime.

The same holds true for countless other, less notorious enslavers who sexually assaulted Black women they held in captivity. Despite what Mr. Carlton said to Jim Brown, many Black people did work in their enslavers' homes, toiling as servants for the white "masters" and "mistresses" in their residences. White supremacy did not require white isolation from Black people.

Stories of racist white people interacting with Black people did not end in the eighteenth century. In 2003, a previously little-known Black woman stood at a lectern in South Carolina wearing a red suit and a scarf. "My name is Essie Mae Washington-Williams," she told the audience. After she explained a bit about her family biography, she revealed a secret to the reporters gathered in the room for the news conference. "My father's name was James Strom Thurmond," she said.

James Strom Thurmond was the full name of the legendary South Carolina segregationist who temporarily broke from the Democratic Party to run for president in 1948 on the States' Rights ticket. The official platform of the party was unambiguously racist: "We stand for the segregation of the races and the racial integrity of each race. . . . We oppose the elimination of segregation, the repeal of miscegenation statutes, the control of private employment by federal bureaucrats called for by the misnamed civil rights program."

It was Thurmond who authored the 1956 Southern Manifesto attacking the Supreme Court's *Brown v. Board of Education* decision and calling on states to "resist forced integration by any lawful means." It was Thurmond who spoke for twenty-four hours and eighteen minutes in opposition to the modest Civil Rights Act of 1957 in the longest solo filibuster in the history of the United States Senate. It was Thurmond who helped lead another filibuster against the Civil Rights Act of 1964 and switched parties to become a Republican to vote for civil rights opponent Barry Goldwater in the 1964 presidential election. It was Thurmond who led the fight against the Voting Rights Act of 1965.

And despite all that, it was Strom Thurmond who fathered a child with a Black woman.

American history is littered with examples of hypocrisy, and some of the more egregious are the legions of white men espousing racist beliefs of white supremacy while engaging in sexual encounters with Black women. In the case of Thurmond, he was twenty-two years old when he fathered a child in 1925 with Carrie Butler, his family's sixteen-year-old Black housekeeper.

In my experiences visiting Mississippi as a child in the 1970s and living in Georgia as a young adult in the 1980s, white racism rarely sought isolation from Black people. African Americans played an integral role in southern society as the servant class for the white elite and the subservient class for ordinary white southerners.

I've written about the experience of working at a mostly white shopping mall outside of Atlanta and living down the street from a former segregationist governor. I can't think of any incident where a white southerner refused to be in my presence, but I do remember feeling a clearly defined racial hierarchy. Black people were not expected to be invisible. They were simply expected to know their place.

That's what makes the "I'm not a racist" argument from some white people so bizarrely irrelevant. Many of them have latched on to the outdated "nonracist by association" theory that suggests that their mere presence in the vicinity of Black people somehow exonerates them from any racial wrongdoing. In one case, a white man who killed a Black man in New York claimed he was not racist because he was "planning a road trip through Africa." In Jordan Peele's 2017 horror thriller *Get Out*, a white character casually tells a Black character, "By the way, I would have voted for Obama for a third term if I could." If they can credibly argue that they know someone Black or feel a connection to someone who is Black, that alone is supposed to prove they cannot be racist.

But given the history of racist enslavers and segregationists who came in close contact with African Americans, proximity to Black people does not disprove accusations of racism.

If white Republicans truly believed that association with Black people proved the absence of racism, then they would also have to stipulate that white Democrats are even less racist because they are more likely than Republicans to campaign in Black communities and work with Black leaders. For that matter, if the number of Black associates disproved one's racism, then by their own logic, they would have to stop calling Black leaders with whom they disagree "racist" because nearly all those leaders not only work closely with Black people in Black communities but also work with white people.

The average white American has only one Black friend, according to data published by the Public Religion Research Institute in 2014. In contrast, the average Black American has eight white friends, the research found. These figures confirm the accuracy of a joke told by comedian Chris Rock years ago. "All my Black friends have a bunch of white friends," he said, but "all my white friends have one Black friend." If having friends of the opposite race is all that it takes to prove that one is not racist, then the average white person is far more racist than the average Black person.

As Black Americans in a largely white country, we have no choice but to encounter white people on a regular basis. Yet the reverse is not true. I remember meeting white people in college who claimed that they had never met a Black person before. It would be virtually impossible to find a Black person who has never met a white person in

America. Because of our proximity to the white majority culture, we tend to know a lot more about white people than white people know about us.

But the larger issue here is that these facile racial arguments of innocence by association contribute to a misunderstanding of racism in America. Racism, anti-Blackness, and white supremacy operate out of a set of beliefs based on biases that don't have to be publicly stated to be present.

Racism is not limited to saying the N-word, wearing a white hood, or burning a cross on a Black person's lawn. Those are extreme forms of racism that have become socially unpopular in recent decades. The old twentieth-century bigotry has evolved and adapted to the twenty-first century, utilizing the internet, social media, and emerging technologies to disseminate racist ideas more efficiently. Today we use tools like artificial intelligence to help determine credit scores, make employment decisions, decide who gets into college, conduct health-care screenings, and predict crime, but "sexism, racism and other forms of discrimination are being built into the machine-learning algorithms that underlie the technology," according to author Kate Crawford, a senior principal researcher at Microsoft.

It's the casual racism that is now more pervasive and pernicious. Most of these less dramatic, more everyday incidents will be buried in the coffins of those who commit them, but a few will survive when the perpetrators are unlucky enough to be exposed.

In 2014, Los Angeles Clippers owner Donald Sterling was banned from the NBA after he was caught on tape complaining that a female companion was "associating with Black people." And in 2021, Dallas Cowboys owner Jerry Jones was criticized after a previously undisclosed photo surfaced showing him with a group of white students who were harassing Black students integrating Little Rock Central High School in 1957.

The NBA and NFL are two of the Blackest professional sports leagues in America. The owners of those teams hire, fire, and trade Black athletes and communicate with them regularly. Both men had proximity to well-known and well-liked successful Black people, and both had questionable histories of racism.

The truth is that many of America's celebrated leaders have complicated histories with racism. President Lincoln met with Black abolitionist Frederick Douglass several times in the White House, yet Douglass later described Lincoln as "preeminently the white man's President, entirely devoted to the welfare of white men." Douglass noted in 1876 that Lincoln was "ready and willing at any time during the first years of his administration to deny, postpone, and sacrifice the rights of humanity in the colored people to promote the welfare of the white people of this country."

President Roosevelt implemented the New Deal but allowed southern Democrats to exclude Black people from some of its benefits. Eisenhower sent federal marshals to integrate public schools in the South but sympathized with the racist white southerners who denounced integration. And Lyndon Johnson, a serial abuser of the N-word, signed the most important civil rights legislation since Reconstruction.

If nothing else comes out of these discussions, it's time to have more sophisticated conversations about race that don't focus on superficial distractions about someone's friends, family, or associates. That rhetoric has been used not only to protect white people from allegations of racism but to elevate certain Black people who enable their racist beliefs.

Even if a best friend, partner, or child is Black, that does not excuse racist behavior from non-Black people. Men marry women and still practice sexism. Why would we assume white people could not marry Black people and still practice racism? If one person is able to form a genuine connection with someone of a different race, that's a valuable life experience, but it does not give that person special insight into an entire race of people. And even if one Black person in proximity is willing to overlook racist behavior, that does not invalidate the experiences of an entire community of Black people who are not.

For white people who do have Black friends and want to respect them, my advice is, don't pimp them out to protect your own hide.

22

People who say they "don't have a racist bone in their body" haven't searched hard enough.

<table>
<tr>
<td>

ARGUMENT

I don't have a Racist bone in my body!

—*Donald Trump,*
July 16, 2019

</td>
<td>

ANSWER

At some point I hope that someone in a similar situation learns to apologize without at the same time trying to claim their remarks are not racist.

—*Milwaukee Independent*
columnist Reggie Jackson,
October 13, 2021

</td>
</tr>
</table>

Earl Butz was the type of guy who just looked like a Republican. As secretary of agriculture, he stood on the column-lined stairs of the White House Rose Garden one day in June 1972 to pose for a photograph with President Richard Nixon and the other members of the cabinet. He fit right in.

Some in the photo, like Donald Rumsfeld, George Shultz, and Caspar Weinberger, would return to serve in future Republican administrations. One person, UN ambassador George Bush, would eventually become president himself. Another, George Romney, had already run for president.

They were the most powerful government officials in the country. And all eighteen people in the photograph—the president, the vice president, and every member of the cabinet—were white men. Nixon never appointed a woman or a person of color to any position in his cabinet. Those were the days when the small minority of white men who ruled nearly every aspect of the country were somehow expected to represent the interests of women, Black people, Latinos, LGBTQ Americans, and other groups of people they knew little about.

Born in a small town in Indiana, raised on a dairy farm, and educated at a high school in a class of only seven students, Butz had very little exposure to America's diversity before he arrived as an undergraduate at Indiana's Purdue University in the 1920s. By the time he reached the Nixon administration nearly five decades later, it appeared as though he had not matured much in his approach to a changing America.

In a speech to a farmers' organization in Illinois in 1973, Butz complained that America's housewives had "such a low level of economic intelligence" that they did not understand "you can't get more by paying less." The following year, at an international food conference in Rome, Butz called for world population control and mocked the pope for opposing the plan by speaking with a fake Italian accent: "He no playa the game, he no maka the rules."

Yet it was a racist comment on a plane ride from Kansas to California in 1976 that generated Butz's biggest controversy. When singer Pat Boone asked Butz why the Republican Party struggled to attract Black voters, Butz responded by mocking the intelligence of African American men. "Coloreds only want three things . . . first, a tight pussy, second, loose shoes, and third, a warm place to shit."

This was a top government official speaking to a fellow Republican in a public space on a commercial aircraft. Farm groups, which President Ford needed for the fall election, continued to support Butz. Allan Grant, the president of the American Farm Bureau Federation, defended the beleaguered government leader. "I know that Secretary Butz is not a racist," Grant said in a statement reported by UPI that tried to position Butz as a victim. "He has already suffered great distress because of his unfortunate remarks made in private, and he has made a public apology for them."

As pressure mounted, however, Butz finally resigned from the cabinet. "This is the price I pay for a gross indiscretion in a private conversation," he said. "The use of a bad racial commentary in no way reflects my real attitude," he added. Even President Ford defended Butz when he accepted his resignation, calling it "one of the saddest decisions of my presidency" and describing Butz as "a close personal friend."

It was Monday, October 4, 1976, and as Butz was leaving the public stage, a new face was entering the arena. Barbara Walters became the first female coanchor of a nightly network newscast that evening, and on her first night she reported on an interview she had just finished with Earl Butz. "You know, Barbara, I'm given to humor," he told her. "I meant this all as a joke." He added that he had told the same joke "many, many times to farmers."

Walters saved Butz's strongest defense for the end, when Butz quoted a friend he said had defended him. "If a Black person were in trouble, Earl Butz would be the first person to pitch in there and help," he said. It was the type of comment white people in trouble often make to juxtapose current racist actions with past nonracist behavior, as if being nice to a Black person one day excused being racist to other Black people another day.

The heavy lifting of defending Earl Butz fell on the shoulders of a twenty-nine-year-old Black man named James E. Bostic Jr., identified by the Associated Press as "the only Black" in the policy-making hierarchy of the Agriculture Department. Bostic, photographed by the AP sitting on his desk in front of a portrait of Abraham Lincoln, unequivocally denied the worst charges against his former boss. "I know my racists," he told a reporter. "And Earl Butz is no racist."

Defining individuals as "racist" is often fraught with difficulty because, quite frankly, even some of the most racist people have good days. If not, they usually can find at least one person in their corner to stand up for them. It is precisely for that reason that some antiracist activists and scholars focus more on racist *actions* than on racist *people*. Even people who don't think of themselves as racist and are not publicly regarded as such can still engage in racist behaviors or make racist statements.

But characterizing Butz as a bigot was not the issue. Regardless of whether Butz's former subordinate employees would consider him to be racist, his "joke" about Black men was unambiguously racist. And nothing in Butz's defense of his remarks suggested he had learned any-thing about antiracism in his brief period of self-reflection. But Bostic went further in defending his ex-boss, telling an AP reporter that Butz "doesn't have a racist bone in his body."

It was one of the first publicly documented instances in which a Black person was called on to defend a white person's racist actions with the phrase that has now become one of the most tired excuses in American racial politics.

Ah, the "racist bone" defense. From a purely biological perspective, we can stipulate that neither Butz nor anyone else in the world has a racist bone in their body. Bones are not racist. People are. Arguing that someone doesn't have a racist bone in their body is like claiming they don't have a sexist blood vessel or a xenophobic artery.

But clearly the argument is more metaphorical than physical, sug-gesting that even at the core of the person's identity, not a trace of rac-ism can be found. But how is this supportable? Unless you know all of a person's thoughts, beliefs, and implicit biases, it's impossible to gauge the absence or presence of bigotry in them.

Personal experience with the individual, no matter how extensive, proves only so much: just because someone is nice to you, or nice to other people when they're in your presence, doesn't mean they're nice to everyone when you're not around. And just because a white person takes a liking to one Black person doesn't mean that white person feels the same way about other Black people. We all know people who hide parts of their identity from the public.

But the bigger problem with the "racist bone" argument is its fail-ure to examine the subtle pervasiveness of racism in America. The basis of the argument is that there are some pure white people who are so untainted by American white supremacy that they manage to live their entire lives without ever experiencing even a fleeting moment of a racist thought.

The additional irony is that the very people who are most often associated with this argument are people who have just been caught engaging in racist behavior, like the loathsome Butz. But the assump-tion of the argument is that the testimony of one person who can vouch for the accused person's history is supposed to outweigh the evidence of the accused's current misbehavior. The person who claims not to be racist is essentially asking a jury—the public—not to believe their own eyes and ears and to focus their attention only on the witness testimony of an interested party.

The defense of Earl Butz was not the first time this strategy had been used in response to racial controversy. In one notable incident in December 1966, twelve Black football players for the Denver Broncos were chastised for boycotting a league event. In response to the protest, the president of the Bronco booster organization was quoted by UPI as saying, "There's not a racist bone in the whole Quarterback Club." Although it is an impressive skill to be able to determine the absence of racism in one individual, it must take a special kind of genius to be able to do so for an entire organization.

Apparently the NFL never got the memo about the problem with this offensive argument, because fifty-five years later it came up again. After he was busted for using racist language in an email about NFL Players Association executive director DeMaurice Smith, Las Vegas Raiders head coach Jon Gruden responded in 2021 with that most predictable reply: "I don't have a racist bone in my body."

The argument was used many times in the years between Butz and Gruden, most notably in the Reagan administration, when right-wing leaders rushed to the Republican president's defense in his numerous controversies. "My own strong impression, based upon 20 years of close observation, is that Reagan hasn't a racist bone in his body," wrote white conservative columnist James Kilpatrick in 1987.

Although public opinion surveys revealed that most Black voters thought of Reagan as racist, white Republican senator Orrin Hatch assured the country in January 1986 that "I know Ronald Reagan very well, and he doesn't have a racist bone in his body." The words were virtually identical to what the Utah senator would say thirty years later in defending another Republican president. "I know Donald Trump," Hatch said after Trump infamously equated racists and antiracists following a deadly August 2017 rally in Charlottesville. "I don't think there's a racist bone in his body."

Perhaps Dr. Hatch needs to examine his rusty stethoscope. Polls showed that the majority of African Americans saw both Reagan and Trump as racist presidents during their administrations, but the testimony of one white guy from Utah was expected to discredit the lived experiences of millions of Black people.

The framing of the racist bone defense was "essential to Reagan's assault on civil rights," according to antiracist scholars Christopher Petrella and Justin Gomer. Writing in the *Washington Post* in July 2019, Petrella and Gomer argued that Reagan's defense "changed the metric from the marginalization of African Americans at a group level to individual misdeeds," thus characterizing racism not as a public problem in need of policy solutions but a personal issue that only could be fixed deep in someone's bones.

The "racist bone" argument also shares parallels with another illogical anatomical defense: the "I know his heart" argument, which is commonly used to prove that a person who has done something egregiously wrong is actually a good person, according to a witness on their behalf.

Jefferson Davis deployed a version of the argument in his first inaugural address as president of the Confederate States in 1861 when he claimed that "he who knows the hearts of men will judge of the sincerity with which we labored to preserve the Government of our fathers in its spirit." In some ways, he was correct. Defenders of the Confederacy were "far from bonkers when they argued passionately that their revolt was consistent with the animating and driving spirit of 1776," wrote historian Gerald Horne in *The Counter-Revolution of 1776*. But Davis's appeal sought to focus on the "hearts" of the people who seceded from the union rather than the actions they took to betray the slowly evolving nation.

A century and a half later, when conservative George Conway wrote a July 2019 op-ed in the *Washington Post* calling the Republican president a racist for telling four women of color in Congress to "go back" to their countries, Conway's wife publicly disagreed with her husband. "I work with this president," said Kellyanne Conway. "I know his heart."

People who say they "don't have a racist bone in their body" haven't searched hard enough.

Yes, the famous nonracist heart and the common nonracist bones work together to protect white people from any possible prejudice.

In Trump's case, it was the same heart that was also defended by Republican House Speaker Paul Ryan in 2017 after Charlottesville. "I know his heart is in the right place," Ryan said at the time.

The people making these arguments suffer from an appalling lack of self-awareness. This country was built on racism and openly embraced anti-Black racial segregation as official government policy until the late 1960s. The idea that a white man born in a lily-white community in Indiana in 1909 (Earl Butz) or a small town in Illinois in 1911 (Ronald Reagan) could live for decades in segregated America and never entertain a single racist idea is so far beyond the realm of possibility as to be farcical.

In fact, I would argue it is impossible to live in America and not be influenced by racism at some level. The failure of white public figures to examine the impact of systemic racism on individual implicit biases reflects a privileged intellectual shallowness that is an indicator of racism itself.

But I extend this observation not only to white Americans but to all Americans. First, I should explain there is a widely held belief in many Black communities that Black people cannot be racist. Racism implies power, the argument goes, and Black people as a group lack such power over white people. Black people can be "prejudiced" but not "racist," according to the people who make this argument.

I've heard this argument almost my entire life from Black people whom I respect, and I fully understand and appreciate the truth of the power imbalance for which it argues. But having said that, I still disagree with it. Although the viewpoint I'm articulating is controversial among some Black people, I honestly believe that everyone, including myself, holds racist thoughts.

I recognize that the presence of racist thoughts need not lead to racist actions, but how could anyone in this country, of any race, not be affected by the anti-Black racism endemic in the larger society? Could any honest, thinking American examine their entire life history of exposure to racist ideas, from childhood to adulthood, and conclude that not a single one of these ideas had ever crossed their mind at some point in their lifetime?

Two points need to made here. First, the very structure of racism in America was designed to force Black people in this country to question our own identity and value. After four hundred years of exposure to racist beliefs, racism is so embedded in the DNA of America that many Black people have internalized these beliefs about our own people.

Second—and this is usually the subject of the greatest pushback from African Americans—it's important to acknowledge that many Black people hold racist beliefs about white people. Nearly all of these beliefs are generated as a response to racism from white people, and for that reason I believe it to be more understandable and relatable than white racism directed at Black people. In addition, *individual racism* of Black people toward white people does not harm most white people in the way that *institutional racism* from white people harms most Black people.

My great-grandfather, who was born in Aberdeen, Mississippi, in 1908, used to tell me stories of the outlandish racist treatment he experienced from white people in his life, and I find it completely understandable that he would hold racist ideas about white people because of that. Even in my own lifetime, in the late twentieth century and early twenty-first century, I've experienced enough anti-Black racism to hold racist ideas about white people as well. Sometimes I am forced to remind myself that not all white people in this country support or defend the racism in the larger society, but this, too, can be difficult.

I've been researching, writing, and speaking about issues of racism for forty years. I've taken implicit bias tests to examine my own prejudices. And I've worked closely with people of all races to examine these issues. But after all that, I cannot deny that I still have some unresolved racial issues toward white people based on the pain that white America has produced for me and my family for generations.

I can only speak for myself about my racial biases, but I've encountered perhaps thousands of other Black people in my life, among my colleagues, friends, and family, who also hold racist beliefs about white people. Many of us don't share these beliefs in public or in mixed company because of the potential repercussions we could experience from our white employers and others who hold power over us, but the beliefs are there.

While I do believe that Black people can be racist, I also think the nature of that racism differs dramatically from white racism. In my experience, Black racism directed at white people is almost always rooted in white racism against Black people. That is to say, Black people become racist because we see white people repeatedly doing racist things to us.

How could a group of people who have been as dehumanized and stigmatized as Black people have been in America not harbor some resentment against white people for all that has been done to us, historically and currently? Even the white people who I believe are allies still benefit from a system that privileges them in nearly every aspect of life, regardless of whether they support such a system.

Here, I must acknowledge the persuasiveness of the "Black people can't be racist" argument because the fundamental difference in the two types of racial prejudice is that Black people, as a group, do lack the power, and usually even the *will*, to translate these racist thoughts into antiwhite racist actions, policies, and laws. I have almost never encountered Black people who sought to impose the same racist policies used against us on white people. In contrast, generations of white Americans have allowed and benefited from anti-Black racist actions, policies, and laws.

The point here is not to equate the two forms of racism or implicate Black people by inclusion but rather to articulate the differences between the two forms of racism in order to indict the shallow white people who claim not to be racist at all. If I as a Black American can acknowledge the existence of racist beliefs in Black communities that have been victimized by white racism, it would strain credulity for any white adult in America to argue that they had somehow managed to escape the tentacles of that same racism for their entire lives.

I'm a realist, and I'm not a doctor, so I don't care what invisible good might be found in any president's bones or heart. Although I appreciate the concept of good-hearted people in positions of power, no internal part of the body can excuse the external actions of the individual. It's not the kindness of a public official's bones or heart that impact Black people; it's the unkind actions of the mouth and pen.

23

Yes, you do see color, and there's nothing wrong with that.

"Toto, I've got a feeling we're not in Kansas anymore."

It's one of the most famous lines in one of the most famous movies of all time. These are the first words spoken by Judy Garland, playing the character of Dorothy Gale, when she steps out of her sepia-toned tragedy and into a Technicolor paradise in the 1939 film *The Wizard of Oz.*

The audience immediately recognizes the difference in her location because the film is shot in black-and-white until Dorothy emerges from her home into the colorful world of Oz.

"We must be over the rainbow," says Dorothy.

It's a testament to the power of color and the vivid imagery that a rainbow evokes. As the scene unfolds, we see red smoke engulfing the Wicked Witch of the West, ruby slippers appearing on Dorothy's feet, and a yellow brick road leading the protagonist on her journey.

Now, imagine Oz without the color—not just the physical mani-festation of color but the representation of various colors as a substitute for diversity. Thinking of Oz without its sundry assortment of characters reduces the film to a story of a girl walking her dog in a park. It's the color of the characters that brings the story to life.

In much the same way, color is what animates our world today. We witness this not just through the physical colors in our universe but from the intersection of various people and cultures from all parts of the world. For better and for worse, our experiences have taught us to associate various qualities with those colors. It is for this reason that we know that Blackness is not just a skin color but also an identity, a culture, a style. We also know that the physical appearance of Blackness varies from person to person, and many of us detect its presence from other cues besides skin color.

Our calculations are sometimes off, as race is not always easily identifiable. Researchers long ago established race as a social construct created by humans, not by biology, but despite its origin as a discriminatory tool to differentiate between the value of various people, race still has a meaning born of shared experience and understanding. There may be no scientific reason to distinguish Black people from white people, but Black people have developed a culture, or cultures, based on our shared history.

So when white people claim that they don't see color, they're effectively denying the unique cultures that Black people have built for ourselves over the course of centuries. The hairstyles, the church services, the music, the dances, the cuisine, the family reunions, the fraternities and sororities, the civic organizations, and the bonds that Black people have built through centuries of oppression are all obliterated by the self-serving fiction of color blindness.

For some uninformed white Americans, I suppose the profession of color blindness could represent a sincere but misguided attempt to assert that they do not subscribe to white supremacy. "As somebody who grew up in a very diverse background as a young boy in the projects, I didn't see color as a young boy and I honestly don't see color now," said the former Starbucks CEO Howard Schultz in 2019 when asked about a 2018 racial profiling incident at a Starbucks location in Philadelphia.

But for many white conservatives today, color blindness has instead become a cudgel to attack race-conscious policy solutions to racism. "I don't see color," conservative commentator Tomi Lahren boasted fatuously to Trevor Noah on *The Daily Show* in 2016. It was familiar conservative rhetoric, reminiscent of a joke told by Stephen Colbert: "I don't see color. People tell me I'm white, and I believe them because police officers call me 'Sir.'"

One of the many problems with the "I don't see color" argument is that it's just not true. Although some people do experience color vision deficiency, which makes it difficult to distinguish between certain colors, total color blindness is very rare among humans.

Clearly, the conservatives who use this line don't mean it literally, though. Instead, they mean to suggest that the differences they perceive in people based on skin color don't register to them as an issue. Even this is difficult to accept from people who repeatedly espouse policies that consistently work to the detriment of people of color. But aside from the politics, it's inconceivable that anyone paying attention in the United States could fail to perceive the differences in the way Black and white people are treated in this country. If you see that, you see color, because skin color in America is directly correlated to either privilege or oppression.

It's not an accident that Black drivers are 20 percent more likely than white drivers to be stopped by police, or that once they've been stopped, they're searched about twice as often as white drivers. Nor is it just a coincidence that white home buyers and appraisers choose to devalue the market rate for residential real estate when the owners selling the property are visibly Black. What this means is that even if you are that rare individual who genuinely cannot see color, everyone else in America does, and their perceptions influence the way Black people are treated.

This was not the doing of Black people. Hundreds of years ago, white society created a concept called race and then fabricated an entire hierarchy based on color, assigning benefits and privileges accordingly.

When thirty-year-old Homer Plessy purchased a first-class ticket and boarded a train in New Orleans in June 1892, his race could not be visibly identified by the train conductor. When asked the question "Are you a colored man?" Plessy, who had a Black great-grandmother, responded "Yes." By the laws of the state of Louisiana, his one-eighth Negro blood made him Black, and his refusal to move to the colored section of the train prompted an arrest, a conviction, an appeal, and, four years later, an infamous US Supreme Court case justifying racial segregation.

White people who claim that they do not—or that other people should not—see color engage in a form of white privilege that enables members of dominant groups to erase the existence of other groups and assign everyone a homogenized identity as a human being. This erasure conceals both our joy and our pain. Because the dominant group created the array of benefits that flow from skin color, asking people not to see color further benefits the dominant group by encouraging people not to see the privilege, the oppression, and the racial disparities associated with those colors.

Many of us as Black Americans want white people and the rest of the world to see our color. "The idea that you are blind to my existing as a Black man doesn't say to me that you lack a bias, or that you are somehow woke," author Jarrett Hill wrote for NBC News in December 2016. "It says to me that you ignore my reality and you choose to do it, because (save for legal blindness) there's no way that you can't actually see me and my melanin." In fact, a Pew Research poll in April 2022 found 76 percent of Black Americans agreed that "being Black is extremely or very important to how they think about themselves."

Many of us want the world to see and celebrate the rich culture we've created, but we also want them to see the racism we experience and do something about it. Facile platitudes about not seeing color don't help us avoid that racism. The security guard who chooses to follow Black people and the taxicab driver who refuses to pick them up on the street both see color. Virtually everyone sees color. Even people with actual color blindness can distinguish other common physical differences between people of various racial groups.

The purpose of creating an inclusive, multiracial society is not to erase color but to understand, respect, and appreciate the complexities of different people. We can create a world that allows us to live together in community rather than uniformity. For this reason, some of us have embraced the idea of America as a *salad bowl* whose various toppings represent our diversity rather than a *melting pot* that assimilates our differences and colors into one bland concoction.

Although *The Wizard of Oz* plunges the viewer into a vibrant, colorful world, it is otherwise limited by its era. The 1930s diversity it presents is mostly an assortment of white people of various heights, genders, and flamboyant costumes. We're introduced to Munchkins, flying monkeys, a brainless scarecrow, a cowardly lion, and a heartless tin man. There's even a green person, the Wicked Witch of the West. Yet there are no Black people in Oz.

The absence of Black people is not surprising given the racism in Hollywood at the time. The film was released the same year that the Black actress Hattie McDaniel played the role of subservient "Mammy" in another Technicolor classic, *Gone with the Wind*, and won a Best Supporting Actress Oscar for her performance. But the Ambassador Hotel, which hosted the Academy Awards ceremony, refused to let her sit at the same table as the white cast members.

The development of *The Wizard of Oz* also indicated how racist ideas were so normalized that they were not a barrier to success for people who espoused them. One such person was L. Frank Baum, the author of the children's novel on which the film was based. In an 1890 newspaper editorial, Baum openly called for the genocide of Indigenous people in America: "The Whites, by law of conquest, by justice of civilization, are masters of the American continent, and the best safety of the frontier settlements will be secured by the total annihilation of the few remaining Indians. Why not annihilation? Their glory has fled, their spirit broken, their manhood effaced; better that they die than live the miserable wretches that they are."

Nearly four decades after *The Wizard of Oz* debuted on the big screen, pop stars Diana Ross and Michael Jackson teamed up for the

1978 film version of the all-Black 1975 Broadway adaptation called *The Wiz*. Finally, in 2015, NBC aired an all-Black live television broadcast of *The Wiz* featuring Stephanie Mills, Mary J. Blige, and Queen Latifah. The reaction was dramatic.

"Minorities act like they're the victims, but can you imagine if we made an all-white version of The Wiz?" wrote one Twitter user. "why are there no whites starring in #TheWiz?" another user posted. "this is racist! Can you imagine if it were the other way?"

After seventy-five years of celebrating a film based on a book written by a racist white man and featuring an all-white cast, the mere reinterpretation of the film with Black people in the same story felt threatening to some white people. This is why many of us want the world to see our color. We relish the opportunity to celebrate the creativity we produce with it, but we also demand the world look and see how we're treated because of it.

24

"All lives matter" is a cheap excuse to avoid saying "Black lives matter."

ARGUMENT

When you say black lives matter, that's inherently racist.

—*Former New York City mayor Rudy Giuliani, July 10, 2016*

ANSWER

Saying "All Lives Matter" as a response to "Black Lives Matter" is like saying the fire department should spray down all houses in a neighborhood, even if only one house is on fire, because all the houses matter. And yes, your house does matter. One hundred percent. But your house is not on fire.

—*Actor Keegan-Michael Key, June 2, 2020*

Black comedian Patrice O'Neal once told a provocative joke about Joran van der Sloot, a Dutch man who is widely thought to have been involved in the mysterious disappearance of an American teen in 2005. "What's the girl in Aruba?" he asks his audience. "Natalee Holloway," they respond immediately. "But he just killed a girl in Peru," he continues. "What's her name?" The audience is silent. "Exactly," said O'Neal, underscoring a point he had just made to the audience. "White women's life is valuable."

When Natalee Holloway disappeared in 2005, the national media coverage was relentless in hunting down clues. Similarly, when twenty-two-year-old Gabrielle Petito disappeared in 2021, that story also became major national news. The emphasis on both stories under-scored the "missing white woman syndrome" that former PBS anchor Gwen Ifill first spoke about in 2004.

In September 2021, a *Washington Post* article described Petito as a "blue-eyed, blonde adventure-seeker" walking barefoot in Kansas, a description that Stanford assistant professor Hakeem Jefferson noted on Twitter "unnecessarily racializes" Petito's disappearance to depict her as "most sympathetic."

Jefferson did not, of course, object to the search for Petito, just as most Black critics of unfair news coverage seek to balance the coverage, not to end it. "The Petito family certainly deserve answers and justice," MSNBC anchor Joy Reid said on her show in September 2021. "But the way this story has captivated the nation has many wondering, Why not the same media attention when people of color go missing?"

Cases involving white middle-class women tend to resonate with assignment editors and news organizations, according to Martin Reyn-olds, co–executive director of the Maynard Institute for Journalism Education, who spoke to the *New York Times* in September 2021. Meanwhile, "the disappearances of people of color tend not to generate the same volume of media interest, despite their occurring at a higher rate," wrote *Times* reporter Katie Robertson. Robertson cited a 2016 study that found that Black people were "significantly underrepre-sented" in media coverage of missing persons cases given their numbers in the FBI's tally of cases.

The point is not that white lives are overvalued but that Black and brown lives are undervalued in America. That's what Black people and our allies mean when we say "Black lives matter." It's an essential state-ment of affirmation in a society that has repeatedly told us that our lives are not important.

For hundreds of years during slavery, our lives were completely meaningless to white society except for purposes of commercial trade and uncompensated labor. During this time, our lives were only deemed valuable insofar as they could improve the quality of white lives. When slavery was finally abolished, for another one hundred years we were relegated to second-class citizenship. And now, from the end of the civil rights era to the present, our lives have been devalued by racial profiling, police brutality, and mass incarceration.

The sad truth is that Black lives have never been valued in America.

Our heartaches are expected. Our pain is ignored. And our suffering is dismissed. Our persistently high unemployment rate rarely causes concern or policy intervention. Our health and mortality disparities fail to elicit the same sympathy directed at white people in crisis. Our crumbling schools don't warrant additional funding from the government or taxpayers. Our underresourced and segregated neighborhoods don't generate investment unless white buyers choose to gentrify them. Our gun-plagued communities aren't given the proper tools to fight crime and violence. Our missing children don't elicit national media coverage. Our overly polluted air and water don't compel government leaders to propose comprehensive solutions. The vast food deserts in our midst don't inspire grocery store chains to open locations in our most struggling communities. And after all that, our families are not safe from the law enforcement officials sworn to protect us.

The tragedies of Black life are taken for granted in America. The cost of buying coffins to bury Black bodies is simply part of the package deal. That is why, in the face of all the obstacles and barriers before us, we proclaim that Black lives matter. We are compelled to do so because society refuses to act as though they do.

It is for this reason that it is not necessary to say "White lives matter" or "All lives matter," because the first is a given and the second is a lie.

Of course white lives matter in America. No observant person could doubt this fact in a society in which white people have dominated virtually every level of power from the founding of the republic to the present. Even if every Black person in America were to chant in unison that "white lives don't matter," it would make little difference to the power structure of a population that has deeply ensconced the privilege of whiteness in this country. Even if Black people wanted to make white lives not matter, which is not the case, we lack the collective power to do it.

Yet some critics complain that saying "Black lives matter" somehow promotes white inferiority. Black actor Terry Crews made this argument in June 2020, shortly after the George Floyd protests began, when he tweeted, "We must ensure #blacklivesmatter doesn't morph into #blacklivesbetter." It's almost as if a Black actor in the 1960s had tried to lecture civil rights activists to ensure that "We shall overcome" doesn't morph into "We shall overpower."

Crews's unwarranted fear of Black supremacy calls to mind the US Supreme Court's concern in 1883 that a civil rights bill passed a few years after the end of slavery might make Black people "the special favorite of the laws." And Crews's rhetoric would later be echoed by Black Republican senator Tim Scott, who told Fox News that "woke supremacy is as bad as white supremacy." Racial supremacy has never been the stated agenda of either the civil rights movement or the Black Lives Matter movement. And even if it were, Black people lack the power and the population to accomplish it.

In contrast, white America does enjoy the collective power to shape and control the lives of Black people. Many white leaders in our history have done so by implementing laws and policies that perpetuate white supremacy and anti-Blackness, while others have done so simply by failing to challenge those laws and accepting that privilege that flows from them.

But the "all lives matter" narrative is also troubling because it promotes a fantasy that belies the true story of America. All lives have never mattered in America.

We saw this illustrated dramatically in May 2020 when Media Matters for America put together a video showing conservatives rationalizing the deaths of tens of thousands of Americans felled by COVID at the exact moment when the caseload seemed to skew toward Black and brown people. "Of course, it's tragic," said Fox News anchor Sean Hannity, "but despite what you hear, the world is not coming to an end." On another show, his colleague Laura Ingraham bravely admitted that the loss of any life is tragic, but the number of people who were dying in one state was still "astonishingly low." And one Fox guest put it most bluntly: "Every single death is tragic," he said, "but also the destruction of the American economy is tragic." I guess all lives matter only when it doesn't affect the bottom line.

All lives did not matter when the founders of the nation deprived Indigenous people of their land, Black people of their freedom, and women of the right to vote. All lives did not matter when the government enacted laws and policies excluding Chinese immigrants and incarcerating Japanese Americans, or when our leaders authorized the use of weapons of mass destruction on innocent civilians in Japan.

All lives certainly did not matter when queer citizens of all colors were rounded up by police officers and arrested for their love. All lives did not matter when the Black victims of the drug crisis were imprisoned while the white victims of the opioid crisis were empowered and supported. All lives did not matter when the nation's leaders ignored the pleas of Black mayors fighting the COVID pandemic or the gun epidemic in their cities. All lives do not matter when cynical politicians exploit the lives of vulnerable trans children for political benefit. And all lives continue not to matter so long as the disproportionate use of state violence against Black bodies remains acceptable and rarely punishable behavior.

We say Black lives matter only because we need to. When George Floyd was murdered by police officers in Minneapolis, his death would have gone unnoticed and unprosecuted were it not for the brave videography of Darnella Frazier. When Ahmaud Arbery was murdered in Georgia, his killers would have been protected were it not for the public pressure that forced the state to investigate and prosecute them. When Breonna Taylor was killed by police in Louisville, almost no one would have been held accountable if the state prosecutor and the Trump administration had remained in charge of the case. This is why activists have to fight to show that Black lives matter.

When a Black person is caught committing a crime, the person usually goes to jail to face prosecution and imprisonment. When a police officer is caught committing a crime against a Black person, however, that officer is almost never charged with a crime unless Black people make it an issue. We have to prove that a Black life matters. And even then, there is no guarantee the officer will be punished, charged, or convicted. In fact, a report from Mapping Police Violence found that "police are almost never charged for excessive force violations" and that between 2013 and 2019, 99 percent of police killings resulted in no charges being filed.

"Black lives matter" is simply a call to arms to pay attention to a neglected community. When white conservatives, or their Black spokespeople, suggest that the use of the phrase somehow diminishes the value of white life, they deploy a sad and predictable deflection tactic, responding to a legitimate issue of Black concern by appealing to a supposedly neutral standard of equality that has never existed in America. When a house is on fire, you respond to the house on fire. Black Lives Matter is not a threat to white lives; it is a cry for help in the face of deadly discrimination against Black lives.

Finally, when I say Black lives matter, I mean all Black lives should matter, even, and perhaps especially, those from vulnerable, marginalized, and oppressed subcommunities. Poor Black lives matter. Black women's lives matter. Black trans lives matter. Black queer lives matter. Black immigrants' lives matter. The lives of Black people with disabilities matter, as do the lives of Black people who are incarcerated. Even the lives of the Black people with whom I strongly disagree matter. Let's protect all of them.

Yet time after time, from the victims of Jeffrey Dahmer in Milwaukee to the victims of Ed Buck in West Hollywood, from the disappearances of Black girls that go unreported in the media to the murders of Black trans women that are ignored by society, from the polluted pipes of Flint, Michigan, to the antiquated infrastructure of Jackson, Mississippi, Black people's lives have never mattered in this country, and they will not unless and until we demand that they do.

25

Yes, everything is about race.

ARGUMENT

Why does everything have to be about race? What difference does that make?

—*Fox News commentator Tomi Lahren, July 26, 2022*

ANSWER

I have found that those who are constantly asking, "Why does everything have to be about race?" are those that do not have to live with race every day. There is not a day that I wake up that I am not aware of my race and how it affects me.

—*Professor Brittany Lee Lewis, January 31, 2016*

So, to answer the question from the white man who spoke to me at a Black History Month event, why does everything have to be about race?

The first twenty-four chapters of this book confront a series of vexing arguments that Black people face every day about race and that refuse to disappear. But at the core of all the questions is the title of this book. Why do Black people continue to talk about race? Why do we focus so much on it? Why can't we just move on?

First, many of us would like nothing better. We're tired of talking about race, writing about it, and speaking about it, but most importantly, we're tired of dealing with it. We're tired of explaining our presence to white people and police officers whenever we're deemed "suspicious." We're tired of waiting in the longest lines to vote. We're tired of hiding our identities. We're tired of burying our loved ones early. And we're tired of constantly having to prove the existence of racism to the very group of people who are responsible for perpetuating it.

But we also know that ignoring the persistent problems of racism and white supremacy in America will not make them go away. We don't talk about racism because we enjoy the experience. We do so because we want racism to end. Whether we talk about it or not, racism exists, but if we don't talk about it, we fail to develop strategies and solutions to eradicate it.

This still does not quite answer the question, Why does everything have to be about race? But Black America may not have that answer: Black Americans did not create a society based on race. White Americans did.

From the very beginning of the country, white America created a vast and extensive system of racial privilege for white people and oppression for Black people. Here's a test. Do a Google search for "the history of racism in" almost any subject you can imagine, and you'll find examples. You can even search for "the history of racism in Google" and discover how search engines themselves were powered by racist algorithms. In fact, every aspect of American life—toys, dolls, schools, colleges, fraternities, sororities, housing, employment, marriage, family, business, finance, insurance, government, hospitals, fire departments, military units, railroads, air travel, media, music, sports, fashion, religion, policing, prisons, farming, tourism, movie theaters, bars, nightclubs, restaurants, grocery stores, shopping malls, public parks, private streets, highways, gated communities, cities, suburbs, cemeteries, and even the pollution in the environment—was set up to perpetuate white supremacy in a way that was often imperceptible to the white beneficiaries but virtually unavoidable for the Black victims.

"Racism is embedded into every facet and crevice of America," according to racial equity consultant Janice Gassam Asare. "Rather than questioning why racialized individuals 'make everything about race,' we should instead be interrogating how these gross inequities are able to continue."

Black Americans experience racial discrimination in ways both mundane (from makeup to bandage colors) and momentous (from redlining to racial profiling). The nation's most contentious twenty-first-century public debates, including abortion, gun control, welfare, taxes, immigration, and police brutality, trace their roots to racist decisions made by policy makers from past centuries that modern society has often forgotten or chosen to ignore. Each generation of America's policy makers has nudged, tweaked, adapted, and refined that racial caste system. But they did not eliminate it.

Despite periods of change—the Reconstruction era of the 1860s and 1870s, the civil rights era of the 1950s and 1960s—America never dismantled the white supremacy that undergirds our republic. We've never had an honest conversation about the history and legacy of racial oppression against African Americans and other people of color and the fundamental changes needed to build a more just society.

Instead of considering the effects of centuries of state-sanctioned racism and anti-Blackness, our nation has swept America's history under the rug and pretended that the passage of a few laws has corrected all our problems. But laws can't change hearts and minds, and they can't stop people who act on their biases quietly, without announcing their prejudices. That change comes only from the hard work of engaging in direct conversations about the rarely acknowledged issue of race, which continues to define and circumscribe our lives, and from developing enduring solutions to create a more perfect union.

As the country moves toward a multiracial society, we should be working together to tear down the barriers and obstacles that prevent us from building a fair and inclusive democracy. Instead, many of our nation's most cynical leaders are engaged in new efforts to whitewash America's past and ban any teaching of our real history.

Let's not forget how we got here. From the beginning, many of the very founders and former leaders we are taught to revere in this country expressed their steadfast beliefs that they *wanted* everything to be about race in America. Race was used to draw the blueprints for the nation's design, to erect the scaffolding that supported its construction, and to make the stones and bricks used to build its foundation. The evidence can be found in the speeches and documents in which they justified their endeavors over the past four centuries.

We cannot ignore this history, which began with the founding of the republic.

Nine months after the first shots were fired at Lexington and Concord in April 1775, the royal governor of the British colony of Virginia, known as Lord Dunmore, issued a proclamation offering freedom to enslaved Black people if they fought for the Crown.

> I do hereby further declare all indentured Servants, Negroes, or others, (appertaining to Rebels,) free that are able and willing to bear Arms, they joining His MAJESTY'S Troops.

Historian Cassandra Pybus has estimated that twenty thousand enslaved Black people ran away to join the British between 1775 and 1782. "Over the course of the war," wrote author Nikole Hannah-Jones in *The 1619 Project*, "thousands of enslaved people would join the British—far outnumbering those who joined the Patriot cause."

Dunmore's offer of freedom to enslaved Black people angered America's white revolutionaries. At the Virginia Convention the following month, the delegates responded by threatening to execute enslaved people who tried to win their freedom with the British.

> WHEREAS Lord Dunmore, by his proclamation . . . hath offered freedom to such able-bodied slaves as are willing to join him, and take up arms, against the good people of this colony . . . it is enacted, that all negro or other slaves, conspiring to rebel or make insurrection, shall suffer death, and be excluded all benefit of clergy.

In 1776, Thomas Jefferson joined in the condemnation of the British move in his original rough draft of the Declaration of

Independence. Although Jefferson was an enslaver himself, he decried what he called the "execrable commerce" and took no personal responsibility as he blamed the king of Great Britain for allowing "a market where MEN should be bought & sold." Jefferson's draft denounced Lord Dunmore's decision to free the enslaved people he claimed to care so much about.

> He is now exciting those very people to rise in arms among us, and to purchase that liberty of which he has deprived them.

The Second Continental Congress reviewed Jefferson's proposed language and deleted the entire section, removing all references to the institution of slavery from the founding document of the new nation. Even as the final version of the declaration proclaimed that "all men are created equal," one-third of the men who signed the document ignored the glaring hypocrisy that they were enslavers themselves. Although the final version completely ignored the moral inconsistency of equality and slavery, it did take a racist swipe at King George's attitudes toward the nation's Indigenous people:

> He has excited domestic insurrections amongst us, and has endeavoured to bring on the inhabitants of our frontiers, the merciless Indian Savages, whose known rule of warfare, is an undistinguished destruction of all ages, sexes and conditions.

In 1788, when the original US Constitution was ratified, the new government explicitly permitted the enslavement of Black people. The Constitution allowed southern states to count enslaved people as three-fifths of a person when determining the number of people in a state for the purpose of federal representation:

> Representatives and direct Taxes shall be apportioned among the several States which may be included within this Union, according to their respective Numbers, which shall be determined by adding to the whole Number of free Persons, including those bound to

Service for a Term of Years, and excluding Indians not taxed, three fifths of all other Persons.

The Constitution also prohibited Congress from banning the importation of enslaved people in the so-called slave trade until at least 1808:

The Migration or Importation of such Persons as any of the States now existing shall think proper to admit, shall not be prohibited by the Congress prior to the Year one thousand eight hundred and eight, but a Tax or duty may be imposed on such Importation, not exceeding ten dollars for each Person.

And the fugitive slave clause of the Constitution required states to return formerly enslaved people to bondage even if they escaped to "free states":

No Person held to Service or Labour in one State, under the Laws thereof, escaping into another, shall, in Consequence of any Law or Regulation therein, be discharged from such Service or Labour, but shall be delivered up on Claim of the Party to whom such Service or Labour may be due.

After declaring its independence from Mexico, the 1836 Texas Constitution banned free Black people and prohibited enslavers from freeing any enslaved people they owned:

Nor shall Congress have power to emancipate slaves; nor shall any slave-holder be allowed to emancipate his or her slave or slaves, without the consent of Congress, unless he or she shall send his or her slave or slaves without the limits of the Republic. No free person of African descent, either in whole or in part, shall be permitted to reside permanently in the Republic, without the consent of Congress.

In his 1837 farewell address to the nation, President Andrew Jackson, a notorious enslaver and "Indian killer," boasted of his decision to sign the Indian Removal Act, which forced Indigenous tribes to leave their lands and resettle in the West.

> The States which had so long been retarded in their improvement by the Indian tribes residing in the midst of them are at length relieved from the evil, and this unhappy race—the original dwellers in our land—are now placed in a situation where we may well hope that they will share in the blessings of civilization and be saved from that degradation and destruction to which they were rapidly hastening while they remained in the States.

In 1856, the US Supreme Court declared in *Dred Scott v. Sandford* that Black Americans, even if they were free, had no rights to citizenship in the United States:

> They are not included, and were not intended to be included, under the word "citizens" in the Constitution, and can therefore claim none of the rights and privileges which that instrument provides for and secures to citizens of the United States. On the contrary, they were at that time considered as a subordinate and inferior class of beings, who had been subjugated by the dominant race, and, whether emancipated or not, yet remained subject to their authority.

In 1858, Abraham Lincoln publicly endorsed the white supremacy embedded in the nation's structure. During a debate with his Democratic Senate opponent in Illinois, Lincoln told the audience,

> I am not, nor ever have been, in favor of bringing about in any way the social and political equality of the white and black races—that I am not nor ever have been in favor of making voters or jurors of negroes, nor of qualifying them to hold office, nor to intermingling with white people; and I will say in addition to this that there is a

physical difference between the white and black races which will ever forbid the two races living together on terms of social and political equality. And inasmuch as they cannot so live, while they do remain together, there must be the position of superior. I am as much as any other man in favor of having the superior position assigned to the white race.

In 1866, one year after Lincoln was assassinated, President Andrew Johnson expressed his own white supremacist views:

This is a country for white men, and by God, as long as I am President; it shall be a government for white men.

In 1882, Republican president Chester A. Arthur signed the Chinese Exclusion Act, banning Chinese immigrants from entering the United States:

Be it enacted by the Senate and House of Representatives of the United States of America in Congress assembled, That from and after the expiration of ninety days next after the passage of this act, and until the expiration of ten years next after the passage of this act, the coming of Chinese laborers to the United States be, and the same is hereby, suspended.

The following year, the Supreme Court limited Congress's right to pass civil rights legislation in the *Civil Rights Cases*. The court ruled that neither the Thirteenth Amendment, abolishing slavery, nor the Fourteenth Amendment, guaranteeing the equal protection of the laws, gave Congress the authority to outlaw discrimination in public accommodations.

It would be running the slavery argument into the ground to make it apply to every act of discrimination which a person may see fit to make. . . . When a man has emerged from slavery, and, by the aid of beneficent legislation, has shaken off the inseparable concomitants

of that state, there must be some stage in the progress of his elevation when he takes the rank of a mere citizen and ceases to be the
special favorite of the laws.

In 1896, in the case of *Plessy v. Ferguson*, the Supreme Court once
again allowed Black Americans to be reduced to second-class status in
their own country, allowing states to segregate them in "separate but
equal" facilities:

> We consider the underlying fallacy of the plaintiff's argument to
> consist in the assumption that the enforced separation of the two
> races stamps the colored race with a badge of inferiority. If this
> be so, it is not by reason of anything found in the act, but solely
> because the colored race chooses to put that construction upon
> it. . . . Legislation is powerless to eradicate racial instincts or to
> abolish distinctions based upon physical differences. . . . If one race
> be inferior to the other socially, the Constitution of the United
> States cannot put them upon the same plane.

But the principle of "separate but equal" proved meaningless, as
three years later, in 1899, the Supreme Court allowed school districts
to exclude Black students from white schools without even offering
alternative schools for the Black kids to attend, in the case of *Cumming
v. Richmond County Board of Education*:

> The substantial relief asked is an injunction that would either
> impair the efficiency of the high school provided for white children
> or compel the board to close it. But if that were done, the result
> would only be to take from white children educational privileges
> enjoyed by them without giving to colored children additional
> opportunities for the education furnished in high schools.

In 1901, the Supreme Court upheld second-class citizenship for
the citizens of Puerto Rico, describing the Hispanic residents as "alien
races" in the case of *Downes v. Bidwell*:

If those possessions are inhabited by alien races, differing from us in religion, customs, laws, methods of taxation and modes of thought, the administration of government and justice, according to Anglo-Saxon principles, may for a time be impossible.

In 1912, when Woodrow Wilson was elected president, he resegregated the federal workforce and dismissed concerns from Black leaders.

Segregation is not humiliating, but a benefit, and ought to be so regarded by you gentlemen. If your organization goes out and tells the colored people of the country that it is a humiliation, they will so regard it, but if you do not tell them so, and regard it rather as a benefit, they will regard it the same. The only harm that will come will be if you cause them to think it is a humiliation.

Wilson also fired fifteen of seventeen Black supervisors and replaced them with white workers. In Georgia, a federal Internal Revenue official boldly fired all Black employees with a warning:

There are no government positions for Negroes in the South. A Negro's place is in the corn field.

In 1921, President Warren G. Harding signed the Emergency Quota Act to impose racial quotas on immigrants and prevent a change in the racial balance of the country:

The number of aliens of any nationality who may be admitted under the immigration laws to the United States in any fiscal year shall be limited to 3 per centum of the number of foreign born persons of such nationality resident in the United States as determined by the United States census of 1910.

In March 1942, one month after President Roosevelt issued an executive order dividing the American West into military areas,

Yes, everything is about race.

General John DeWitt announced restrictions on the movements of Japanese Americans in those areas:

> Commencing at 12:00 midnight, P. W.T., March 29, 1942, all alien Japanese and persons of Japanese ancestry who are within the limits of Military Area No. 1, be and they are hereby prohibited from leaving that area for any purpose until and to the extent that a future proclamation or order of this headquarters shall so permit or direct.

In 1944, in the case of *Korematsu v. United States*, the Supreme Court allowed the federal government to execute the racist policy of incarcerating Japanese Americans:

> We deem it unjustifiable to call them concentration camps, with all the ugly connotations that term implies—we are dealing specifically with nothing but an exclusion order. To cast this case into outlines of racial prejudice, without reference to the real military dangers which were presented, merely confuses the issue.

Two days after the Supreme Court's historic 1954 decision ending racial segregation in public schools in *Brown v. Board of Education of Topeka*, President Eisenhower was asked if he agreed with the ruling. He declined to endorse the court's decision and instead only spoke of his legal duty to enforce it:

> The Supreme Court has spoken, and I am sworn to uphold the constitutional processes in this country; and I will obey.

Five years later, in January 1959, Judge Leon Bazile of the Circuit Court of Caroline County, Virginia, convicted Mildred Jeter and Richard Loving for violating the state's ban on interracial marriage and justified the separation of the races based on religious intent:

> Almighty God created the races white, black, yellow, malay and red, and he placed them on separate continents. And but for the

interference with his arrangement there would be no cause for such marriages. The fact that he separated the races shows that he did not intend for the races to mix.

When Congress debated the 1964 civil rights bill, South Carolina's segregationist senator Strom Thurmond, copying the language of the Supreme Court's 1883 decision in the Civil Rights Cases, claimed the new law would "bestow preferential rights on a favored few." Thurmond's rhetoric about law and order and his warnings about giving power "to government bureaucrats" would be adopted and embraced by the Republican Party for the next six decades:

Submitting to intimidation will only encourage further mob violence to gain preferential treatment. The issue is whether the Senate will pay the high cost of sacrificing a precious portion of each and every individual's Constitutional rights in a vain effort to satisfy the demands of the mob.

Congress passed the bill anyway, but many white southern leaders resisted. The Citizens Council in Jackson, Mississippi, issued a call for widespread disobedience in 1964:

"Civil rights" bills have been enacted against the South before, and they have been beaten back—not through supine acquiescence but through organized socioeconomic and political unity! . . . Integration cannot be imposed upon an unwilling white majority by the business community in Jackson, or anywhere else.

As recently as 2002, Senate Republican Leader Trent Lott of Mississippi seemed to endorse racial segregation when he celebrated Senator Strom Thurmond's one hundredth birthday. Thurmond ran for president in 1948 as a Dixiecrat opposed to the "social intermingling of the races," and more than fifty years later, Lott praised that racist campaign:

Yes, everything is about race.

I want to say this about my state: When Strom Thurmond ran for president, we voted for him. We're proud of it. And if the rest of the country had followed our lead, we wouldn't have had all these problems over all these years.

Six years later, Barack Obama's election as president didn't stop the racist attacks on his identity. In March 2011, future presidential candidate Donald Trump launched a five-and-a-half-year campaign challenging the authenticity of the first Black president's birth certificate, which had been duly issued by the State of Hawaii:

I have a birth certificate. People have birth certificates. He doesn't have a birth certificate. He may have one but there is something on that birth certificate—maybe religion, maybe it says he's a Muslim, I don't know. Maybe he doesn't want that. Or, he may not have one.

In 2013, a 5–4 majority of the Supreme Court substituted its judgment for that of the United States Congress, which had just reauthorized the 1965 Voting Rights Act with a Senate vote of 98–0 in 2006. Despite all the evidence to the contrary, the court's conservative majority acted as though racial discrimination in voting was an outdated issue and no longer a serious threat in America:

Our country has changed, and while any racial discrimination in voting is too much, Congress must ensure that the legislation it passes to remedy that problem speaks to current conditions.

Within twenty-four hours of the Supreme Court's voting rights decision, Texas, Mississippi, and Alabama began implementing new racially biased voting restrictions. Other states quickly followed. In July 2016, in the case of *North Carolina State Conference of the NAACP v. McCrory*, the United States Court of Appeals for the Fourth Circuit, noting the "inextricable link between race and politics in

North Carolina," ruled that a new Republican state voter ID law was unconstitutional:

> Before enacting that law, the legislature requested data on the use, by race, of a number of voting practices. Upon receipt of the race data, the General Assembly enacted legislation that restricted voting and registration in five different ways, all of which disproportionately affected African Americans. . . . The new provisions target African Americans with almost surgical precision.

In January 2017, President Trump issued an executive order following up on his campaign promise to impose a "a total and complete shutdown of Muslims entering the United States." The order stated,

> I hereby proclaim that the immigrant and nonimmigrant entry into the United States of aliens from countries referred to in section 217(a)(12) of the INA, 8 U.S.C. 1187(a)(12), would be detrimental to the interests of the United States, and I hereby suspend entry into the United States, as immigrants and nonimmigrants, of such persons for 90 days from the date of this order.

And in August 2020, Trump returned to birtherism when he refused to quash baseless rumors that Democratic senator Kamala Harris, the first Black woman on a major party ticket, was somehow ineligible to run for vice president:

> I just heard it today that she doesn't meet the requirements, and by the way, the lawyer that wrote that piece is a very highly qualified, very talented lawyer.

This is not a complete account of every racist policy or comment made by America's leaders in the past few centuries. It would take volumes to include them all. But these are just a few examples of the ways in which our nation's founders intended to create a system of white supremacy and racial subjugation and how every generation of successors has perpetuated that very same system.

Despite this long history of racism, Black conservative Thomas Sowell has argued that racism is only "kept alive" because of "politicians, race hustlers and people who get a sense of superiority by denouncing others as 'racists.'" It's an odd statement considering the frequency with which white conservatives repeatedly denounce Black civil rights leaders as "racist," but it's shameful and intellectually dishonest to claim that racism only exists because the people who are fighting against it continue to talk about it.

Sowell's commentary reflects centuries of paternalistic racial gaslighting designed to convince Black people and other marginalized groups that their oppression is only in their heads. If Black people feel targeted by state-sanctioned segregation, it is "solely because the colored race chooses to put that construction upon it," the Supreme Court said in 1896. If African Americans feel humiliated by racial discrimination, it's only because a civil rights organization "goes out and tells the colored people" to believe this, said President Wilson in 1912. If Japanese Americans object to being shipped to concentration camps, it's only because they don't realize that the policy is not about "racial prejudice," said the Supreme Court in 1944.

The real "race hustlers" (if I may borrow that pejorative term, which conservatives love to deploy as an attack) are not the civil rights advocates fighting for justice. There is no "hustle" in standing up for victims of police brutality or racial discrimination in America. Rather, the real "race hustlers" are the Black conservatives who allow themselves to be used as mouthpieces for the perpetuation of white supremacy. That's where the money is these days.

Black commentators don't stand out by being one of the many African Americans demanding racial justice. That line is too crowded. Instead, you make a name for yourself as a Black conservative by denying the existence of racial injustice. That gets you the lucrative book deals and speaking engagements and regular appearances on Fox News and right-wing media.

Many of America's white racists need affirmation from their Black enablers who provide them political cover. They quote Black people like Sowell and Candace Owens and others, who stand virtually alone as outliers in the larger Black community. White racists find vindication by elevating a small but vocal group of Black people who are not only unrepresentative but flatly contradict the sentiment expressed in most Black communities.

Since the founding of the country, white racists have celebrated Black people who help perpetuate their white supremacy. In fact, the only Black people whom white racists tend to uplift are those who disagree with the majority of Black people. The reward—financial and otherwise—comes from being the contrarian.

As a Black man in America, I've been writing about race since I was a high school student. I've done so to address a persistent problem in our society, not to get rich off it. But if I wanted to make a lot of money, the easiest thing to do would be to switch sides, claim to be a Black conservative, and begin making statements that contradict the beliefs of the majority of Black people. My income and exposure would rise immediately and exponentially. But I'll leave that to the real "race hustlers."

The simple answer to the question of why everything is about race is not that Black people want it to be so but that white America designed it to be so. The only way we can move forward to a place where everything does not have to be about race is by honestly acknowledging the pervasive role that race has already played in our country's past and continues to play in the present, and then taking positive, concrete, and comprehensive steps to change the future. So let us begin.

Readings

Michelle Alexander, *The New Jim Crow: Mass Incarceration in the Age of Colorblindness* (New York: New Press, 2010).

James L. Bacon, *The Ties That Bind: From Slavery to Freedom* (self-pub., CreateSpace, 2016).

Derrick Bell, "*Brown v. Board of Education* and the Interest-Convergence Dilemma," *Harvard Law Review* 93, no. 3 (January 1980): 518–533.

Keith Boykin, *Race Against Time: The Politics of a Darkening America* (New York: Bold Type Books, 2021).

Ta-Nehisi Coates, "The Case for Reparations," *The Atlantic*, June 2014.

Kimberlé Crenshaw, "Mapping the Margins: Intersectionality, Identity Politics, and Violence Against Women of Color," *Stanford Law Review* 43, no. 6 (July 1991): 1241–1299.

Lani Guinier and Gerald Torres, *The Miner's Canary: Enlisting Race, Resisting Power, and Transforming Democracy* (Cambridge, MA: Harvard University Press, 2002).

Nikole Hannah-Jones, Caitlin Roper, Ilena Silverman, and Jake Silverstein, eds., *The 1619 Project: A New Origin Story* (New York: One World, 2021).

Cheryl I. Harris, "Whiteness as Property," *Harvard Law Review* 106, no. 8 (June 1993): 1707–1791.

Jesse J. Holland, *Black Men Built the Capitol: Discovering African-American History In and Around Washington, D.C.* (Guilford, CT: Globe Pequot Press, 2007).

Gerald Horne, *The Counter-Revolution of 1776: Slave Resistance and the Origins of the United States of America* (New York: New York University Press, 2014).

Ibram X. Kendi, *Stamped from the Beginning: The Definitive History of Racist Ideas in America* (New York: Bold Type Books, 2016).

Clint Smith, *How the Word Is Passed: A Reckoning with the History of Slavery Across America* (New York: Little, Brown, 2021).

Acknowledgments

Writing a book is a collaborative effort. Although I take responsibility for any shortcomings in this published work, I share the credit with many others.

First, this work would not have been possible without the support of my agent, Jane Dystel, and my editor and publisher, Clive Priddle.

Second, I'm grateful to Lyric Renee Truth for reading early drafts of this book and assisting with the research and the bibliography. And I appreciate the ideas I got from Pierre Sherrill on "white centering" and from Renauld Clarke on "wokeness." Also, thanks to my copyeditor, Erin Granville, for helping me to view the text through the eyes of the reader, and to my publicists, Jocelynn Pedro, Flo McAfee, and Janelle Grai, for helping to spread the word on my recent published works.

Third, thanks to the many independent bookstores, Black-owned bookstores, and commercial chain bookstores that have carried my books and welcomed me to book signings in their cities.

Fourth, I appreciate the many friends and family members who allowed me the space to complete this work, including my mom, Shirley Parker, who was completely supportive when I skipped Thanksgiving and Christmas in 2022 while I was on deadline.

Fifth, I give thanks to Brandon Adams, Krystal Adams, Michael Adams, Esteban Antoine, Kyeng Beeman, Donna Brazile, Jericho

Brown, Lorin Brown, Clay Cane, Jasmyne Cannick, Corece, Ivan Daniel, Keith Dickerson, Reginald Dickerson, Robert Dickerson, Jardin Douglas, Maurice Franklin, Julia Gordon, Jeremy Graves, James E. Grooms, Robin Harrison, Sylvia A. Harvey, Neil Henriques, Krishna Henry, Jarrett Hill, George M. Johnson, Sean Johnson, Cameron Jones, Cheryl Jones, Malcolm Kenyatta, Don Lemon, Alphonso Morgan, Lori Newberry, Allen Orr, Mike Ramsey, Joy Reid, Rashad Robinson, Maiysha Simpson, Kevin E. Taylor, Rochelle Teague, Joanna Varikos, Juan Walker, Savoy Walker, Emil Wilbekin, Nathan Hale Williams, David Wilson, Ted Winn, and Leah Wright Rigueur.

Finally, I thank Elon Musk for making the Twitter experience so unbearable in November 2022 that he broke my thirteen-year addiction to my favorite social media platform, allowing me the time to write this book.

Bibliography

A Brief Chronology

Horne, Gerald. *The Dawning of the Apocalypse*. New York: Monthly Review Press, 2020.

Nell, William Cooper. *The Colored Patriots of the American Revolution*. Boston: Robert F. Wallcut, 1855.

Naturalization Act of 1790, ch. 3, § 1, 1 Stat. 103, 103–04 (repealed 1795).

Texas Const., General Provisions, § 9.

Douglass, Frederick. *My Bondage and My Freedom*. New York: Miller, Orton and Mulligan, 1855.

Plessy v. Ferguson, 163 U.S. 537 (1896).

Trump, Donald. Remarks at news conference, New York, August 15, 2017. Transcript: "Full Text: Trump's Comments on White Supremacists, 'Alt-Left' in Charlottesville." Politico, August 15, 2017. www.politico.com/story/2017/08/15/full-text-trump-comments-white-supremacists-alt-left-transcript-241662.

Introduction

Morrison, Toni. "A Humanist View." Speech at Portland State University, Portland, OR, May 30, 1975. Transcript at www.mackenzian.com/wp-content/uploads/2014/07/Transcript_PortlandState_tMorrison.pdf.

PART ONE
Erasing Black History

Mazzei, Patricia, and Anemona Hartocollis. "Florida Rejects A.P. African American Studies Course." *New York Times*, January 19, 2023.

Coscarelli, Joe, and Reggie Ugwu. "What Kanye West Said About Slavery, Obama and Mental Health in His New Interviews." *New York Times*, May 1, 2018.

@doorbender. "When Harriet Tubman was born Thomas Jefferson was alive . . ." TikTok video, 00:12. May 30, 2021. www.tiktok.com /@doorbender/video/6968288531156438277.

1. Barack Obama's election does not compensate for hundreds of years of racism.

Sonmez, Felicia. "McConnell Says He's Against Reparations for Slavery: 'It Would Be Pretty Hard to Figure Out Who to Compensate.'" *Washington Post*, June 18, 2019.

Obama, Barack. Remarks at press conference, July 9, 2016. Transcript: "Press Conference by President Obama After the NATO Summit." Press release. July 9, 2016. https://obamawhitehouse.archives .gov/the-press-office/2016/07/09/press-conference-president-obama -after-nato-summit.

2. Critical race theory is not indoctrinating school kids to be "woke."

Communications Office of the Governor of Florida. "Governor DeSantis Announces Legislative Proposal to Stop W.O.K.E. Activism and Critical Race Theory in Schools and Corporations." Press release. December 15, 2021. www.flgov.com/2021/12/15/governor-desantis -announces-legislative-proposal-to-stop-w-o-k-e-activism-and-critical -race-theory-in-schools-and-corporations/.

Crenshaw, Kimberlé. "Kimberlé Crenshaw on Confronting America's Racism." Interview by Molly Kaplan for *At Liberty: The ACLU Podcast*. YouTube video, 6:30, quote at 3:06. Posted by ACLU on August 6, 2021. https://youtu.be/Jih7ZbB8OLE.

Bernstein, Fred. "Derrick Bell, Law Professor and Rights Advocate, Dies at 80." *New York Times*, October 6, 2011.

Dawsey, Josh, and Jeff Stein. "White House Directs Federal Agencies to Cancel Race-Related Training Sessions It Calls 'Un-American Propaganda.'" *Washington Post*, September 5, 2020.

Vought, Russell. Memorandum M-20-34, "Training in the Federal Government." White House, Office of Management and Budget, Information and Guidance. September 4, 2020. www.whitehouse.gov/wp-content /uploads/2020/09/M-20-34.pdf.

Exec. Order No. 13950, 85 FR 60683, September 22, 2020. https:// trumpwhitehouse.archives.gov/presidential-actions/executive-order -combating-race-sex-stereotyping/.

King, Martin Luther, Jr. "I Have a Dream." Speech at the March on Washington for Jobs and Freedom, Lincoln Memorial, Washington, DC, August 28, 1963. Transcript: "Read Martin Luther King Jr.'s 'I Have a Dream' Speech in Its Entirety." NPR, January 16, 2023. www.npr .org/2010/01/18/122701268/i-have-a-dream-speech-in-its-entirety.

Fortin, Jacey. "Critical Race Theory: A Brief History." *New York Times*, November 8, 2021.

Craig, Tim, and Lori Rozsa. "In His Fight Against 'Woke' Schools, DeSantis Tears at the Seams of a Diverse Florida." *Washington Post*, February 7, 2022.

The Daily Show. "Unsolved Mysteries: Do Any Republicans Know What Critical Race Theory Actually Is?" YouTube video, 3:40, quote at 1:49. Posted by The Daily Show on June 29, 2021. www.youtube.com /watch?v=6ofjZH80y3g.

Reyes, Ronny. "Florida Bans 54 of Its School Math Textbooks for 'Trying to Indoctrinate Students': Half of the Prohibited Titles Feature Critical Race Theory." Daily Mail.com, April 16, 2022. www.dailymail .co.uk/news/article-10724369/Florida-bans-28-math-textbooks -school-fight-Critical-Race-Theory.html.

Harriot, Michael. @michaelharriot. "Critical Race Theory took my guns and give them to the transgenders." Twitter, June 18, 2021, 5:07 a.m. https://twitter.com/michaelharriot/status/1405859591456538627.

Marshall, Josh. @joshtpm. "Critical race theory ate my homework." Twitter, June 21, 2021, 5:44 a.m. https://twitter.com/joshtpm/status /1406956210927067142.

Gotanda, Neil, Gary Peller, and Kimberlé Crenshaw, eds. *Critical Race Theory: The Key Writings That Formed the Movement*. New York: New Press, 1995.

3. Dr. King didn't say America should be color-blind.

Associated Press. "Reagan Quotes King Speech in Opposing Minority Quotas." *New York Times*, January 19, 1986.

King, Martin Luther, Jr. Speech. Date and location unknown. Clip: "Somebody Told a Lie—MLK That's Never Quoted." YouTube video, 2:17, quote at 2:08. Posted by Black Independence Day on June 9, 2011. https://youtu.be/UGtjAaJeUWY.

King, Martin Luther, Jr. "I Have a Dream." Speech at The March on Washington for Jobs and Freedom, Lincoln Memorial, Washington, DC, August 28, 1963. Transcript: "Read Martin Luther King Jr.'s 'I Have a Dream' Speech in Its Entirety." NPR, January 16, 2023. www.npr.org/2010/01/18/122701268/i-have-a-dream-speech-in-its-entirety.

Seale, Colin. "MLK's 'I Have a Dream' Speech and Rejecting Colorblindness for Today's Children." *Forbes*, January 20, 2020.

King, Martin Luther, Jr. *Why We Can't Wait*. New York: Signet, 1964.

Kornbluh, Felicia. "Dr. King Sought Affirmative Action." *New York Times*, January 12, 1996.

King, Peter H. "Dr. King: Quote, Unquote." *Los Angeles Times*, March 5, 2019.

King, Martin Luther, Jr. "Where Do We Go from Here?" Speech before the Southern Christian Leadership Conference, Atlanta, GA, August 16, 1967. Transcript available from the Martin Luther King, Jr. Research and Education Institute at Stanford University, https://kinginstitute.stanford.edu/where-do-we-go-here.

Newport, Frank. "Martin Luther King Jr. Revered More After Death Than Before." Gallup News Service, January 16, 2006.

Clines, Francis X. "Reagan's Doubts on Dr. King Disclosed." *New York Times*, October 22, 1983.

Yang, John E., and Sharon LaFraniere. "Bush Picks Thomas for Supreme Court." *Washington Post*, July 2, 1991.

Bensinger, Ken. "Christian Walker Lashes Out on Twitter After Father's Georgia Senate Loss." *New York Times*, December 7, 2022.

4. Republicans are no longer the "party of Lincoln."

Fox News. @FoxNews. ".@RealBenCarson: Who started the KKK? That was the Democrats." Twitter, November 6, 2016, 7:58 a.m. https://twitter.com/foxnews/status/795294320278417409.

Goldwater, Barry. Speech on US Senate floor, June 19, 1964. Transcript: "Text of Goldwater Speech on Rights." *New York Times*, June 19, 1964.

Schwartz, Ian. "CNN's Keith Boykin: Man Who Called Trump 'First Black President' an 'Uncle Tom.'" RealClearPolitics, February 27, 2020. www.realclearpolitics.com/video/2020/02/27/cnns_keith_boykin_man_who_called_trump_first_black_president_an_uncle_tom.html.

Morrison, Toni. "Comment." *New Yorker*, September 27, 1998.

Milbank, Dana. "In Which Trump Discovers Some Guy Named Frederick Douglass." *Washington Post*, February 1, 2017.

Wagner, John. "Trump: Most People Don't Know President Lincoln Was a Republican." *Washington Post*, March 22, 2017.

Mintz, Morton. "Warren Book Blames Ike for '50s Strife." *Washington Post*, March 13, 1977.

King, Martin Luther, Jr. "The Rising Tide of Racial Consciousness." Speech at the Golden Anniversary Conference of the National Urban League, New York, September 6, 1960. Transcript available from the Martin Luther King, Jr. Research and Education Institute at Stanford University, https://kinginstitute.stanford.edu/king-papers/documents/rising -tide-racial-consciousness-address-golden-anniversary-conference.

King, Martin Luther, Jr. Speech, Los Angeles, October 27, 1964. Clip: "KTLA News: 'Martin Luther King, Jr. Urges People to Vote.'" You-Tube video, 8:43. Posted by UCLA Film & Television Archive on September 6, 2016. www.youtube.com/watch?v=9tRhyqhC_7o.

Texas Observer. "Goldwater's Policies, Kennedy's Style." October 30, 1964.

Moyers, Bill D. "What a Real President Was Like." *Washington Post*, November 13, 1988.

Perlstein, Rick. "Exclusive: Lee Atwater's Infamous 1981 Interview on the Southern Strategy." *The Nation*, November 13, 2012.

Truman, Harry S. Speech at the Democratic National Convention, Philadelphia, July 15, 1948. Transcript available from the American Presidency Project, UC Santa Barbara, www.presidency.ucsb.edu/documents /address-philadelphia-upon-accepting-the-nomination-the-democratic -national-convention.

Boykin, Keith. *Race Against Time: The Politics of a Darkening America*. New York: Bold Type, 2021.

Boykin, Keith. "Either Party Can Win the Loyalty of Black Voters Moving Forward. Here's How." *Washington Post*, September 23, 2021.

Boykin, Keith, and Michael Steele. "I Keep the Flame Burning on What Republicanism Is: With Guest Keith Boykin." *The Michael Steele Podcast*, October 2021. www.spreaker.com/user/11313090/100821-msp -keith-boykin.

5. The Civil War was about slavery, not states' rights.

Davis, Jefferson. *The Rise and Fall of the Confederate Government*. New York: D. Appleton, 1881.

Mississippi Declaration of Secession Convention. "A Declaration of the Immediate Causes Which Induce and Justify the Secession of the State of Mississippi from the Federal Union." *Journal of the State Convention and Ordinances and Resolutions Adopted in January 1861* . . . Jackson, MS: E. Barksdale State Printer, 1861.

Amateau, Rod, dir. *The Dukes of Hazzard.* Season 1, episode 1, "One Armed Bandits." Aired January 26, 1979, on CBS.

Nolasco, Stephanie. "'Dukes of Hazzard' Star John Schneider on General Lee, Cancel Culture: 'We Don't Belong in That Country Club.'" Fox-News.com, November 26, 2021. www.foxnews.com/entertainment /dukes-of-hazzard-john-schneider-general-lee-cancel-culture-poker -run-christmas-in-tune.

Stutz, Colin. "Kendrick Lamar Responds to Geraldo Rivera: 'Hip-Hop Is Not the Problem, Our Reality Is.'" Billboard.com, July 2, 2015. www.billboard.com/music/rb-hip-hop/kendrick-lamar-responds -geraldo-rivera-alright-bet-awards-6620035/.

Faust, Drew Gilpin. "Death and Dying." National Park Service website. Accessed June 2, 2023. www.nps.gov/nr/travel/national_cemeteries /death.html.

Lee, Robert E. Letter to Mary Randolph Custis Lee, December 27, 1856. *Encyclopedia Virginia.* https://encyclopediavirginia.org/entries/letter-from -robert-e-lee-to-mary-randolph-custis-lee-december-27-1856/.

McPherson, James M. *This Mighty Scourge: Perspectives on the Civil War.* New York: Oxford University Press, 2007.

Furst, Jenner, and Julia Willoughby Nason, dirs. *Rest in Power: The Trayvon Martin Story.* Paramount, 2018.

South Carolina Declaration of Secession Convention. "Declaration of the Immediate Causes Which Induce and Justify the Secession of South Carolina from the Federal Union." December 24, 1860. https://avalon .law.yale.edu/19th_century/csa_scarsec.asp.

Virginia Convention. "An Ordinance to Repeal the Ratification of the Constitution of the United States of America by the State of Virginia, and to Resume All the Rights and Powers Granted Under Said Constitution." April 17, 1861. www.battlefields.org/learn/primary-sources /declaration-causes-seceding-states#virginia.

Cleveland, Henry. *Alexander H. Stephens, in Public and Private: With Letters and Speeches, Before, During, and Since the War.* Philadelphia: National Publishing Company, 1886.

Congress of the Confederate States of South Carolina, Georgia, Florida, Alabama, Mississippi, Louisiana, and Texas. "Constitution of the Confederate States." March 11, 1861. Avalon Project, Yale Law School. Accessed June 7, 2023. https://avalon.law.yale.edu/19th_century/csa_csa.asp.

Agiesta, Jennifer. "Poll: Majority Sees Confederate Flag as Southern Pride Symbol, Not Racist." CNN.com, July 2, 2015. www.cnn.com/2015/07/02/politics/confederate-flag-poll-racism-southern-pride/index.html.

Smith, Jenny. "Commentary: Who Were the United Daughters of the Confederates?" *Jefferson City (MO) News Tribune*, September 28, 2020.

Serwer, Adam. "The Myth of the Kindly General Lee." *The Atlantic*, June 4, 2017.

Cole, Devan. "Tom Cotton Describes Slavery as a 'Necessary Evil' in Bid to Keep Schools from Teaching 1619 Project." CNN.com, July 27, 2020.

Obama, Michelle. Address at the Democratic National Convention, Wells Fargo Center, Philadelphia, July 25, 2016. Clip: "Michelle Obama: 'I Wake Up Every Morning in a House That Was Built by Slaves." YouTube video, 1:10. Posted by PBS NewsHour on July 25, 2016. www.youtube.com/watch?v=zHnJ2sTIVUI.

Victor, Daniel. "Bill O'Reilly Defends Comments About 'Well Fed' Slaves." *New York Times*, July 27, 2016.

Prasad, Ritu. "The Awkward Questions About Slavery from Tourists in US South." BBCNews.com, October 2, 2019. www.bbc.com/news/world-us-canada-49842601.

Sullivan, Sean. "Ben Carson: Obamacare Worst Thing 'Since Slavery.'" *Washington Post*, October 11, 2013.

Elder, Larry. Interview by Ainsley Earhardt, Brian Kilmeade, and Steve Doocy, *Fox & Friends*. Fox News, April 9, 2019. Transcript: "Fox & Friends Guest: Black Families Were Better Off as Slaves." Media Matters for America. www.mediamatters.org/fox-friends/fox-friends-guest-black-families-were-better-slaves.

Arizona v. Mayorkas, 598 U.S. _____ (2023).

Tarlo, Shira. "Tucker Carlson Guest Tells Black Americans 'You Need to Move On' from Slavery on Fox News." Salon, February 22, 2019. www.salon.com/2019/02/22tucker-carlson-guest-tells-black-americans-you-need-to-move-on-from-slavery-on-fox-news/.

Calhoun, John C. "The Southern Address." *Charleston Courier*, February 1, 1849.

6. Black History Month is still needed in a society that denies Black contributions.

Ruffin, Amber. "Why We Need a White History Month." *The Amber Ruffin Show*. Aired February 5, 2021, on Peacock. Clip available on YouTube,

posted by The Amber Ruffin Show on February 5, 2021. www.youtube
.com/watch?v=jdRAuBuZMNQ.

Johnson, Angela. "Black Twitter Goes Off on Jeopardy Contestants Who
Didn't Know Ketanji Brown Jackson." *The Root*, November 11, 2022.
www.theroot.com/black-twitter-goes-off-on-jeopardy-contestants-
who-didn-1849772339.

Sanders, Linley. "How Much Do Americans Think They Know About
Black History?" YouGov.com, February 17, 2021. https://today.yougov
.com/topics/society/articles-reports/2021/02/17/americans-think
-they-know-about-black-history.

Crowley, Michael, and Jennifer Schuessler. "Trump's 1776 Commission Cri-
tiques Liberalism in Report Derided by Historians." *New York Times*,
January 18, 2021.

1836 Project Advisory Committee. *The 1836 Project: Telling the Texas
Story*. December 2022. https://tea.texas.gov/sites/default/files/1836
-document-telling-the-Texas-story-final.pdf.

Kaur, Harmeet. "Kanye West Just Said 400 Years of Slavery Was a Choice."
CNN.com, May 4, 2018. www.cnn.com/2018/05/01/entertainment
/kanye-west-slavery-choice-trnd/index.html.

Woodson, Carter G. *The Mis-education of the Negro*. Washington, DC: Associated Publishers, 1933.

Freeman, Morgan. Interview by Mike Wallace, *60 Minutes*. CBS, December 18, 2005. Transcript: *Showbiz Tonight*, December 19, 2005. https://
transcripts.cnn.com/show/sb/date/2005-12-19/segment/01.

PART TWO
Centering White Victimhood

Johnson, Andrew. "Proclamation 179, Granting Full Pardon and Amnesty to
All Persons Engaged in the Late Rebellion." December 25, 1868. www
.loc.gov/resource/rbpe.23602600/?st=text.

7. Affirmative action is not "reverse discrimination."

Will, George. "Reverse Discrimination Is, by Any Other Name, Still Ugly."
Free Lance-Star (Fredericksburg, VA), November 18, 1976.

Fish, Stanley. "Reverse Racism, or How the Pot Got to Call the Kettle Black."
The Atlantic, November 1993.

Mansky, Jackie. "The Origins of the Term 'Affirmative Action.'" *Smithsonian
Magazine*, June 22, 2016.

Exec. Order No. 10925, 3 CFR, 1959–1963 Comp. p. 448, March 6, 1961. www.presidency.ucsb.edu/documents/executive-order-10925 -establishing-the-presidents-committee-equal-employment-oppor tunity.

Regents of Univ. of California v. Bakke, 438 U.S. 265 (1978).

Clinton, Bill. Speech on affirmative action at the National Archives, Washington, DC, July 19, 1995. Transcript: "Excerpts from Clinton Talk on Affirmative Action." *New York Times*, July 20, 1995.

Crenshaw, Kimberlé W. "Framing Affirmative Action." *Michigan Law Review First Impressions* 105 (2006): 123–133.

Massie, Victoria M. "White Women Benefit Most from Affirmative Action— and Are Among Its Fiercest Opponents." Vox, June 23, 2016. www.vox .com/2016/5/25/11682950/fisher-supreme-court-white-women -affirmative-action.

Johnson, Lyndon B. "To Fulfill These Rights." Commencement address at Howard University, Washington, DC, June 4, 1965. Transcript available from the American Presidency Project, UC Santa Barbara, www .presidency.ucsb.edu/documents/commencement-address-howard -university-fulfill-these-rights.

Fowle, Daniel G. Letter to Colonel E. Whittlesey, assistant commissioner of the Bureau of Refugees, Freedmen, and Abandoned Lands, April 5, 1866. In *Executive Documents Printed by Order of the House of Representatives during the First Session of the Thirty-Ninth Congress, 1865–'66*, 7–8. Washington, DC: Government Printing Office, 1866.

Civil Rights Cases, 109 U.S. 3 (1883).

King, Peter H. "Dr. King: Quote, Unquote." *Los Angeles Times*, October 27, 1996.

Students for Fair Admissions, Inc. v. University of North Carolina, 600 U.S. ____ (2023). www.supremecourt.gov/opinions/22pdf/20-1199_l6gn .pdf.

8. Even the poorest white people have white privilege.

Von, Theo. "White Privilege." YouTube video, 2:02. Posted by Theo Von on August 22, 2017. www.youtube.com/watch?v=MvzwmoZaNHQ.

McIntosh, Peggy. "White Privilege: Unpacking the Invisible Knapsack." *Peace and Freedom*, July/August 1989.

James, Lois. "The Stability of Implicit Racial Bias in Police Officers." *Police Quarterly* 21, no. 1 (March 2018): 30–52.

Gumbinner, Liz. @Mom101. "No one looks at your bank account before pulling a gun on you for a traffic violation." Twitter, April 13, 2021, 10:18 a.m. https://twitter.com/Mom101/status/1382020415040655368.

Harris, Cheryl I. "Whiteness as Property." *Harvard Law Review* 106, no. 8 (June 1993): 1707–1791.

Madison, James. "On Property." *National Gazette*, March 29, 1792.

Zitser, Joshua. "Black Family Receives a Home Appraisal $259k Higher than Original After Asking a White Neighbor to Present It for Them, Report Says." *Business Insider*, November 19, 2022. www.businessinsider.com/seattle-black-family-whitewashes-home-get-appraisal-259k-higher-report-2022-11.

Du Bois, W. E. B. *Black Reconstruction in America, 1860–1880*. New York: Oxford University Press, 1935.

Stepansky, Joe, Larry McShane, and Jason Sheftell. "Actor Forest Whitaker Gets Stopped and Frisked Leaving Morningside Heights Deli." *New York Daily News*, February 16, 2023.

Cooper, Helen, and Abby Goodnough. "Over Beers, No Apologies, but Plans to Have Lunch." *New York Times*, July 30, 2009.

Landon, Michael, and Ed Friendly, exec. producers. *Little House on the Prairie*. Season 3, episode 18, "The Wisdom of Solomon." Aired March 7, 1977, on NBC.

9. Yes, European immigrants struggled, but they were not slaves.

Wilkey, Robin. "Tea Party Leader's Tweet Suggests Blacks Stop 'Bitching and Moaning' About Slavery." *Huffington Post*, December 18, 2013. www.huffpost.com/entry/tea-party-racist-tweet_n_4467221.

Amend, Alex. "How the Myth of the 'Irish Slaves' Became a Favorite Meme of Racists." Hatewatch, Southern Poverty Law Center, April 19, 2016. www.splcenter.org/hatewatch/2016/04/19/how-myth-irish-slaves-became-favorite-meme-racists-online.

Baker, Peter. "A Half-Century After Wallace, Trump Echoes the Politics of Division." *New York Times*, July 30, 2020.

Ambinder, Marc. "'This Is Alabama. We Speak English.'" *The Atlantic*, April 26, 2010.

King, Martin Luther, Jr. "The Other America." Speech at Grosse Pointe High School, Grosse Pointe, Michigan, March 14, 1968. Transcript available from Grosse Pointe Historical Society, www.gphistorical.org/mlk/mlkspeech/.

Abramitzky, Ran, and Leah Boustan. *Streets of Gold: America's Untold Story of Immigrant Success*. New York: PublicAffairs, 2022.

Haddad, Diane. "Debunking Three Myths About Your Immigrant Ancestors." *Family Tree Magazine*. Accessed June 3, 2023. https://familytreemagazine .com/records/immigration/three-myths-immigrant-ancestors/.

Wilkerson, Miranda E., and Joseph Salmons. "'GOOD Old Immigrants of Yesteryear,' Who Didn't Learn English: Germans in Wisconsin." *American Speech* 83, no. 3 (2008): 259–283.

Hogan, Liam. "Debunking the Imagery of the 'Irish Slaves' Meme." Medium, September 14, 2015. https://limerick1914.medium.com/the-imagery-of -the-irish-slaves-myth-dissected-143e70aa6e74.

Stack, Liam. "Debunking a Myth: The Irish Were Not Slaves, Too." *New York Times*, March 17, 2017.

Hogan, Liam, et al. "Open Letter to Irish Central, Irish Examiner and Scientific American About Their 'Irish Slaves' Disinformation." Medium, March 8, 2016. https://limerick1914.medium.com/open-letter-to-irish -central-irish-examiner-and-scientific-american-about-their-irish -slaves-3f6cf23b8d7f.

Kendi, Ibram X. *Stamped from the Beginning: The Definitive History of Racist Ideas in America*. New York: Nation, 2016.

Alexander, Michelle. *The New Jim Crow: Mass Incarceration in the Age of Colorblindness*. New York: New Press, 2010.

Naturalization Act of 1790, 1 Stat. 103, 103–104. March 4, 1790.

Guinier, Lani, and Gerald Torres. *The Miner's Canary: Enlisting Race, Resisting Power, Transforming Democracy*. Cambridge, MA: Harvard University Press, 2002.

Harris, Cheryl I. "Whiteness as Property." *Harvard Law Review* 106, no. 8 (June 1993): 1707–1791.

Hunter, Tera W. "Slaves Weren't Immigrants. They Were Property." *Washington Post*, March 9, 2017.

Merica, Dan. "Carson: 'There Were Other Immigrants Who Came in the Bottom of Slave Ships, Who Worked Even Longer, Even Harder, for Less.'" CNN.com, March 7, 2017. www.cnn.com/2017/03/06/politics /ben-carson-immigrants-slavery/index.html.

Perkins, Madeleine. "Ben Carson Clarifies Remarks on Slaves as Immigrants, Calls Them 'Two Entirely Different Experiences.'" *Business Insider*, March 6, 2017.

X, Malcolm. "The Ballot or the Bullet." Speech in Washington Heights, New York, March 29, 1964. Transcript available from AMDOCS:

Documents for the Study of American History. www.vlib.us/amdocs/texts
/malcolmx0364.html.

King, Martin Luther, Jr. "Letter from a Birmingham Jail." April 16, 1963.
Available from the University of Pennsylvania's Africa Center. www
.africa.upenn.edu/Articles_Gen/Letter_Birmingham.html.

Baldwin, James. *The Price of the Ticket: Collected Nonfiction, 1948–1985*.
Boston: Beacon, 1985.

10. White Americans still benefit from the legacy of slavery.

Bennett, Kaitlin. @KaitMarieox. "No one alive today was ever a slave." Twitter, February 25, 2020, 6:05 p.m. https://twitter.com/KaitMarieox
/status/1232486759700656129.

Smith, Clint. Interview by Terry Gross, *Fresh Air*. NPR, June 1, 2021. Transcript (partial): "Slavery Wasn't 'Long Ago': A Writer Exposes the
Disconnect in How We Tell History." NPR.org, June 1, 2021. www
.therg/2021/06/01/1001243385/slavery-wasnt-long-ago-writer-exposes
-the-disconnect-in-how-we-tell-history.

Rock, Chris. "'Kill the Messenger': Neighborhood." YouTube video, 0:58.
Posted by HBO on January 29, 2009. www.youtube.com/watch?v
=53hXBg-U-ac.

DeSpain, Lynn Bryant. Public testimony to the Oregon Senate Committee
on Judiciary and Ballot Measure 110 Implementation, March 10, 2021.
Oregon Legislative Information System. https://olis.oregonlegislature
.gov/liz/2021R1/Downloads/PublicTestimonyDocument/15185.

Walker, Herschel. "Written Statement on Reparations." US House Sub-
committee Hearing on Slavery Reparations, February 17, 2021. www
.congress.gov/117/meeting/house/111198/witnesses/HHRG-117
-JU10-Wstate-WalkerH-20210217.pdf.

Desmond, Matthew. "In Order to Understand the Brutality of American
Capitalism, You Have to Start on the Plantation." *New York Times
Magazine*, August 14, 2019.

Smith, Ryan. "Ruth Odom Bonner, Who Rang the Freedom Bell with President Obama, Passes Away at 100." *Smithsonian Magazine*, September
1, 2017.

Trent, Sydney. "At 88, He Is a Historical Rarity—the Living Son of a Slave."
Washington Post, July 27, 2020.

Liptak, Adam, and Michael Wines. "Strict North Carolina Voter ID Law
Thwarted After Supreme Court Rejects Case." *New York Times*, May
15, 2017.

11. Being called a "Karen" is not comparable to being called the N-word.

Sarnoff, Eva. @EvaSarnoff. "Yes. The K-word is stronger than the n-word, at least currently." Twitter, April 7, 2020, 6:41 a.m. https://twitter.com /EvaSarnoff/status/1247519775963537412.

Chideya, Farai. *The Color of Our Future: Race in the 21st Century.* New York: HarperCollins, 1999.

Barr, Andy. "Roger Stone Claims Michelle Obama 'Whitey' Video Will Soon Surface." *The Hill*, June 2, 2008. https://thehill.com/blogs /blog-briefing-room/news/campaigns/41096-roger-stone-claims -michelle-obama-whitey-video-will-soon-surface/ajax/aggregate/.

Trump, Donald J. @realDonaldTrump. ".@MarkBurnettTV called to say that there are NO TAPES of the Apprentice." Twitter, August 13, 2018, 6:50 p.m. https://twitter.com/realDonaldTrump/status /1029183344397955074.

Fitzpatrick, Alex. "President Trump Calls Omarosa 'That Dog' as He Denies Using the N-Word." *Time*, August 14, 2018.

Watts, Marina. "Domino's Pizza Drops 'Calling All Karens' Free Pizza Give-away After Backlash." *Newsweek*, July 29, 2020.

Chase, Chevy, and Richard Pryor. "Word Association." *Saturday Night Live.* Aired December 13, 1975, on NBC. Clip available on YouTube, posted by Saturday Night Live on October 4, 2013. www.youtube.com /watch?v=yuEBBwJdjhQ.

Bump, Philip. "Calling Someone a White Supremacist Is Not Equal to Using the N-word." *Washington Post*, May 18, 2023. www.washingtonpost .com/politics/2023/05/18/marjorie-taylor-greene-jamaal-bowman/.

PART THREE
Denying Black Oppression

Willis, Kiersten. "Why Steve Harvey Says Everyone Should Fly First Class." *Atlanta Black Star*, November 13, 2018.

12. Complying with the police does not protect us.

Klemko, Robert. "Much of America Wants Policing to Change. But These Self-Proclaimed Experts Tell Officers They're Doing Just Fine." *Washington Post*, January 26, 2022.

Kendi, Ibram X. "Compliance Will Not Save Me." *The Atlantic*, April 19, 2021.

Vandell, Perry. "Unsealed Court Records in Muhaymin Case Reveal Officer Explanation Behind Arrest." *Arizona Republic*, December 8, 2021.

azcentral.com and The Arizona Republic. "Phoenix Has Its Own 'I Can't Breathe' Case, Footage of Muhammad Muhaymin Jr and Police in 2017." YouTube video. Posted on June 5, 2020. https://youtube /-FPrK13-sBU.

Cramer, Maria, and Hurubie Meko. "Al Sharpton Eulogizes Jordan Neely at Funeral in Harlem." *New York Times*, May 19, 2023.

Alexander, Leslie, and Michelle Alexander. "Fear." In *The 1619 Project: A New American Origin Story*, created by Nikole Hannah-Jones, 97–124. New York: Random House, 2021.

New York Civil Liberties Union. "Stop-and-Frisk Data." Accessed April 26, 2023. www.nyclu.org/en/stop-and-frisk-data.

Edwards, Frank, Hedwig Lee, and Michael Esposito. "Risk of Being Killed by Police Use of Force in the United States by Age, Race, Ethnicity, and Sex." *Proceedings of the National Academies of Sciences* 116, no. 34 (2019): 16793–16798.

Morin, Rich, and Renee Stepler. *The Racial Confidence Gap in Police Performance*. Pew Research Center, September 29, 2016. www.pewresearch .org/social-trends/2016/09/29/the-racial-confidence-gap-in-police -performance/.

Levenson, Eric. "How Minneapolis Police First Described the Murder of George Floyd, and What We Know Now." CNN.com, April 21, 2021. www.cnn.com/2021/04/21/us/minneapolis-police-george-floyd -detheindex.html.

Duvall, Tessa. "Louisville Police Release the Breonna Taylor Incident Report. It's Virtually Blank." *Louisville (KY) Courier Journal*, June 10, 2020.

Kaufman, Liz. "6 James Baldwin Quotes About Race." PBS.org, August 4, 2020. www.pbs.org/wnet/americanmasters/6-james-baldwin-quotes -race/15142/.

Weisman, Jonathan, and Reid J. Epstein. "G.O.P. Declares Jan. 6 Attack 'Legitimate Political Discourse.'" *New York Times*, February 4, 2022.

13. No, we're not going back to Africa.

Stracqualursi, Veronica. "Rep. Ilhan Omar on Trump's Racist Attack: 'He Spreads the Disease of Hate.'" CNN.com, September 23, 2020. www.cnn.com/2020/09/23/politics/ilhan-omar-trump-attacks -pennsylvania-rally/index.html.

Cabral, Amilcar. *Return to the Source: Selected Speeches by Amilcar Cabral*. Edited by Africa Information Service. New York: Monthly Review Press, 1973.

Lincoln, Abraham. "Address on Colonization to a Deputation of Negroes." Speech at White House, Washington, DC, August 14, 1862. In *The Collected Works of Abraham Lincoln*, vol. 5. Ann Arbor, MI: University of Michigan Digital Library Production Services, 2001. https://quod.lib.umich.edu/l/lincoln/lincoln5/1:812?rgn=div1;view=fulltext.

King, Timmia. "Two Views: Marcus Garvey the Leader and the Threat." *Rediscovering Black History* (blog), National Archives, March 14, 2017. https://rediscovering-black-history.blogs.archives.gov/2017/03/14/two-views-marcus-garvey-the-leader-and-the-threat/.

Rosenberg, Jacob. "'Love It or Leave It' Has a Racist History. A Lot of America's Language Does." *Mother Jones*, July 20, 2019.

14. Black people don't have to prove our patriotism.

Arkansas Democrat-Gazette (Little Rock). "More NFL Players on Knee After Trump Urges Firings." September 25, 2017.

Noah, Trevor. @Trevornoah. "This! IG: kimberlylatricejones & djonesmedia." Twitter, June 6, 2020, 8:34 a.m. https://twitter.com/Trevornoah/status/1269291643842289666.

Kaepernick, Colin. Remarks at press conference, January 27, 2013. Clip: "Super Bowl Arrival Press Conferences—Colin Kaepernick." YouTube video, 12:46. Posted by Fortyniners LakersSpin on January 28, 2013. https://youtu.be/YG—S_0fj68.

Trump, Donald. "FACT CHECK: Donald Trump's Republican Convention Speech, Annotated." NPR, July, 21, 2016. www.npr.org/2016/07/21/486883610/fact-check-donald-trumps-republican-convention-speech-annotated.

Payne, Marissa. "Colin Kaepernick Refuses to Stand for National Anthem to Protest Police Killings." *Washington Post*, August 27, 2016.

Trudo, Hanna. "Obama: Kaepernick 'Exercising His Constitutional Right to Make a Statement.'" Politico, September 5, 2016. www.politico.com/story/2016/09/obama-colin-kaepernick-protest-227731.

Perez, A. J. "Donald Trump: NFL Players' Anthem Protests 'a Lack of Respect for Our Country.'" *USA Today*, September 12, 2016.

Graham, Bryan Armen. "Donald Trump Blasts NFL Anthem Protesters: 'Get That Son of a Bitch off the Field.'" *The Guardian*, September 23, 2017.

West Virginia State Board of Education v. Barnette, 319 U.S. 624 (1943).

King, Martin Luther, Jr. "I Have a Dream." Speech at the March on Washington for Jobs and Freedom, Lincoln Memorial, Washington, DC, August 28, 1963. Transcript: "Read Martin Luther King Jr.'s 'I Have a Dream' Speech in Its Entirety." NPR, January 16, 2023. www.npr .org/2010/01/18/122701268/i-have-a-dream-speech-in-its-entirety.

Phillip, Abby. "O'Reilly Told Trump That Putin Is a Killer. Trump's Reply: 'You Think Our Country Is So Innocent?'" *Washington Post*, February 4, 2017.

Noah, Trevor. "When Is the Right Time for Black People to Protest?" *The Daily Show*. Aired September 25, 2017, on Comedy Central. Clip available on the Comedy Central website, posted on September 26, 2017. www .cc.com/video/nujtiv/the-daily-show-with-trevor-noah-when-is-the-right -time-for-black-people-to-protest.

Morley, Jefferson. "Even Republicans Should Care About the Racist History of 'The Star-Spangled Banner.'" *Washington Post*, August 28, 2020.

Baldwin, James. Interview by Dick Cavett, *The Dick Cavett Show*. ABC, May 16, 1969. Clip: "James Baldwin Discusses Racism | The Dick Cavett Show." YouTube video, 17:08. Posted by The Dick Cavett Show on June 24, 2020. www.youtube.com/watch?v=WWwOi17WHpE.

Resnikoff, Paul. "Former Congressman Calls Stevie Wonder 'Another Ungrateful Black Multi-Millionaire.'" Digital Music News, September 24, 2017. www.digitalmusicnews.com/2017/09/24/stevie-wonder -kneel-trump-racist/.

Sullivan, Emily. "Laura Ingraham Told LeBron James to Shut Up and Dribble; He Went to the Hoop." *The Two-Way* (blog), NPR, February 19, 2018. www.npr.org/sections/thetwo-way/2018/02/19/587097707/laura -ingraham-told-lebron-james-to-shutup-and-dribble-he-went-to-the -hoop.

Campbell, Randolph B. "Mike." "Slavery." *The Handbook of Texas*, Texas State Historical Association. Accessed May 21, 2023. www.tshaonline .org/handbook/entries/slavery.

15. We will never reach equality without reparations.

Barrett, Ted. "McConnell Opposes Paying Reparations: 'None of Us Currently Living Are Responsible' for Slavery." CNN.com, June 19, 2019. www.cnn.com/2019/06/18/politics/mitch-mcconnell-opposes -reparations-slavery/index.html.

Coates, Ta-Nehisi. "The Case for Reparations." *The Atlantic*, June 2014.

Bacon, James L. *The Ties That Bind: From Slavery to Freedom*. Self-published, CreateSpace, 2016.

Tichy, Susan. "William & Matilda Bowie." Magruder's Landing website. November 17, 2011. Accessed June 7, 2023. https://magruderslanding .com/slavery/john-s-magruder-mcgregor-wills/william-matilda-bowie/.

Brown, DeNeen L. "D.C. Emancipation Day: 3,000 Slaves in the Nation's Capital Cried and Cheered When They Learned They Were Freed." *Washington Post*, April 15, 2017.

Chase, Salmon P. Letter to Schuyler Colfax, Speaker of the House of Representatives, with accompanying report, February 16, 1864. In *Executive Documents Printed by Order of the House of Representatives during the First Session of the Thirty-Eighth Congress, 1863–'64*, 9:1–11. Washington, DC: Government Printing Office, 1864.

Sherman, William T. "Special Field Orders, No. 15, Headquarters, Military Division of the Mississippi, by Major General W. T. Sherman . . ." January 16, 1865. Mss83434, box 3, item 256. William A. Gladstone Afro-American Military Collection, Manuscript Division, Library of Congress. https://tile.loc.gov/storage-services/service/gdc/gdccrowd/mss /mss83434/256/256.txt.

Perry, Miranda Booker. "No Pensions for Ex-slaves: How Federal Agencies Suppressed Movement to Aid Freedpeople." *Prologue* magazine, Summer 2010. www.archives.gov/publications/prologue/2010/summer/slave -pension.html.

Student Nonviolent Coordinating Committee. "Jim Forman Delivers Black Manifesto at Riverside Church." Timeline, SNCC Digital Gateway. Accessed June 4, 2023. https://snccdigital.org/events /jim-forman-delivers-black-manifesto-at-riverside-church/.

New York Review of Books. "Black Manifesto: The Black National Economic Conference." July 10, 1969.

Robinson, Randall. *The Debt: What America Owes to Blacks*. New York: Plume, 2000.

X, Malcolm. Interview, March 1964. Clip: "Malcolm X- On Progress." YouTube video, 0:20. Posted by mrholtshistory on April 21, 2008. www .youtube.com/watch?v=cReCQE8B5nY.

Haley, Alex. "Alex Haley Interviews Martin Luther King, Jr." *Playboy*, January 1965.

Sutton, Belinda. "Belinda Sutton's 1783 Petition (Full Text)." February 14, 1783. Royall House and Slave Quarters website. https://royallhouse .org/belinda-suttons-1783-petition-full-text/.

Schuessler, Jennifer. "Columbia Examines Its Long-Ago Links to Slavery." *New York Times*, May 13, 2015.

Obama, Michelle. Address at the Democratic National Convention. Wells Fargo Center, Philadelphia, July 25, 2016. Clip: "Michelle Obama: 'I Wake Up Every Morning in a House That Was Built by Slaves.'" YouTube video, 1:10. Posted by PBS NewsHour on July 25, 2016. www.youtube.com/watch?v=zHnJ2sTIVUI.

Holland, Jesse J. *Black Men Built the Capitol: Discovering African-American History in and Around Washington, D.C.* Guilford, CT: Globe Pequot, 2007.

Washington Post. "J.P. Morgan Discloses Past Links to Slavery." January 21, 2005.

Faulkner, William. *Requiem for a Nun*. New York: Random House, 1951.

Harris, Cheryl I. "Whiteness as Property." *Harvard Law Review* 106, no. 8 (June 1993): 1707–1791.

PART FOUR
Myths of Black Inferiority

Ducey, Kenny. "Cincinnati Coach Tommy Tuberville Claps Back at Heckler: 'Go to Hell, Get a Job.'" *Sports Illustrated*, November 5, 2016.

Edmondson, Catie. "Senator-Elect Tommy Tuberville Flubs Basics of the Constitution, World War II and the 2000 Election." *New York Times*, November 13, 2020.

Associated Press. "Senator: Dems Back Reparations for Those Who 'Do the Crime.'" October 9, 2022.

16. There are more white people than Black people on welfare.

Gamboa, Suzanne. "Santorum: 'I Don't Want to Make Black People's Lives Better by Giving Them Somebody Else's Money.'" *AFRO News*, January 4, 2012. https://afro.com/santorum-i-dont-want-to-make-black-peoples-lives-better-by-giving-them-somebody-elses-money/.

Sit, Ryan. "Trump Thinks Only Black People Are on Welfare, but Really, White Americans Receive Most Benefits." *Newsweek*, January 12, 2018.

Scott, Janny. Interview by Terry Gross, *Fresh Air*. NPR, May 3, 2011. Transcript (partial): "The 'Singular Woman' Who Raised Barack Obama." NPR.org, May 3, 2011. www.npr.org/2011/05/03/135840068/the-singular-woman-who-raised-barack-obama.

Scott, Janny. *A Singular Woman: The Untold Story of Barack Obama's Mother*. New York: Riverhead, 2011.

Washington Star. "'Welfare Queen' Becomes Issue in Reagan Campaign." *New York Times*, February 15, 1976.

Brockell, Gillian. "She Was Stereotyped as 'the Welfare Queen.' The Truth Was More Disturbing, a New Book Says." *Washington Post*, May 21, 2019.

Levin, Josh. *The Queen: The Forgotten Life Behind an American Myth.* New York: Little, Brown, 2019.

US Census Bureau. "About Program Income and Public Assistance." October 3, 2022. www.census.gov/topics/income-poverty/public-assistance /about.html.

O'Connor, Carroll, and Jean Stapleton. "Those Were the Days." Theme song for *All in the Family,* airing 1971–1979 on CBS.

Floyd, Ife, LaDonna Pavetti, Laura Meyer, Ali Safawi, Liz Schott, Evelyn Bellew, and Abigail Magnus. *TANF Policies Reflect Racist Legacy of Cash Assistance: Reimagined Program Should Center Black Mothers.* Center on Budget and Policy Priorities, August 4, 2021. www.cbpp.org/sites /default/files/8-4-21tanf.pdf.

King, Martin Luther, Jr. "The Other America." Speech at Stanford University, April 14, 1967. Clip: "Martin Luther King: How White People Got Their Land and Wealth." YouTube video, 1:15. Posted by Black Wall Street International on January 18, 2016. https://youtu.be /Fmv103saaEk.

Atkins, Norman. "Governor Get-a-Job; Tommy Thompson." *New York Times,* January 15, 1995.

Elliot, Debbie. "'Food Stamp President': Race Code, or Just Politics?" *Morning Edition,* NPR, January 17, 2012. www.npr.org/2012/01/17/145312069 /newts-food-stamp-president-racial-or-just-politics.

Blow, Charles M. "Paul Ryan, Culture and Poverty." *New York Times,* March 21, 2014.

Rank, Mark. "Poverty in America Is Mainstream." *New York Times,* November 2, 2013.

Wetts, Rachel, and Robb Willer. "Privilege on the Precipice: Perceived Racial Status Threats Lead White Americans to Oppose Welfare Program." *Social Forces* 97, no. 2 (December 2018): 793–822.

17. "Black-on-Black crime" is an outdated media trope.

Suen, Brennan. "Fox News Revives 'Black-on-Black Crime' Canard to Dismiss Black Lives Matter Movement." Media Matters for America, September 3, 2015. www.mediamatters.org/sean-hannity/fox-news-revives -black-black-crime-canard-dismiss-black-lives-matter-movement.

Taylor, Zariah. "Reasons Why 'Black-on-Black Crime' Is Not a Valid Argument Against the Black Lives Matter Movement." VOX ATL, March 18, 2022. https://voxatl.org/vox-5-reasons-why-black-on-black-crime-is-not-a-valid-argument-against-the-black-lives-matter-movement/.

St. Louis Post-Dispatch. "Alarm Leads Police to Victim." June 1, 1980.

Thompson, Derek. "Six Reasons the Murder Clearance Rate Is at an All-Time Low." *The Atlantic*, July 7, 2022.

Wynter, Sylvia. "'No Humans Involved': An Open Letter to My Colleagues." *Forum N.H.I.: Knowledge for the 21st Century* 1, no. 1 (Fall 1994).

Ifill, Gwen. Panel at Unity: Journalists of Color conference, Washington, DC, August 5, 2004. Clip: "Gwen Ifill Coins the Term 'Missing White Woman Syndrome.'" C-SPAN.org. Quote at 00:20. www.c-span.org/video/?c4666788/user-clip-gwen-ifill-coins-term-missing-white-woman-syndrome.

Purnell, Derecka. "The 'Missing White Woman Syndrome' Still Plagues America." *The Guardian*, September 29, 2021.

Rivers, Erika M. "About OBG." Our Black Girls. Accessed May 8, 2023. https://ourblackgirls.com/about-our-black-girls/.

Joyce, Eric. "'Stop the Violence' March Seeks to Continue to Help Reduce Violent Crime in Saginaw." *Saginaw (MI) News*, October 29, 2010.

Williams, Juan. "The Trayvon Martin Tragedies." *Wall Street Journal*, March 27, 2012.

Coates, Ta-Nehisi. "Why Don't Black People Protest 'Black-on-Black Violence'?" *The Atlantic*, April 2, 2012.

Obama, Barack. State of the Union address, Washington, DC, February 12, 2013. Transcript: "Remarks by the President in the State of the Union Address." Press release. February 12, 2013. https://obamawhitehouse.archives.gov/the-press-office/2013/02/12/remarks-president-state-union-address.

18. Black families are not broken.

Wemple, Erik. "Amid His Own Troubles, Bill O'Reilly Denounces Dissolution of Black Families." *Washington Post*, March 1, 2016.

West, Cornel. Interview by Bill O'Reilly, *The O'Reilly Factor*. Fox News, August 20, 2015. Transcript: "Assessing Black Lives Matter's [sic] Agenda." FoxNews.com, January 24, 2017. www.foxnews.com/transcript/assessing-black-lives-matters-agenda.

Pan, Deanna, and Jennifer Berry Hawes. "In 1944, George Stinney Was Young, Black and Sentenced to Die." *Post and Courier* (Charleston, SC), March 25, 2018.

Blow, Charles M. "How White Women Use Themselves as Instruments of Terror." *New York Times*, May 27, 2020.

Richardson, James M. "The Geo. Stinney Case." *Greenville (SC) News*, June 14, 1944.

ESPN.com. "Report—Jets Owner Woody Johnson Investigated for Alleged Racist, Sexist Comments." July 22, 2020. www.espn.com/nfl/story /_/id/29517259/report-jets-owner-woody-johnson-investigated-racist -sexist-comments.

Glaister, Dan. "Abort All Black Babies and Cut Crime, Says Republican." *The Guardian*, October 1, 2005.

Hill, Curtis. "Curtis Hill: Black Lives Matter Movement Should Prioritize Black Fatherhood to Improve Black Lives." FoxNews.com, July 10, 2020. www .foxnews.com/opinion/black-lives-matter-black-fatherhood-curtis-hill.

Moynihan, Daniel Patrick. *The Negro Family: The Case for National Action*. Office of Policy Planning and Research, US Department of Labor, March 1965. www.dol.gov/general/aboutdol/history/webid-moynihan.

Livingston, Gretchen, and Kim Parker. "Chapter 1. Living Arrangements and Father Involvement." In *A Tale of Two Fathers: More Are Active, but More Are Absent*, Pew Research Center, June 15, 2011. www.pewresearch .org/social-trends/2011/06/15/chapter-1-living-arrangements-and -father-involvement/.

Jones, Jo, and William D. Mosher. "Fathers' Involvement with Their Children: United States, 2006–2010." *National Health Statistics Reports* 71, December 20, 2013. US Centers for Disease Control and Prevention, Division of Vital Statistics.

Sherman, Shantella Y. "Dispelling the Myth of Derelict Black Fathers." *Washington Informer*, June 13, 2018.

Levs, Josh. "No, Most Black Kids Are Not Fatherless." *HuffPost*, July 26, 2016. www.huffpost.com/entry/no-most-black-kids-are-no_b_11109876.

Blow, Charles. "Black Dads Are Doing Best of All." *New York Times*, June 8, 2015.

Smith, Clint. *How the Word Is Passed: A Reckoning with the History of Slavery Across America*. New York: Little, Brown, 2021.

19. Black cities struggle because of decisions by white policy makers.

Waldman, Paul. "Trump's Attack on 'Democrat Cities' Is Right Out of the GOP Playbook." *Washington Post*, September 2, 2020.

Badger, Emily. "'Democrat Cities' Aren't as Partisan or as Powerful as the President Suggests." *New York Times*, September 2, 2020.

Feldman, Brian S. "How America's Coastal Cities Left the Heartland Behind." *The Atlantic*, April 18, 2016.

Koza, Patricia. "President Reagan's Transportation Budget Contains Massive Cuts in Highway." United Press International, February 18, 1981.

Turner, Margery Austin, and Solomon Greene. "Causes and Consequences of Separate and Unequal Neighborhoods." Structural Racism Explainer Collection, Urban Institute. Accessed June 4, 2023. www.urban.org /racial-equity-analytics-lab/structural-racism-explainer-collection /causes-and-consequences-separate-and-unequal-neighborhoods.

Brownstein, Ronald. "It's Not Just Voting and Covid: How Red States Are Overriding Their Blue Cities." CNN.com, June 8, 2021. www.cnn .com/2021/06/08/politics/red-states-blue-cities-counties/index.html.

Mathers, Matt. "Trump Retweets Call to Let 'Democrat Cities Rot' over Video of NYC Protesters." *The Independent*, August 18, 2020.

Metropolitan Police Department (St. Louis, MO). "2023 Homicide Analysis." Accessed May 22, 2023. www.slmpd.org/images/Homicide _Stats_for_Website.pdf.

New York Police Department. "Citywide Seven Major Felony Offenses, 2000–2021." Historical New York City Crime Data, Crime Statistics, NYPD. Accessed June 4, 2023. www.nyc.gov/assets/nypd /downloads/pdf/analysis_and_planning/historical-crime-data/seven -major-felony-offenses-2000-2021.pdf.

Fox, Justin. "New York City Is a Lot Safer Than Small-Town America." Bloomberg.com, June 7, 2022. www.bloomberg.com/opinion/articles /2022-06-07/is-new-york-city-more-dangerous-than-rural-america.

PART FIVE
Rebranding Racism

Moore, Jason, dir. "Everyone's a Little Bit Racist," *Avenue Q*. 2003. Clip: "Everyone's a Little Bit Racist—Avenue Q—Original Broadway Cast." YouTube video, 5:42. Posted by Broadway Classics on February 2, 2013. www.youtube.com/watch?v=RXnM1uHhsOI.

Bell, Derrick A., Jr. "*Brown v. Board of Education* and the Interest-Convergence Dilemma." *Harvard Law Review* 93, no. 3 (January 1980): 518, 523.

20. There is no "race card."

Lee, Traci G. "Palin to Obama: Stop 'Playing the Race Card.'" NBCNews .com, January 20, 2014. www.nbcnews.com/id/wbna54127234.

Blow, Charles M. "Stop Playing the 'Race Card' Card." *New York Times*, March 19, 2015.

Vicens, AJ, and Natalie Schreyer. "Donald Trump Once Told NBC News He Would Have Done Better as a Black Man." *Mother Jones*, June 20, 2016.

Kaur, Harmeet. "Kanye West Just Said 400 Years of Slavery Was a Choice." CNN.com, May 4, 2018. www.cnn.com/2018/05/01/entertainment /kanye-west-slavery-choice-trnd/index.html.

21. Black friends do not immunize people from racism.

Luciano, Michael. "Newsmax's Greg Kelly Airs Photos of Trump with Rosa Parks and Michael Jackson in Effort to Prove He's Not Racist, Casually Adds That Allegations Against King of Pop 'Are Fake.'" Mediaite+, May 23, 2022. www.mediaite.com/tv/greg-kelly-says-donald -trump-isnt-racist/.

Belfield-Martin, Leenika. "Hey, Your 'Black Friend' Here—Stop Using Me." Yahoo!Life, June 8, 2020. www.yahoo.com/lifestyle/having-black -friends-doesnt-automatically-204630757.html.

King, Regina, dir. *One Night in Miami . . .* Culver City, CA: Amazon Studios, 2020.

Jefferson, Thomas. *Notes on the State of Virginia*. Philadelphia: Pritchard and Hall, 1788.

Foston, Nikitta A. "Strom Thurmond's Black Family." *Ebony*, March 2004.

States Rights Democratic Party. Platform, adopted in Oklahoma City, August 14, 1948. Available from the American Presidency Project, UC Santa Barbara. www.presidency.ucsb.edu/documents/platform-the -states-rights-democratic-party.

102 Cong. Rec. 4515–4516 (1956).

Ramirez, Isabella. "Daniel Penny: I'm Not Racist, I Was Planning a Trip to Africa Before Chokehold Death." *Daily Beast*, May 20, 2023. www .thedailybeast.com/daniel-penny-im-not-racist-i-was-planning-a-trip -to-africa-before-chokehold-death.

Peele, Jordan, dir. *Get Out*. Universal City, CA: Universal Pictures, 2017.

Ingraham, Christopher. "Three Quarters of Whites Don't Have Any Non-white Friends." *Washington Post*, August 25, 2014.

Crawford, Kate. "Artificial Intelligence's White Guy Problem." *New York Times*, June 25, 2016.

Golliver, Ben. "NBA Investigating Clippers Owner Donald Sterling for Alleged Racist Comments." *Sports Illustrated*, April 26, 2014.

Brown, DeNeen L. "Frederick Douglass Delivered a Lincoln Reality Check at Emancipation Memorial Unveiling." *Washington Post*, June 27, 2020.

Douglass, Frederick. Speech at the dedication of memorial to Abraham Lincoln, Washington, DC, April 14, 1876. Transcript available from Knowledge of Freedom Seminar, Dickinson College and the Teagle Foundation. https://housedivided.dickinson.edu/sites/teagle/texts /frederick-douglass-speech-at-dedication-of-emancipation-memorial -1876/.

22. People who say they "don't have a racist bone in their body" haven't searched hard enough.

Fabian, Jordan. "Trump: I Don't Have a Racist Bone in My Body." *The Hill*, July 16, 2019.

Jackson, Reggie. "My Head Might Explode If I Hear Another White Person Say They Don't Have a Racist Bone in Their Body." *Milwaukee Independent*, October 13, 2021. www.milwaukeeindependent.com /reggie-jackson/head-might-explode-hear-another-white-person-say -dont-racist-bone-body/.

Goldstein, Richard. "Earl L. Butz, Secretary Felled by Racial Remark, Is Dead at 98." *New York Times*, February 4, 2008.

Tribune Wire Services. "Pope Refuses Comment on Butz' Controversial Remark." *South Bend (IN) Tribune*, November 29, 1974.

"Butz Resigns over Slur." *Capital Times* (Madison, WI), October 4, 1976.

United Press International. "Earl Butz Resigns in Wake of Slur." October 4, 1976.

New York Times. "Texts of Butz Statement and Letter and Ford's Reply." October 5, 1976.

ABC News. Barbara Walters discusses Earl Butz. Aired October 4, 1976, on ABC. YouTube video, 28:57. Posted by NewsActive3 on July 12, 2015. https://youtu.be/dQHQ7nfwK4I.

Robbins, William. "Butz Is Confident That His Policies Will Be Continued." *New York Times*, October 7, 1976.

Associated Press. "Butz Not a Racist, Black Ex-aide Says." *Los Angeles Times*, October 7, 1976.

United Press International. "Denver Fete Boycotted by Negroes." *Boston Globe*, December 7, 1966.

Simmons, Myles. "Jon Gruden Undercuts His Apology with Tired 'Racist Bone' Expression." Pro Football Talk, NBCSports.com, October 8, 2021.

https://profootballtalk.nbcsports.com/2021/10/08/jon-gruden-under cuts-his-apology-with-tired-racist-bone-expression/.

Kilpatrick, James. "Reagan Resents Marshall's Criticism." A Conservative View (column). *Honolulu Star-Bulletin*, September 16, 1987.

Chicago Tribune. "Reagan No Racist, Sen. Hatch Asserts." January 20, 1986.

Washington Post. "Sen. Hatch on Trump: 'I Don't Think There's a Racist Bone in His Body.'" August 17, 2017.

Patrella, Christopher, and Justin Gomer. "'Not a Racist Bone in His Body': The Origins of the Default Defense Against Racism." *Washington Post*, July 16, 2019.

Davis, Jefferson. "First Inaugural Address." Speech in Montgomery, AL, February 18, 1861. Transcript available from the Papers of Jefferson Davis at Rice University. https://jeffersondavis.rice.edu/archives/documents /jefferson-davis-first-inaugural-address.

Horne, Gerald. *The Counter-Revolution of 1776: Slave Resistance and the Origins of the United States of America*. New York: New York University Press, 2016.

Conway, George. "Trump Is a Racist President." *Washington Post*, July 15, 2019.

Samuels, Brett. "Kellyanne Conway: 'I Totally Disagree' with Husband's Op-Ed Calling Trump Racist." *The Hill*, July 16, 2019.

Wang, Mary. "Racism Doesn't Matter If Your Heart Is in the Right Place, According to Paul Ryan." *Vogue*, October 1, 2017.

23. Yes, you do see color, and there's nothing wrong with that.

Lahren, Tomi. Interview by Trevor Noah, *The Daily Show*. Comedy Central, November 29, 2016. Clip: "Tomi Lahren—Giving a Voice to Conservative America on 'Tomi.'" YouTube video, 14:08. Posted by The Daily Show on December 1, 2016. https://youtu.be/F2xv4fba65U.

Fleming, Victor, dir. *The Wizard of Oz*. Beverly Hills, CA: Metro-Goldwyn-Mayer, 1939.

Dart, Tom. "Former Starbucks CEO Howard Schultz Criticized for Saying 'I Don't See Color.'" *The Guardian*, February 13, 2019.

Quindlen, Kim. "23 Hilarious 'Stephen Colbert' Quotes That Are Just Ridiculous Enough to Prove a Point." Thought Catalog, September 15, 2015. https://thoughtcatalog.com/kim-quindlen/2015/09/23-hilarious -stephen-colbert-quotes-that-are-just-ridiculous-enough-to-prove -a-point/.

Gates, Henry Louis, Jr. "'Plessy v. Ferguson': Who Was Plessy?" *Henry Louis Gates Jr.'s 100 Amazing Facts About the Negro* (blog), PBS, September 18, 2013. www.pbs.org/wnet/african-americans-many-rivers-to-cross /history/plessy-v-ferguson-who-was-plessy/.

Hill, Jarrett. "Dear 'White Allies,' Stop Saying That You 'Don't See Color.'" NBCNews.com, December 1, 2016. www.nbcnews.com/news/nbcblk /opinion-dear-tomi-lahren-please-stop-saying-you-dont-see-n690801.

Cox, Kiana, and Christine Tamir. *Race Is Central to Identity for Black Americans and Affects How They Connect with Each Other.* Pew Research Center, April 14, 2022. www.pewresearch.org/race-ethnicity/2022 /04/14/race-is-central-to-identity-for-black-americans-and-affects -how-they-connect-with-each-other/.

Sutherland, JJ. "L. Frank Baum Advocated Extermination of Native Americans." *The Two-Way* (blog), NPR.org, October 27, 2010. www.npr.org /sections/thetwo-way/2010/10/27/130862391/l-frank-baum-advocated -extermination-of-native-americans.

Enriquez, Justin. "The Wiz Live's All-Black Cast Sees Twitter Explode over 'Lack of Whites.'" DailyMail.com, December 4, 2015. www.dailymail .co.uk/tvshowbiz/article-3345408/Social-media-flooded-racist-tweets -black-Wiz-Live-musical-special-kicks-off.html.

24. "All lives matter" is a cheap excuse to avoid saying "Black lives matter."

Twohey, Megan. "Rudolph Giuliani Lashes Out at Black Lives Matter." *New York Times*, July 10, 2016.

Key, Keegan-Michael. Interview by James Corden, *The Late Show with James Corden.* CBS, June 1, 2020. Clip: "Keegan-Michael Key Is Finding Optimism in Signs of Unity." YouTube video, 5:47. Posted by The Late Late Show with James Corden on June 2, 2020. https://youtu.be /agr7W7SgBT4.

O'Neal, Patrice. "Patrice O'Neal on 'Missing White Women.'" YouTube video, 8:14. Posted by LaughPlanet on October 14, 2022. https: //youtu.be/vnJ1Q5rHv8k.

Shepherd, Katie. "A 22-Year-Old and Her Boyfriend Set Out on a Cross-Country Road Trip in Their Van. Now, She's Missing." *Washington Post*, September 14, 2021.

Jefferson, Hakeem. @hakeemjefferson. "'This info is hardly pertinent to the story . . .' unnecessarily racializes the missing person . . ." Twitter,

September 16, 2021, 8:12 a.m. https://twitter.com/hakeemjefferson/status/1438521230361968646.

Robertson, Katie. "News Media Can't Shake 'Missing White Woman Syndrome,' Critics Say." *New York Times*, September 22, 2021.

D'Zurilla, Christie. "Terry Crews Widely Criticized (Again) for #blacklivesbetter Tweet." *Los Angeles Times*, June 30, 2020.

Civil Rights Cases, 109 U.S. 3 (1883).

Lanum, Nikolas. "Tim Scott Responds to MSNBC's Joy Reid: 'Woke Supremacy Is as Bad as White Supremacy.'" FoxNews.com, March 9, 2021. www.foxnews.com/media/tim-scott-joy-reid-woke\-supremacy-prop-republicans.

Media Matters. @mmfa. "How Fox News dismisses tens of thousands of Americans dying: 'Every death is tragic, but . . .'" Twitter, May 21, 2020, 7:56 a.m. https://twitter.com/mmfa/status/1263483930889588737?s=21.

Higgins, Tucker, and John W. Schoen. "These 4 Charts Describe Police Violence in America." CNBC.com, June 4, 2020. www.cnbc.com/2020/06/01/george-floyd-death-police-violence-in-the-us-in-4-charts.html.

25. Yes, everything is about race.

Lahren, Tomi. "Yale Med School Professor Blames White Supremacy for Biden Working While Sick." *Fox News Commentary with Tomi Lahren*, July 26, 2022. https://radio.foxnews.com/2022/07/26/yale-med-school-professor-blames-white-supremacy-for-biden-working-while-sick/.

Lewis, Brittany. "Unapologetically Black: Reflections on My Childhood and Assimilation." *Washington Times*, January 31, 2016.

Asare, Janice Gassam. "Why Does Everything Have to Be About Race?" *Forbes*, October 28, 2021.

Murray, John (Earl of Dunmore). "Lord Dunmore's Proclamation, 1775." November 7, 1775. Gilder Lehrman Institute of American History. Accessed June 4, 2023. www.gilderlehrman.org/history-resources/spotlight-primary-source/lord-dunmores-proclamation-1775.

Hannah-Jones, Nikole. "Democracy." In *The 1619 Project: A New American Origin Story*, created by Nikole Hannah-Jones, 7–36. New York: Random House, 2021.

Pendleton, Edmund. "Virginia Assembly's Response." December 14, 1775. Digital History, University of Houston. Accessed June 4, 2023. www.digitalhistory.uh.edu/active_learning/explorations/revolution/virginia_assembly.cfm.

Jefferson, Thomas. "Jefferson's 'Original Rough Draught' of the Declaration of Independence." Declaring Independence: Drafting the Documents (exhibition), Library of Congress. Accessed June 4, 2023. www.loc.gov /exhibits/declara/ruffdrft.html.

Jefferson, Thomas. "Declaration of Independence: A Transcription." America's Founding Documents, National Archives website. Accessed June 4, 2023. www.archives.gov/founding-docs/declaration-transcript.

US Const. art. I, § 2, cl. 3.

US Const. art. I, § 9, cl. 1.

US Const. art. IV, § 2, cl. 3.

Texas Const., General Provisions, § 9.

Jackson, Andrew. "Farewell Address." March 4, 1837. Transcript available from the American Presidency Project. www.presidency.ucsb.edu /documents/farewell-address-0.

Dred Scott v. Sandford, 60 U.S. 393 (1856).

Lincoln, Abraham. Fourth debate with Stephen A. Douglas. Charleston, IL, September 18, 1858. Transcript available from Lincoln Home, National Historic Site Illinois, National Park Service. www.nps.gov /liho/learn/historyculture/debate4.htm.

Trickey, Erick. "'Kill the Beast': The Impeachment Trial That Nearly Took Down a President 150 Years Ago." *Washington Post*, May 16, 2018.

Chinese Exclusion Act of 1882. 22 Stat. 58 (Chapter 126).

Civil Rights Cases, 109 U.S. 3 (1883).

Plessy v. Ferguson, 163 U.S. 537 (1896).

Cumming v. Richmond County Board of Education, 175 U.S. 528 (1899).

Downes v. Bidwell, 182 U.S. 244 (1901).

Barnett, Randy. "Expunging Woodrow Wilson from Official Places of Honor." *Washington Post*, June 25, 2015.

Wormser, Richard. *The Rise and Fall of Jim Crow*. New York: St. Martin's, 2003.

Emergency Quota Act of 1921. 42 Stat. 5 (Pub. Law 67-5).

DeWitt, J. L. Public Proclamation No. 4, 7 Fed. Reg. 2601 (March 27, 1942).

Korematsu v. United States, 323 U.S. 214 (1944).

Caplan, Lincoln. "A President, a Chief Justice and the Politics of Segregation." *New York Times*, June 12, 2018. www.nytimes.com/2018/06/12 /books/review/eisenhower-vs-warren-james-f-simon.html.

Loving v. Virginia, 388 U.S. 1 (1967).

Thurmond, Strom. "Senator Hubert Humphrey (D-MN) and Senator Strom Thurmond (D-SC), Debate on the Civil Rights Act, March 18, 1964."

Debates over the Civil Rights Act of 1964, Teaching American History website. Accessed June 4, 2023. https://teachingamericanhistory.org/document/the-civil-rights-act-1964/.

New York Times. "Civil Rights Act: How South Responds." July 12, 1964.

Edsall, Thomas B., and Brian Faler. "Lott Remarks on Thurmond Echoed 1980 Words." *Washington Post*, December 11, 2002.

Kessler, Glenn. "A Look at Trump's 'Birther' Statements." *Washington Post*, April 28, 2011.

N.C. State Conference of the NAACP v. McCrory, 831 F.3d 204 (4th Cir. 2016).

Exec. Order No. 13769, 3 C.F.R. 272 (2017).

BBC News. "Trump Stokes 'Birther' Conspiracy Theory About Kamala Harris." BBC, August 14, 2020. www.bbc.com/news/world-us-canada-53774289.

Sowell, Thomas. @ThomasSowell. "Racism is not dead, but it is on life support . . ." Twitter, August 18, 2019, 10:27 a.m. https://twitter.com/ThomasSowell/status/1163140385532776449?lang=en.

Index

Index

Index

Index

Index

Index

Index

Credit: Sean Howard

Keith Boykin is a *New York Times*–bestselling author, TV and film producer, and former CNN political commentator. A graduate of Dartmouth College and Harvard Law School, Boykin served in the White House, cofounded the National Black Justice Coalition, cohosted the BET talk show *My Two Cents*, and taught at the Institute for Research in African-American Studies at Columbia University in New York. He's a Lambda Literary Award–winning author and editor of seven books. He lives in Los Angeles.